Hong Kong
Metamorphosis

歷變中看香港

黎敦義

Hong Kong
Metamorphosis

Denis Bray

香港大學出版社
HONG KONG UNIVERSITY PRESS

Hong Kong University Press
14/F Hing Wai Centre
7 Tin Wan Praya Road
Aberdeen
Hong Kong

First published 2001
Reprinted 2002

ISBN 962 209 550 X

A CIP catalogue record for this book is available from
the British Library.

Secure On-line Ordering
http://www.hkupress.org

Printed and bound by Condor Production Ltd., Hong Kong, China.

Contents

Claimer

A claimer is the opposite of a disclaimer. This is not a work of fiction. All the characters are, or were, real people. All the events took place.

On the other hand, my memory is not infallible. I once had a long argument with a newspaper columnist, Kevin Sinclair, about the year in which the communists arrested three yachts sailing from Hong Kong to Macau over Chinese New Year. I was sure of my date. A few days later Kevin sent me a newspaper cutting of the event dated a year earlier. So I am prepared for people to say I got something wrong.

This all started in 1993 with a request from the Hong Kong Branch of the Royal Asiatic Society for a talk about my childhood. This was published by the Society, under the title, *Growing up in China,* in its Journal Vol. 32, 1992. That is the origin of Chapter 1. I also used what I had written for Chapter 5 in another talk to the Society in 2000. In 1999, the Centre of Asian Studies, at the University of Hong Kong, mounted a seminar entitled 'Hong Kong, British Crown Colony, Revisited' at which a few of us were each given the floor for two hours. I wrote far too much but the text of what I had to say is published by the Centre in a book of the same title. Material now in Chapters 4–9, 10 and 11 started life in that seminar. By the time I had done all that I felt I had enough to start on this book.

The disclaimer is that this is not intended to be a well researched, definitive history. Many areas are lightly touched on. It is simply an anthology of recollections that have come to me as I sit at my computer in a contented retirement.

Robin Hutcheon very kindly gave me some tips. He did the Index, and in record time. Thanks very much. My wife, Marjorie, read the text with many helpful suggestions. Old friends have, consciously or not, reminded me of long forgotten details. Sadly, all the governors that I served under have died. Either in correspondence or chat Lord Wilson, Sir Y. K. Kan and Mr Yung Wah Kan, formerly of the Belgian Bank, showed that my memory was indeed flawed. In fact, I began to be afraid that if I talked to many more people I should have to start all over again. Errors you may still find are mine alone.

To the best of my knowledge, the rights of the photographs, which I have had for twenty to fifty years, have been respected and acknowledged. If omissions exist, and are brought to my attention, these will be remedied in later editions.

Denis Bray
Hong Kong
August 2001

The Bray family in England, 1934.

Left to right: Jeremy, Barbara, Mrs Muriel Bray, Denis, Eleanor, Kathleen Banks, Matron of the Foshan Hospital.

Last visit to Foshan: The Bray family, 1938.

Left to right: Eleanor, Mrs Muriel Bray, Barbara, Denis, Rev Arthur Bray and Jeremy.

Holiday from Chefoo in Foshan, 1938.

Photo by Stearn & Sons.

Colquhoun Sculls, Cambridge, 1946.

Photo by George Bushell and Son.

Jesus College, Cambridge beating Leander Club in the first heat of
the Grand Challenge Cup, Henley Royal Regatta, 1947.

Denis, in glasses, teaching engineering drawing. HMS *Caledonia*, 1948.

No. E.5

30 SEP 1949 19

This is to Certify that Instructor Lieutenant D.C. BRAY RN has served as an Instructor Officer in HM Ship under my command, from the 4th day of October 1947, to the 26th day of September 1949, during which period he has conducted himself To my entire satisfaction. An able instructor officer who has made the most of his time in the service.

{ Captain
H.M.S. Caledonia

*Here the Captain is to insert in his own handwriting the conduct of the Officer

Certificate of service on release from the National Service.

Cold beer on *Wind Song*.

Ceil III, Skipper Bill Turnbull.

One of the six out of sixty-three boats to finish in Class III of the Fastnet Race, 1979.
Winner in the Restricted Division.

All but one of the 1947 Jesus College crew celebrating the 50th anniversary of winning the Grand Challenge Cup at Henley, 5 July 1997.

From left to right: Denis, John Whalley, David Odhams, Chris Barton, Des Harriss (cox, kneeling), Geoff Thomas, Bym Rogers, Larry Whalley (Captain).

Denis and Marjorie visiting Father Poletti at his Fan Ling Church.

A fine Catholic priest who devoted his life to the people of South China and Hong Kong.

Wedding day – 19 February 1952 at St John's Cathedral, Hong Kong.

Lord Wilson of Tillyorn and Lady Wilson came to our 40th wedding anniversary party.

Marjorie photographs the family at the dawn of the new millennium, Fiji, 1 January 2000.
From left to right: Denis, Gemma (granddaughter), Diana (daughter), Lucy (daughter),
Fred (son-in-law), Andrew (grandson), Alison (daughter) and Katharine (granddaughter).
Jennifer (daughter) and Ben (grandson) were not there.

'. . . an endless chain of paddles . . .' Irrigation on Lantau, 1950.

'. . . threshed into large tubs on the spot . . .' Tai Po, 1950.

Harvesting the second rice crop below Lion Rock in the Sha Tin valley, 1950.
Today 600,000 people live in Sha Tin.

Tolo Harbour from near the Lookout.
Taken in 1954 before the devastation caused by taking fill for the Plover Cove dam.
Photo by Liu Yan Sum, a keen photographer and VR of Sheung Shui.
He had exhibited the photo and gave it to me after the exhibition.

Denis, as District Officer of Tai Po, witnesses the swearing in of the officers of the Sha Tin Rural Committee, Chairman Ng Chung Chi, centre, with hand raised, 14 April 1956.

Acting Governor, Claude Burgess, visits the Islands in 1959.

Left to right: Denis, Deputy District Commissioner, Kong Ping Yau, His Excellency, Ronald Holmes, District Commissioner, James Hayes, District Officer.

The Governor lunches at Island House with staff in the New Territories, 1971.

Left to right: Reggie Remedios, Patrick Williamson, Harnam Grewal, Ken Rolfe, Harold Kwok, Gloria Barretto, Ian Macpherson, Denis, Sir David Trench, Marjorie, Tony Eason, (unknown in background), Billy Estrada, Haider Barma, C. C. Lo.

The Governor attends Tin Hau Festival celebrations in Yuen Long.

Taken at the home of Mr Chiu Lut Shau, a prominent rural leader in the district, 1972. Left to right: Mrs Chan Yat Sun, Chan Yat Sun, Chairman of the Heung Yee Kuk, Chiu Lut Shau, Mrs Chiu, Sir David Trench, Leonard Chiu, Mrs Stephen Chiu, Stephen Chiu, Ann Macpherson, Mrs Leonard Chiu, Ian Macpherson, Denis.

Denis as Commissioner of
Transport and Cheung Yan Lung
at the inauguration of the Lantau
Bus Company Limited, 1966.

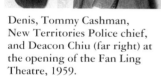

Denis, Tommy Cashman,
New Territories Police chief,
and Deacon Chiu (far right) at
the opening of the Fan Ling
Theatre, 1959.

Left to right: Father Lerder,
Chow Li Ping and Denis on
Cheung Chau Island at a Caritas
low-cost housing project, 1972.

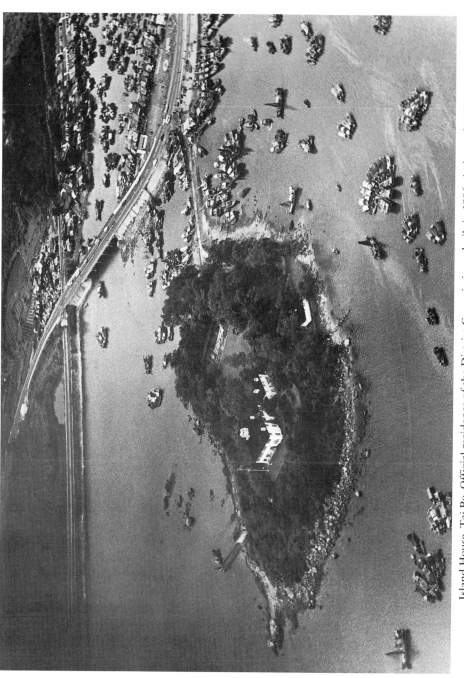

Island House, Tai Po, Official residence of the District Commissioner built in 1906. As it was in 1972.

Lord MacLehose of Beoch escorts Marjorie as Chairman of
the Juvenile Care Centre Charity Ball, 1973.

Queen Elizabeth's visit to Aberdeen.
Left to right: Marjorie, Mrs K. S. Lo, Lord MacLehose, K. S. Lo, Queen Elizabeth, Prince Philip,
Ted Nichols, Director of Fisheries, Lady MacLehose, Denis, Lady-in-Waiting.

Sir Edward Youde meeting the Chairman of the New York and Hong Kong Stock Exchanges.
Left to right: Denis, Ronald Li, Sir Edward Youde, John Phelan Jr., 1986.

Eric Ho, Bim Davies, John Chan and Denis at the Temple of Heaven, December 1984.

Left to right: Ms Suen Fong-chung, Mrs Chan Fung Chau, Lu Ping, Denis, Hilton Cheong-Leen, Woo Hon Fai, Mok Wah Chiu and K. S. Lo at the signing of the Joint Declaration on the future of Hong Kong, Beijing, December 1984.

1

Growing up in China

A few years ago, I was asked to speak to the Royal Asiatic Society in Hong Kong about growing up in Hong Kong. I said I did not grow up in Hong Kong but in China. The change of title did not seem to bother them. To compose a talk on the first thirteen years of your life, when there are practically no books to consult and friends from those days are scattered or gone, was a challenge. To the challenge was added an audience much more knowledgeable than I on the history of the area. I hoped I could get away with it because nobody could check on much that I had to say. This challenge started me on writing about past recollections. It turned out to be quite fun.

I was born

I did not start life in China but in Hong Kong — at the Matilda Hospital in Hong Kong. My father was working in the Methodist Mission in Foshan at the time, running Wah Ying School. This school was founded in 1903 near to a hospital, also run by the mission, which was founded in 1881. The hospital, now known officially as the Number One People's Hospital, but spoken of as the *Chun Do Yi Yuen*, or Methodist Hospital, celebrated its hundredth anniversary in 1982. The school, now known as the Number One Middle School but spoken of still as *Wah Ying*, celebrated its ninetieth anniversary in December 1993.

January 1926 was towards the end of the General Strike, when all Chinese were urged to boycott any form of service for foreigners, and was accompanied by incidents of unrest in China and in Hong Kong itself. It was no time for a pregnant woman to remain in China unless it was essential. So my mother had come to the comparative safety of Hong Kong for the birth.

I cannot recall the event though by a curious coincidence my first memories are of the Matilda Hospital. I was four at the time and had developed a roaring appendix. It had to come out.

Now a journey up the Peak by the Peak Tram was no great novelty, but to go up by a Peak Car was a great adventure. We went to the hospital, and there I went through the traumatic experience of being gassed by having ether poured on a mask while I was held down against my protesting hands. No doubt a more modern anaesthetic would have been less traumatic but it would also have been less memorable.

The events surrounding this experience allow me to take you to Cheung Chau for it was to Cheung Chau that I was taken for convalescence.

Cheung Chau and summer holidays

Cheung Chau lies a few miles to the west of Hong Kong and throughout the 1930s, was a rest resort for missionaries from South China. In these days of universal air-conditioning, it is difficult to appreciate the trials of the summer in Hong Kong, let alone the hotter and more humid conditions in South China. The typical tour for a missionary was five years followed by a furlough in England during which the missionary toured the country speaking about his experiences. During the hot summers, missionaries' families would descend on the resorts of Hong Kong. Two were particularly popular — Cheung Chau and Sunset Peak high on Lantau, a much larger, mountainous island west of Hong Kong.

On Lantau, a number of bungalows had been built and are still there. They are at the top of the mountain to enjoy the lower temperatures which the wealthy sought on the Peak on Hong Kong Island. We slept in our bungalows but had our meals in the common dining-room which was also used for meetings and services. As children, we spent the whole time out of doors swimming in pools in the streams. My most vivid memory of Lantau was being there in a typhoon. We must have had some warning of the approach of the typhoon as the shutters were closed, so that the lamps had to be lit — there was no electricity of course. We did not have long to wait before the storm hit. The noise was terrific and the wind blew quantities of water under the door into the bungalow. It seemed to go on for a long time. The next day the shutters were opened, the lamps put out and we emerged into a battered but recognizable environment.

On the whole we preferred Cheung Chau, and it was to Cheung Chau that I was taken after my appendix operation. During my stay in hospital when I had to stay in bed for some time, I had forgotten how to walk or even stand up! I protested that I could not possibly walk up to the bungalow on Cheung Chau so a sedan chair was sent for. I had not seen one on Cheung Chau before, though they were a common sight in Hong Kong and were used to carry children up Lantau Peak. I was lured out of my invalid bed by the present of some stunning bathing shoes. These were brightly coloured rubber shoes that were meant to protect your feet from stones on the beach. I do not remember ever actually using such shoes but, with the sound of the waves lapping on the beach, they were enough to remind me of the delights of swimming, and messing about in the sand, and playing with model boats — the largest of which had been made specially by the building contractor in Foshan.

Swimming played a central part in our lives on Cheung Chau. I can remember my first unaided swim which was rewarded by the present of a trumpet — much regretted by my parents in subsequent days. The beach was the highlight of our lives. We would walk through the thick pine woods across the island from our bungalows, down through the screw pine to the beach. The smells of the pine trees, of the screw pine and of the beach and the sea still evoke the thrill of arriving at the beach and dashing into the sea.

Some of the grown-ups were able to swim out to a large rock off the Evening Beach (Kwun Yam Wan) to which the Residents' Association had fixed some iron rungs for climbing out. I was only able to achieve such an exploit when I had come back to work in 1950, but by then the iron rungs had rusted away. The association also arranged with some fishermen, who fished at night, to anchor their boat in the bay and fix steps and a diving-board for us to use by day. This did come in reach and I can still recall the thrill of climbing up the steps after the swim-out. The boat had a delicious smell of fish and sea water and was swarming with little black creatures with lots of legs. It was a great place to play as well as being an excellent diving-platform.

The Morning Beach (Nam Tam Wan) was much smaller but it too had a large rock equipped with rungs to climb out on. We did not go often to the Police Beach (Tung Wan), which adjoined the Evening Beach, though I do remember seeing their diving-boat there washed up high and dry after a typhoon.

The village had not changed much when I first visited it after the war. The walk up to the bungalows was past the market and through the narrow lanes with their shops selling fishing tackle, torches, salt fish, groceries and other odds and ends. We passed the power station of the Cheung Chau Electric Company which thumped away at night. We never had electricity in our bungalows because it was too expensive. Once out of the village, the scene was one of devastation for all the pine trees, which had covered the island before the war, had been felled for fuel.

The village was confined to the narrow isthmus so that once you left this behind and climbed up, you found yourself among small hills and scattered bungalows. I can remember the building of the community hall which was used as a chapel and meeting place. The only sounds round the bungalows were the wind in the trees and the waves on the beaches and rocks. From the bungalow that we used most often there was a magnificent view over towards Ling Ting Island. On our last visit in 1938, we were able to see the Royal Navy's motor torpedo-boats travelling at fantastic speeds with a most impressive roar.

The mission compound at Foshan

Cheung Chau was for holidays but our real life was in Foshan. We lived in a spacious house, known still as the White House, on the edge of the compound and adjoining a small creek and paddy-fields. When I saw the house again in 1987, it had shrunk! The mission contained a hospital and nurses training school, a primary and secondary school with workshops for the boys, an innovation which was years ahead of its time. Nearly all the staff were Cantonese but a doctor, Dr Philip Early, the head nursing sister, Kathleen Banks, and a few of the teachers were from England. Only the English knew English and they were all taught Cantonese full-time for two years on arrival. I often regret that I was unable to enjoy this period of study. This time was sufficient for students to learn not only to speak but also to read the classics, or the Bible, and write speeches or sermons depending on your calling — missionary or Hong Kong Government Cadet.

As children, our first language was Cantonese and we always used this among ourselves. We spoke to our parents in English. When we were on furlough in 1933, my sister and I slept in the same bedroom. After the lights were out, we used to chatter away in Cantonese, much to the amusement of the relatives listening outside the door.

All our social contacts were with Chinese associated with the school or hospital. Agnes Chan was a jolly nursing sister; Dr Mary Chan was one of the first Western-trained doctors who was still alive at the age of eighty-three when my brother and I visited in 1987. She was as sprightly as ever, crying out, as we climbed the stairs to her room, 'Denis, you look like your father and Jeremy like your mother!'

The Foshan household was quite large with an amah to look after us children (who many years later also looked after my own children), a cook, who was husband of the amah, and one or two others to help with the washing and housework. When the time came, I went to the primary school with all the other children of my age — a single very fair head among a sea of black. I can visualize the classroom in which we had our lessons and the playground outside. The textbooks were very thin and had paper covers so that it was possible for the history master to roll one up and give us a good clip over the head if we were being particularly stupid. English was not taught in the primary school, only to the senior students in the secondary school. I was sent to sit among the senior girls to learn my English grammar from my mother who taught the subject.

We had school uniforms of a sort still seen in Hong Kong, but the school only supplied the material to ensure that everybody had the same colour. Ours was a beautiful pale blue only slightly darker than the Cambridge blue. Quantities of the new material would arrive and then be made up into the smartest of outfits.

Paddy-fields and dragon boats

We would walk to school through paddy-fields which for most of the year were flooded for the rice. Small fish abounded in these fields though I never caught any. The cycle of the rice crops was familiar to everybody. First, a scattering of seeds in a small patch, then, when the seedlings were about six inches above the water, the planting out of the seedlings. Then nothing much until harvest — and there were two harvests a year. Water was supplied to the paddy-fields by a complicated irrigation system that involved pumping water up from the creeks. These pumps were an endless chain of paddles which were pulled up a trough, whose lower end was in the creek, and which discharged into the fields. Some pumps were small and driven by a man using his arms as extensions of long wooden handles attached to extended spokes of the upper wheel round which the chain of paddles rotated. Others were driven by three or four men treading spokes protruding from the axle of the driving wheel. For the winter harvest, the water was drained out so that the rice could be cut and threshed into large tubs on the spot. Where there had been acres of water, now there were dry fields of stubble and stacks of rice straw drying out. As the fields dried, we would take short cuts across them. We also found that the mud was soft enough to make into the mud equivalent of snowballs. This led to splendid games in which factions would build forts with the straw and bombard the enemies with mud balls.

As children, we did not go often into the town except to walk to church. This we did along streets paved with enormous stone slabs laid five at a time along the road and then five across. The roads were elevated above the fields and along the creeks with which the whole delta is riddled. In times of flood, these dykes protected the fields. Occasionally they would be breached. A general alarm would then be raised, as the whole population rushed to repair the damage before the countryside was flooded.

The creeks, one of which passed at the foot of our garden, carried the commerce of the villages and, in the fifth month, the dragon boats. The festival of the fifth moon is of equal importance to the Mid-Autumn Festival and only slightly less than that of the New Year. It commemorates the life of a righteous official (*Wat Yuen* in Cantonese) who, in 314 BC, drowned himself in despair at the iniquity of the authorities. Dragon boats are the descendants of the boats of the villagers seeking to comfort the spirit of their fallen hero. For weeks before the actual festival, dragon boats would be paddled along the creeks of the delta and, from time to time, one would pass our garden. These were magnificent vessels bearing only superficial resemblance to those used today for racing in Hong Kong. The largest had over 100 paddlers. In the centre was an enormous drum with two drummers. Gongs were placed at other points. Large ornamental, cylindrical umbrellas were beautifully embroidered and with little mirrors as added decoration. They had a frightful time negotiating the bend in the creek outside our house, a feat which was only accomplished with tremendous shouting that added to the cacophony already supplied by the percussion. As the fifth month approached, we were on the lookout for the dragon boats which we could hear long before we could see them. With the first sounds of the drums and gongs, we would drop everything and rush down to the gap in the bamboo hedge from which we had a grandstand view.

Last visit to Foshan

All these events occurred in the period from about 1928 to 1933. After that, we went on leave from which I returned to school in North China. I did, however, make one last journey to Foshan in the spring of 1938. Normally our long school holidays were in the winter but, with the Japanese war starting in 1937, we had a short holiday that winter — when we nearly all stayed at school — and a long holiday in the following spring. It was wonderful to return to the old house and try and pick up a bit of Cantonese again. Canton was under attack by the Japanese who would fly over and bomb the city from time to time. We were close enough to hear the bombs but not to suffer from them. Nevertheless, we had a sandbagged air raid shelter in the garden. Out of curiosity, I went into this gloomy recess one day only to scurry out as soon as I was able to make out my surroundings. I have never seen such a dense cloud of mosquitoes. Thank goodness we never had to use this shelter.

Our departure for Hong Kong that spring was dramatic. From the hospital, we took the ancient hospital motor boat down the creeks to Canton. We found the river steamer for Hong Kong moored in the fast-flowing stream. It was surrounded by an impenetrable mob of sampans carrying people fleeing from the Japanese attack on Canton which was expected any day. Our motor boat could not get to the gangway so we transferred to a sampan. We approached the ladder from downstream as most of the boats were tied to the steamer upstream. We soon found out why because as each sampan cast off from the ladder, another — aided by the stream — pushed its way in from upstream. We could make no headway. The only possible approach was from the bows. As we worked our way slowly down, we saw that the captain was getting worried by the crowds swarming on board. He had to sail or be swamped. Our luggage was manhandled across the intervening sampans, but my father would not allow us to be passed along in the same way, which I thought was a pity. The captain saw us and waited only until our sampan at last made the steps. He then gave the order for his crew to chop through the mooring ropes of all the sampans still tied on. Once freed of these, he weighed anchor and set off for Hong Kong — an overnight journey.

P&O to England: Canadian Pacific to China

In 1933 my father was due for leave, so the whole family, now comprising four children and parents, set off on the P&O *Rawalpindi*, a ship which was later converted to be an armed merchantman during the war and was sunk by a U-boat after a gallant action. Travel by sea was the most commonly used way to reach Europe. From about 1933, one could go faster by taking the Trans-Siberian railway. Fast mail was marked 'Via Siberia' on the envelopes. The sea journey took five weeks. Going by sea, we started with four days at sea to Singapore and trips to the Botanical Gardens there. Then on to Penang, Colombo, Aden, through the Suez Canal perhaps with a stop at Marseilles, where some in a hurry got on the train through France to England, a stop at Gibraltar and thence to Plymouth where we got off for a train to Herefordshire. Most passengers went on to Tilbury in London.

There was a leisurely routine about the trip. Beef tea was served on the deck mid-morning and tea in the afternoon. An enterprising steward rounded up a number of children to help him gather up the cups and plates and rewarded us with magnificent Orders of Chivalry. We usually found some acquaintance in the ports or fellow missionaries. Aden was a coaling port where a ceaseless stream of labourers carried basket after basket of coal on board. We had to keep portholes shut to keep the coal dust out — and the heat in, for there was no air-conditioning. At sea, we had a good deal of freedom and were taken on exploratory trips to such places as the bridge and the engine-room. On the bridge, we were shown the compass that a sailor was steering by. This mystified me because there was no compass needle, just a card with the points of the compass. It was many years before I understood that the magnets were suspended below the card and the trick was to keep a black line at the front of the compass lined up with a mark on the card, indicating the course to be steered. In the engine-room, we saw the huge pistons of the steam engine driving the propeller shaft and walked down to the very end of the tunnel in which it turned. The heat was terrific.

In 1934, leave was up. My father and I returned early to get me into school in September. The two of us travelled by the scenic route, first on the Canadian Pacific ship, the *Duchess of Bedford* which we boarded at Liverpool and which took us across the Atlantic to Montreal, passing, but not hitting an iceberg off Newfoundland, shaped like the headdress of a Native American. Then by Canadian Pacific Railway for three days and four nights across Canada to Vancouver. That was a glorious journey. The first day was through pine forests and by lakes. The second was across endless prairie country and the third through the Rocky Mountains. At the back of the train, there was an observation coach from which we had an excellent view of the scenery. Each evening, beds were made up and each morning they were folded up.

From Vancouver we sailed on another Canadian Pacific ship, the *Empress of Asia,* to Shanghai — a long journey which must have included a stop in Japan. Some of the sailors began to pull my leg by recounting how the men going to the crows nest, high on the foremast, had to leap from the rigging which only reached the mast well above the lookout point. Often they would fall to the deck and be killed, I was told, to be washed overboard in the morning. I got so concerned about this that it was only after I was taken to the compartment in the bows and saw the men actually climbing up inside the mast that I was convinced that the story was a fairy tale.

A funny thing about sojourns with my father was that he introduced me to simple gastronomic delights. During my convalescence in the Matilda Hospital from appendicitis it was kippers and on the Trans-Pacific trip it was celery, curry and Worcestershire sauce in the soup to prevent seasickness. All have been favourites ever since! And he patiently read from *The Swiss Family Robinson* each evening.

Chefoo schools

From Shanghai we took a coastal steamer north to Chefoo. Chefoo is the name of a small village on a bluff of land connected to the mainland of the Shandong peninsula by a sand spit. The school was named after this village, though the town, in which it lies, is now called Yantai after the nearby walled city dating from the Ming dynasty. The China Inland Mission had established primary and secondary schools for European and American children from all over China. There were about 100 children in the primary school, 100 boys in the Boys' School and 100 girls in the Girls' School. The Prep School, as the primary school was called, was in an old building and I can well remember the misery of homesickness. After tea at six o'clock we were sent to bed, which seemed ridiculous. My father stayed a few days before sailing for Hong Kong but I saw very little of him. When he left, I felt abandoned. Others even younger suffered the same fate but seemed to survive.

In fact, these schools were run by a most devoted staff of missionaries who took great care of us — body and soul. They were of a fundamentalist persuasion and expected very high moral behaviour from all of us. The standard of teaching was high and the students got good marks in the Oxford School Certificate Examinations. Pa Bruce was the headmaster of the Boys' School but it is Gordon Martin, a classics scholar, who I remember best. He had rowed at Oxford and had had two boats built for competition, the *Hero* and *Leander*. The boat race between these two crews was one of the highlights of the celebrations of Lammemuir Day — marking the day a ship of that name sailed from England carrying the first China Inland Mission missionaries in the nineteenth century. I cannot help feeling that it was one of his lantern-slide lectures about Oxford and its rowing that planted in my mind a seed of desire to participate in this excellent sport. He was also an accomplished artist at illustrating stories that he would write. In those days, we had no radio or television entertainment so he would read books to us. I particularly remember his keeping us enthralled in his reading of *The Cloister and the Hearth* though I cannot remember the story itself.

The four seasons

School life was regulated to fit the climate. The winters were bitter and so cold that one year we came back from holidays to find the sea frozen over. We walked from the docks to school over the sea. The summers were glorious. I suppose they were hot as I remember hearing of temperatures of 100°F (38°C) or more but the air was dry and on the whole not so hot as Hong Kong. The sea was perfect for swimming, which was allowed once it had reached the temperature of 64°F (18°C) for three successive days. Spring and autumn were intermediate — considerably colder than the summer but not the freezing temperatures of the winter. To cope with these extremes in climate, we had three sets of clothing — khaki shirts and shorts for summer, wool jackets and shorts for spring and autumn and thick wool jackets and plus-fours for the winter. The school buildings were also designed to cope with these extremes. The spacious verandahs round the playground of the Boys' School kept the hall and common rooms cool in the summer. In the winter, wooden frames with glass were put up in the arches of the verandahs giving an extra layer of insulation while the central heating was going full blast.

There was always some excitement with each change of season. Watching the removal of the glass frames on the verandahs heralded the abandonment of our plus-fours. The production of khaki shirts and shorts meant swimming and rowing was not far off. I can remember so clearly gazing out of the bedroom window across the glassy calm sea in the early mornings, wondering if it had reached the magic 64°. In the autumn, the halcyon summer days would end abruptly with the 'breaking-up storm', a wild blow whose climatic explanation I cannot remember. Then came the first snow and the wooden frames for the verandahs were brought out again.

When I was at the school, a new building was completed for the Prep School and a new classroom block was built where the boys from the Boys' School and the girls from the Girls' School could take coeducational lessons. Reading Jean Moore's account of her days at Chefoo, I learnt that boys and girls were not only kept apart in their sleeping accommodation but also for lessons. This had been dropped by the time I went, so it was strange to find myself in a school for boys only when I went to England later on. We only mixed for lessons and church (where we sat apart except those in the choir — which I joined) and for the rest we existed in entirely separate schools.

In this school, we were also kept pretty isolated from the local population. We did not learn the Shandong language, though the teachers were entirely bilingual. We did not go into town but would come across Chinese on our walks in the hills. Here we would see men pushing incredible loads on huge wheelbarrows, the goods carried on platforms on either side of the massive central wheel. The handles of the barrow were joined by a strap which the men carried over their shoulders. Others carried great loads on bamboo poles. Mules were also beasts of burden. There were no motorable roads outside the town.

When the Japanese overran Chefoo, they set up a roadblock right outside the school and we would try to engage the soldiers in chat. The Japanese controlled the town but the hills were infested with guerrillas and we could occasionally hear firing in the night. The Japanese left us alone at that time for they were not at war with Britain. I had left China before Pearl Harbour, but once the Japanese were at war with the British and Americans, the school was closed down and students and teachers shipped off to another location as part of a prison camp.

Out of school

In the Prep School, our lives were confined to the school area and, in the summer, the beaches in front. We also went for long hikes in the hills behind the schools, but it was the beach that was most fun. On Sundays, we walked in crocodile the couple of miles along the waterfront to a church in the town — most going to the Union Church but some went to the Church of England. I do not recall any Roman Catholics among us and doubt whether I had heard of them then. Only recently I met a lady whose mother went to a Catholic school at Chefoo and attended a Catholic church there.

1935 was a memorable year because it was the Silver Jubilee of King George V. The British Consul in Chefoo put on a great fair to which we all went. Here we were given banknotes specially drawn for the occasion, which entitled us to rides and ice-cream and so forth. The banknotes were so attractive that I could not bring myself to spend them all and kept some for years.

From time to time, ships of the Royal Navy called at Chefoo and there would be sure to be some entertainment. Sometimes, it was open day on the ship; once they dressed up as pirates and came ashore on our beaches and gave us a party there. We also played football against them. The main port for the Royal Navy was Wei Hai Wei (now Weihai), some sixty miles down the coast. Chefoo was the summer home for the American fleet, who would have come up from the Philippines, and who also took us on boating expeditions to nearby islands.

Holidays at school

After two years in the Prep School, I was old enough to go to the Boys' School. The transfer took place during the summer holidays which I, like many others, was spending at school. As I said, children came to these schools from all over China. Most were children of missionaries, but businessmen also sent their children there. Some came from nearby — Qingdao, or Tianjin, or Shanghai. These children could go home for the month-long summer holidays and some even went for the two weeks at Easter. A party of us came from Hong Kong and South China. As it would take us ten days to get to Foshan, we only made the journey once a year during the two-month long winter holidays. Others came from so far away in Yunnan Province that they never went home. So there were always a good many children in the schools during the holidays.

These holidays were made very enjoyable times for us. In the summer, it would be swimming and tennis. In the winter, some went skating but at all times the staff would think of amusements and games, hobbies and outings which came in great variety.

In 1937 my father had planned a trip to Peking, but the outbreak of hostilities with the Japanese prevented this. Instead, my mother came to Chefoo for the summer holidays and we all stayed at the Missionary Home. This was a simple hostel where we had our meals and slept, but that was about all. There was an Anglican church nearby and I recall the atmosphere of peace and reverence at my first Evensong there. During the day, we would be off to the beach annex of the Chefoo Club where there were rowing-boats and canoes. From nine in the morning until lunch-time and all afternoon, a crowd of us were in and out of the water, rowing out to the raft which was a converted junk with diving-boards. I got so brown that summer that the mark of the swimming trunks was still visible at Christmas time.

Holidays at home

A great part of school life was the holidays at home. Home at this time was in Tung Shan Terrace off Stubbs Road in Hong Kong, when my father was building the Chinese Methodist Church in Wan Chai — the triangular red brick building that stood at the junction of Hennessy Road and Johnston Road. This was home not in a flat but a three-storey house, with a garden overlooking Happy Valley. At the back, we had access to Bowen Road which was a safe place to play as there were no motor vehicles. Those holidays I remember chiefly for rambles up to Sir Cecil's Ride and a major hike over to Tai Tam from Wong Nei Chung Gap. And we went to a school pantomime at the Central British School (now King George V School) where the bad guy called himself 'ZBW my middle name is Trouble You' — ZBW being the call-sign of the embryo Radio Television Hong Kong. We had our first family car here, an Austin Seven with a folding roof, and went for picnics to the beaches at Repulse Bay and Big Wave Bay and at Stanley where a new prison was being built. Although it was winter in Hong Kong, the climate was comfortable for us from the north and we had no hesitation in swimming.

Our journeys home in the winter holidays were considerable undertakings. Of course, there was no air travel; nor was rail travel possible. Instead, we went by sea on the B&S ships of the China Navigation Line. These were coasters of about seven thousand tons which made their way up and down the China coast, carrying cargoes of all sorts, a small number of passengers in cabins and a much larger number of deck passengers. Sometimes, we were able to get a ship that went all the way from Chefoo to Hong Kong, but often we had to get off in Shanghai and wait in the China Inland Mission hostel for a suitable connection. Some luckless schoolmaster had to accompany some twenty or so children — more as far as Shanghai — on these journeys. They were carefree days and I have often wondered how we all survived. We would sit up on the taffrail undeterred by the possibility of toppling over into the sea. I remember getting into frightful trouble from practising throwing a penknife into the cabin bulkhead. In the ports we watched the loading and unloading of cargo, listening to the varied languages of the coast in Fuzhou, Xiamen and Shantou. It was always a thrill to catch the odd Cantonese phrase as we neared home. At one port, we took on board a large number of pigs which were housed in pens on the deck forward of the accommodation. The loading of these pigs involved tremendous squealing generated by the beating of the pigs to make them move. We thought this was cruel so, in the evening, when the loading was finished, several of us sought out the bamboo poles that had been used for beating the pigs and threw them overboard. At sea we would come across massive fishing fleets. On one occasion, our ship was in collision with one of these fishing junks and took the crew on board. We heard that one man had been lost but the rest rescued, including the family of the owner. They looked a miserable wet group on board. I imagine there was a good deal of argument about whose fault the collision was and bargaining about compensation. In any event, the ship was stopped for several hours before the fishermen were taken off by one of the other boats.

Storms and pirates

These journeys were made in the winter so there was no danger from typhoons, but the north-east monsoon produces almost continuous gales in the Taiwan Strait and China Sea. This monsoon sped us on our way south but held us up on the way back. The little ships bucketed about all over the place, but any seasickness was soon over. It was great fun hanging over the very bows in a big sea watching the ship's stem come right out of the water and plunge back. The year when the sea froze over we found the first ice in the form of tiny plates like fish-scales. These got larger and larger until we found drifts of serious ice. The ship had to take one or two runs at some of these drifts and we had a great struggle to get alongside when we reached the port in Chefoo.

Pirates were common on the China coast, but only once was a school party involved in a piracy. This was the Shanghai party travelling back to school on the *Tungchow* in, I think, January 1936. The pirates, believing that this ship had a load of silver, got on board in Shanghai as deck passengers. The deck passengers were segregated from the cabin area and bridge by bars and locked gates while armed White Russian guards patrolled the decks near the bars day and night. Once at sea, the pirates killed the White Russian guard and took over the ship. The ship disappeared for days. Nobody had any idea where on the thousands of miles of China coast to look for her. As time wore on, the distance she could travel extended until it could be anywhere from Tianjin to Hanoi. The Royal Navy had an aircraft-carrier based in Hong Kong and this was drafted into the hunt. An aircraft from HMS *Hermes* spotted a ship like the *Tungchow* anchored in Bias Bay (Daya Bay) which was a well-known haunt of China coast pirates. It was indeed the *Tungchow* and the pirates, seeing the plane swoop over, realized that they had better decamp. Once they were away, the Captain sailed for Hong Kong where he arrived a few hours later. Although the pirates escaped, they had a frustrating piracy. They had got the wrong ship. The silver was on another ship which delivered its cargo safely. The *Tungchow* carried no silver but a cargo of oranges. The pirates broke open the crates in their hunt for the silver so that the ship was running with oranges which the boys gathered in quantities. The pirates did no harm to the children but at first kept them shut up in the passenger accommodation. You can imagine what tales the Shanghai party had to tell when we all got back to school.

We leave China

In 1939, my father's tour was up and he decided, after twenty-five years, to retire from the mission field. He was in his mid-fifties and few stayed so long. Today, this sounds an early retiring age but today we have the untold advantage of constant air-conditioning to temper the severity of our summers, and much greater control over diseases. The advance of the Japanese and the threatening war situation in Europe may well have influenced his decision too.

In any event, my parents and our younger sister set off from Foshan while my brother, other sister and I set off from Chefoo on the last of our journeys on a B&S coaster for Shanghai. My parents travelled up from Hong Kong on a Canadian Pacific steamer, the *Empress of Russia,* which we joined in Shanghai. We had a few days' wait when we took advantage of the mountainous inflation. My purchase was a tennis racket at the old price of only a few dollars. By this time, Shanghai had been occupied by the Japanese though they were still at peace with Britain and America. In the occupied parts of the city, security was tight, especially round the docks, and we had to pass through several checkpoints manned by pretty rough soldiers. Once at sea, those worries were left behind, but as a postscript, when we sailed from Yokohama a few days later, we found ourselves in the midst of large-scale manoeuvres by the Japanese fleet with accompanying aircraft firing at and bombing targets not far from us.

Now, more than fifty years later, I find myself living on Bowen Road along which we used to play in the winter holidays. For some years, my wife and I lived across the valley from the Matilda Hospital where I was born and where I forgot how to walk. The other day my brother and I went on a visit to Foshan. The bungalow where we often stayed on Cheung Chau was still there last time I visited the island. In all these places, I have seen traces of the past. I have yet to get back to Chefoo.

2

Sojourn in Britain

Peacetime in the English countryside

We landed in England in the middle of August 1939 and went straight to a thatched cottage near my father's sister, who lived in the small village of Eastnor in Herefordshire. The house was out in the country, up a drive not fit for cars. There was no electricity and only one tap in the kitchen. It was two miles from the town of Ledbury where my father had been born and in which he had relatives yet. The harvest was in full swing with the binders circling the ever smaller patch of wheat and, at the last, the rabbits bounding out to be clobbered by the youth for supper.

On Sunday, we went into the Methodist Church in Ledbury where we met more relatives, in particular a couple of handsome young men, Bob and Jack, sons of my father's cousin. They each tipped me half a crown — untold wealth. As August came to an end, the blackberries were ready for picking and we spent hours tackling the blackberry bushes all round. Our pickings were kept for the call of the fishmonger who weighed them out and paid us three farthings a punnet. Farthings, a quarter of a penny, had dropped out of common use though they still existed. If his calculations showed we needed a farthing in payment, we got it.

This was still a time of peace and a more peaceful scene than the heart of the pre-war English countryside would be difficult to imagine. There was no sign of war. There was no talk of war, at least to us children. Then on the first Sunday in September, war was declared at eleven o'clock.

We were at church and my father was preaching. It was one of his sermons that I remember. He recounted the horrors of the war that had been going on in China for two years and graphically brought home to these good country people the barbarity of the massacre of Nanjing. They were a sombre lot at the usual gossip after the service.

We did see some army trucks from time to time and I am sure the radio was full of war talk. The only manifestation I recall was when a cousin of mine called to ask my father to marry her to this fine young man before he went off to the Royal Air Force. Then the fishmonger, an old man of forty-one, was called up. The young men had gone already and in Ledbury we heard that children evacuees had arrived from London to be safe from the expected air raids.

I had more important things on my mind. I was being fitted up to go to school. For weekdays we were expected to wear sports jackets and flannel trousers. At the age of thirteen, I insisted on long trousers to show I was grown-up. For Sundays we had to wear black jackets and black pinstriped trousers. A trunk was packed with all the requirements from a list supplied from the school and sent off by rail PLA — Passenger's Luggage in Advance. I was given clear instructions on how to change stations at Birmingham and board the special train for school. I had one suitcase and sure enough someone offered to carry it for me from one station to another — a stranger who expected sixpence for his trouble.

The special train duly came in and I boarded, a new boy, among a great many others returning from their summer holidays.

Boarding school

The school was Kingswood School, a Methodist foundation for sons of Methodist parsons, though most of the boys were not. Its premises at Bath were requisitioned by the Admiralty and the school was evacuated to the tiny school town of Uppingham in Rutland, the smallest county in England. This operation was only possible through the generosity of the headmaster of Uppingham School, who said he could provide classrooms and accommodation for a school of our size and offered to share the use of the school chapel and assembly hall. The gymnasium became our dining-room. Uppingham was a much grander school than ours. They wore black jackets and pinstriped trousers every day, morning coats and boaters on Sundays.

The two schools in fact had little contact. Even though we lived in one of their houses, our studies were separate. Both schools had to have two or more boys to a study, thus breaking an old tradition that Uppingham boys each had his own study.

School was pretty rough until I settled in and made a few friends. I had been at boarding school in China so was spared the pangs of homesickness that affected some of the other new boys. I was soon introduced to the mysteries of rugby football — not that the rules were explained. I knew roughly what it was about but had no idea what I was expected to do. When the ball landed in my hands, I was so terrified that I gave it a colossal kick which fortunately went miles up the field and found touch right near the oppositions goal-line. Everybody cheered. I thought this was fun. It became even more fun when a senior boy in our house said, 'I think you will make a fine hooker.' I had no idea what a hooker was, but he taught me that it was my job to be in the middle of the front row of forwards in the set scrums and hook the ball back to our side. From then on, I thought most of the game was pretty rough with a few brilliant sprinters on the wings and the rest rather clumsy louts. Refinement was being the hooker and getting the ball back in the scrums.

To take the rugby story to its end, I found myself in the Under Fourteen's school team, then the Colts, Under Sixteen's, eventually the second and finally the First Fifteen. In the latter, we played other nearby schools. This involved wonderful bus journeys to strange places, huge teas after the matches and singsongs in the bus on the way home in the dark. There were other great schools nearby who would not give us fixtures with their First Fifteens but only their Second Fifteen. I only remember Oundle was one such who entertained us royally. When we trounced their Second Fifteen by pushing their scrum over the five-yard line, they gallantly vouchsafed us a game against their First Fifteen. We were duly humiliated by a brilliant wing three quarter who could run twice as fast as any of us.

Being a boarding school, we had a good deal of spare time and considerable freedom in how we spent it. My two favourite pastimes were playing the piano and doing woodwork. I had started the piano at school in China and found that I liked it and could do it well enough to enjoy practising without thinking it was a chore. At Kingswood, we had a music master who encouraged us to look at all sorts of music we had not seen — all classical but catholic in choice. You could hum a tune to ask if you could learn that piece. He would try a few bars of various pieces until he got the one you wanted and then rolled off in ecstasy until he woke up to see you still waiting. There was a music school at Uppingham which we could use. It was a small two-storey building crammed with cubicles just big enough for a piano and there I spent hour after hour either polishing up a piece for my lesson or exploring any music I found lying around. I remember particularly a book that had lost its cover with some music that was marvellous but anonymous. I fumbled through page after page. It was some time later that I found that this was a collection of some of the easier Beethoven Sonatas.

The carpentry shop was another favourite spot. The carpentry master was a little Welshman who encouraged us to make useful things in the traditional way, each job just a little more difficult than the last. He would award a couple of new chisels for the best work. I remember the excitement when I saw in the show at the end of term, that a magazine rack that I had made contained two fine gleaming chisels.

Cycling was another favourite pastime. During the war, there were few motor vehicles on the Rutland roads so that we had no hesitation in riding our bikes as far as we liked. A naughty thing I did a few times was to ride over to Corby where there was a fine cinema. Cinemas were forbidden territory, but it was fun to buy a ticket and a Mars Bar and settle down for an afternoon's forbidden pleasure. The longest journey I did in one day was to cycle across England to Ledbury in Herefordshire, a distance of 108 miles. I did not find it particularly exhausting but felt pretty stiff the next day. Our bikes had no gears but we used to cycle long distances as a matter of course. One summer, several in our family cycled from Aberystwyth on the Cardiganshire coast of Wales to Oxford over a few days.

The school had a custom of having two whole holidays about a month after the beginning of term and a month before the end. The day was not fixed. The headmaster would look out at the weather. If it really looked as though it was going to be a fine day, the school would be summoned to the hall soon after lessons started. There we were told that today was a whole holiday. We could do as we pleased so long as we were back in time for the evening meal. Sandwich lunches were being prepared. Before we were turned out, the headmaster would give us some ideas of what we could do. He set us a challenge. Could we walk thirty miles? Could we explore various famous spots nearby? Cycling to out-of-the-way places was my pleasure, the longest trip was to Spalding, about a sixty-mile round trip. Picnics by a nearby river, exploring a new reservoir, these were the sort of rather unenterprising ways I remember spending these whole holidays. There was no question of home exeats in wartime so these holidays were our only break from school routine. Home was the best part of a day's train journey away.

After I had arrived, it was found that I was ahead of one class in some subjects but behind in others, so it was decided that I should be allocated to the lower one. The classes were split into groups of boys taking the same subjects. We had a classics class, a modern languages class and a science with Latin class. It was to the last that I went and it was science that I revelled in. The point of Latin was that you could not get into either Oxford or Cambridge without having passed Latin at the sixteen-year-old exam, called then School Certificate. I am afraid several of us failed Latin the first time round, but we were able to take the exam again at Christmas, on the same set books. We bought English translations of our books and learnt them off by heart. I can still remember the opening sentence of Virgil's *Aeniad*, Volume II — 'Unspeakable O Queen are the wonders we have to tell . . .'. We passed second time round.

I was still continuing with a general science course in the Sixth Form until it was realized that instead of being able to take the Cambridge Scholarship exams in the third year of the sixth form, my age made it necessary to do so after only just over one year. With great anguish, I gave up chemistry and concentrated on mathematics and physics. The maths teacher, Francis Tongue, thought I might just make it if I really worked. He gave me hours of personal tuition, taking me through the most complicated trigonometrical equations, introducing me to the wonders of calculus and advanced Euclidean geometry. This was all before modern maths. Many of our textbooks were originally written in Victorian times. They were so good that Lamb's Calculus was still a standard text at least twenty-five years later. I hope it still is. It gave me tremendous pleasure and stimulation.

Three terms after this decision to specialize, I went to Cambridge for the Scholarship Exams. Tongue had been to Jesus College so it was there I went to meet his tutor. I thought the college food, which we had in the fine old hall, the oldest dining-hall in Cambridge, was magnificent after wartime school food. I enjoyed the maths exams which were really tough, but I made a mess of the general essay we had to write. I did not get the scholarship though my tutor said that they would admit me. Had my father been a Church of England parson instead of a Methodist, my tutor said, he could have got me a Rustat Scholarship. The system was full of these delightful curiosities, all ancient and very mysterious. I went back to school not unduly anxious though I had no idea what fees an undergraduate without a scholarship would need. The following summer we took our Higher School Certificate exams. Someone found that government assistance was available to science students as Sate Bursaries. I was lucky enough to get one of these which enabled my father to afford to let me take up the place offered at Jesus College.

University

University life was a marvellous opening up to the world. No longer were we subject to the tight timetables of school. We lived independently in rooms near the college. There was a bewildering array of sporting and other activities. Undergraduates could attend any lecture in the university, but my tutor, Alan Pars, made a practical selection of those he thought would be useful. They did not take up all day. As I had played in the school rugger fifteen, I went for the rugger club. This immediately introduced me to a crowd of friends, many of whom were, like me, in our first year. There was, I am glad to say, no tradition of giving freshmen the sort of unpleasant time that is common in some universities. We went to various buildings for lectures by great mathematicians. Pars would give two of us weekly tutorials in the college. Pars was typical of the teaching fellows. He was a bachelor and lived in college. He would entertain us as well as look out for our welfare. Even married fellows lived in college, going home at weekends but dining in hall during the week and often asking a few of their students up for coffee after dinner. Pars heard of a shipment of used clothing from America for impoverished students and gave me my first dinner-jacket.

I found I had spare time for this was still during the war and the university sports world held itself in check in the time it demanded of its sportsmen. We played rugger every Saturday but that was all. I found that the boat club welcomed anyone who wanted to try his hand at rowing. I could not commit myself to row in a crew for my Saturdays were booked. I could however take out a sculling boat and this is what I did. At first, the boat was a rather heavy, clinker-built boat. Even so, it was unstable enough to tip me out just when I thought I had got the hang of it. I read books about rowing by that magnificent coach Steve Fairbairn and began to see something of the rowing fraternity. In the summer term there was no rugger, so I joined a crew and was put into second May Boat. This was a new experience. We had an outing three times a week, all that was allowed by the university rules, and on the intervening afternoons I got back into my sculling boat. Work and rowing and rugger. I scarcely did anything else. It was a full life, full of social activity as well as a striving for results both academic and sporting. I was very pleased to get a First Class in the Part I Maths Tripos. One of the books I chose as a prize was a history of the Jesus College Boat Club. It stopped in 1929 but was a marvellous account of some of the great days of Jesus College rowing. By a quirk of history, I found myself doing the typesetting for a later history of the Boat Club for the period 1962–94. I did not try any novelty but carefully copied all the signs and symbols of the earlier book.

Serious physics

In my second year, I was required by my bursary to drop maths and switch to physics. This was tough. The last physics I had done was the Sixth Form exam at school and I was plunged straight into Part II Cambridge physics. I never felt the enthusiasm for the subject that I had had for maths. I found it hard-going and must admit that I found it rather beyond me. In particular, I found the lack of guidance in the experimental work bewildering. I simply had no idea what I was attempting to discover. There was still time for sport. I was reluctant to give up rugger for I had become Secretary of the College Club. I had found rowing such fun that I did not want to give that up either. One Saturday afternoon I rowed in the Freshmen's sculls, jumped out of the boat at the finish, handed it over to a friend and rode his bicycle back to college in time for a game of rugger. Young and fit though I was, I found this just a bit too much. It was rugger that went.

Serious rowing

The war finished in the summer of 1945, so the University Boat Club debated whether to lift the wartime restrictions to three days a week for rowing. The Jesus College people led a rebellion against the powers of the University Boat Club in favour of abolishing the time limits and we won the day. From then on, we rowed six days a week. The outing took no more than an hour or two, so there was still plenty of time for work

— but not much else. I found that this sport came to dominate my spare time. After the outings, we would often gather in one or other sets of rooms for tea and dissection of the day's outing. The mornings and evenings were for work. Percy Bullock, the College Boatman, was a marvellous guide and mentor not only in rowing but in life in general. Jesus had a strong tradition of following its own style of rowing pioneered by Steve Fairbairn who had been at the college in the 1880s. The 1930s had seen the college at the Head of the River over and over again. We were daggers drawn against the orthodox school of rowing manifest most strongly in Trinity College and in the University Boat Club. The difference in style was most noticeable in the junior boats. Jesus crews concentrated on working the oar and paid little attention to beautiful body form. The orthodox crews looked much prettier but did not go so fast. I did not make the First May Boat in my second year. They went up four places in the May Races, which, of course, take place in June, and won the Ladies Plate at Henley. The first serious race in the Michaelmas term was the coxswainless fours. As their name implies, these boats have four oarsmen and no coxswain. They were steered by one of the crew who had wires from the rudder fastened to one of his clogs which he could move from side to side. As we rowed with our backs to the way we were going, the steerer had to know the course backwards. I was put at bow and steerer of the second four. The first four were clearly the favourites but we did not yield much to them. We won our first race easily and found ourselves up against the First & Third Trinity first four. This crew had won the Visitors Cup at Henley that year. They were ultra-orthodox so we were out for their blood. They came right up on us at the beginning but, bit by bit, we rowed them down and beat them by a comfortable fifteen seconds. What a humiliation for the orthodox camp for Trinity to be beaten by the Jesus second four! We did not feel our triumph in any way diminished by being beaten the following day by our own college first four who went on to win the finals.

I suppose rowing came to be more and more fascinating. After the coxswainless fours, I went in for the Colquhoun Sculls, the principal university sculling race. This was really ridiculous because I weighed two stone less than the competition. Still I reached the finals in 1945. I tried again in 1946 but was again beaten in the finals.

We rowed in every sort of boat there was. I had a memorable row in a pair down to Ely, some eighteen miles below Cambridge. The two of us seemed to hit it off with great precision. In double sculls, with another partner, we did not distinguish ourselves. And there were all sorts of less serious races. One was a sculling boat race that took place after we had broken training from the Fairbairn Cup race in December. It was in the same format, that is a row for three miles between the locks. Everyone put their name down for this race and we drew lots for the boats. Several of us rowed in fancy dress, mine being my dinner-jacket. My boat was a very old, pre-war one of immense length that was fashionable then. I noticed a small hole in the stern canvas but thought nothing of it. The boat was so fine that the stern would almost go under water at the beginning of each stroke. This did not matter until I found myself rowing into a slight head wind which was kicking up some small waves. These came over the canvas, but still I did not worry until I found the stern of the boat slowly getting lower and lower in the water. About halfway down the course, the stern finally disappeared. I got to the bank just before the boat sank.

The serious stuff was in the eights and by now I was in the first boat. Although we won the Fairbairn Cup in 1945, we lost it by 4/5 second the next year. The Lent Races at the end of the Lent, or spring, term and the May Races are bumping races where individual college boats start in the order determined by the finishing order of the year before. The boats start with a length and a half between them. The cox of each boat hangs onto a chain from the bank until the start. A gun is fired four minutes before the start and another one with sixty seconds to go. The scene on the river during the few seconds before start of a bumping race is breathtaking. Sixteen boats are pushed out from the bank in dead silence, broken only by the coaches counting down the seconds. The boatmen using their long poles, and years of fine judgement, ease the boats out to the extreme length of the chain in the cox's hands. Then the gun goes and 140 men instantly dig in their oars and race. The coaches shout encouragement and the crowd goes wild.

The object is to bump the boat in front. We started as the head boat at the front of all. For three nights, which is what we called the afternoons, we had no difficulty in keeping ahead of the boat behind us. On the Saturday, we were being chased by Christ's College who had already made three bumps and were striving to dislodge us from the headship. We were a bit nervous at the start but had no difficulty in keeping well away from them. In the way these things go, I met Martin Clemens, who had coached the Christ's boat, some fifty years later. He had rowed pre-war and was over from Australia, staying with a pre-war Jesus oarsman, Alan Burrough, at Henley during the regatta. I need hardly say that his version of the race was that they all but bumped us.

In the Easter holidays, we rowed in the Head of the River Race in London. This is a timed race with the boats starting at fifteen-second intervals in the order they finished the year before. The course is over the four-and-a-quarter mile Boat Race course but rowed in the opposite direction, from Mortlake to Putney. In 1947, there were some 300 entrants and we started third. The winter had been particularly severe and now the snows were melting. Enormous volumes of water poured down the Thames. Although the river is tidal, there was so much water flowing down that, for a time during our training, the direction of flow was out to sea whether the tide was flooding or ebbing. We started in a strong following wind and went off at a splendid pace. It was not long before we passed the second boat which happened to be the Isis crew, the Oxford University second boat. As we passed under Hammersmith Bridge, where the river bends through almost 180 degrees, we found that the fine following wind had become a strong head wind, kicking up great waves against the tide. Water started coming in over both sides of the boat. Much more of this and we should sink. We noticed that London Rowing Club, who were behind us, and were much more experienced in the ways of the Thames, moved over nearer to the bank to avoid the roughest water. Quite improperly, several started shouting at the cox to do likewise. He didn't. He kept in the fastest part of the stream for he could see that the rough water did not last for long. The upshot was that we won in a record time, faster than any University Boat Race at that time, and some twenty seconds ahead of London who were second. There were some three or four inches of water in the boat at the finish — an inch more and we would have sunk.

That May, or summer, term we were determined to go Head of the River in the May Races. Having gained four places in 1946, we started second. We soon made our bump on the first night and held the position without serious challenge. After the end of term, the crews of the first two boats moved down to Marlow where there is an annual regatta over quite a short course. It served as a warm-up for Henley Royal Regatta two weeks later. In one heat of the major race, we were drawn against the Oxford Head of the River crew and anticipated a tough struggle. Imagine our amazement when we had a length's lead after only ten strokes. Cambridge rowing was so far ahead of that at Oxford at that time. Cambridge won the Boat Race with boring regularity — even though they rowed in that awful orthodox style.

The Henley Grand

We won the Grand Challenge Cup at Marlow and prepared for Henley. After the weekend, we rowed up the river to Henley and stayed there at an hotel in the middle of town. We did some hard work at Henley but also a good deal of light work. In particular, we practised changing our rate until we could go from less than twenty strokes a minute, to forty, in one or two strokes. It was impressed on us that when we reached the hole in the wall, a landmark about forty strokes from the end of the regatta course, we were to jack up the rate of striking as we had been practising.

The Grand Challenge Cup at Henley is the premier rowing event in Britain and has always attracted many of the best crews in the world. In historical times, several of these were English club crews or Cambridge College crews, seldom Oxford crews. American, continental and Australian crews would come if they thought they could win. Leander Club usually made up a crew of the best from Oxford and Cambridge colleges. Today, the Challenge attracts only a handful of national crews, still including Leander being the best from England.

At the draw for the starting orders in Henley Town Hall, the first name out of the hat for the Grand Challenge Cup was Jesus. This was greeted with some cheering and some jeering. When the second was Leander, the shouting became delirious. The Leander crew was the winning Cambridge University crew of that year, selected from all the colleges in the university, with the strengthening of a pre-war stroke and an Oxford Blue. Our own Jesus Blue came back to row for the college. Leander were the champions of orthodoxy. Now we should see which style would triumph. I can remember sitting at the start and hearing the Oxford Blue in the Leander crew, rowing at two, saying to his neighbour, 'Look at that bow. He only weighs nine stone nine pounds!' That got me mad. It is true that we had two very light men in the bows with the number two weighing ten stone ten pounds, but we could move the boat. We got a slight lead at the start but Leander came back and held us all the way down the course so that we were level when we got to the hole in the wall. Here we put in our spurt and won by half a length.

That was all we came to Henley for! True, there were now foreign crews to do battle with, but we had achieved all that we set out to do — to demonstrate the superiority of the Fairbairn style over the orthodox. In the semi-finals we were against a Swiss crew from Zurich. They were a beautiful crew but perhaps a little older than us. Just to demoralize us as we came up to them near the start, the stroke tapped his oar twice and, without a single word of command, the crew went off into the smoothest paddle. We were more relaxed for this race. This row was our best. Again, we approached the enclosures level with the opposition. I heard later that the old orthodox stalwarts in the grandstands could not bring themselves to cheer for Jesus, their old rivals, but cheered for England. Our final spurt was too much for the Swiss whom we beat by half a length.

In the final, we were up against a strong Dutch university crew weighing a stone a man more than us. We still could not leave them in the early stages of the race. Our blood was up so we started our spurt earlier than before and won by a length and a quarter.

I have never seen so many red and black Jesus caps at the boat landing. They were jumping with excitement. We had not won the Grand since 1885 though coming close to it several times in the late 1930s. These men picked up our boat and put it away for us. What was even more astonishing was to see the Dutch crew rushing up with their wooden clogs filled to the brim with champagne. I had heard of drinking champagne out of a dancing girl's slipper but these clogs held much more!

You may think that writing so much about rowing in university life shows an unbalanced memory. Perhaps it does. All I can say is that what has remained of university days in afterlife is the time I spent with those friends on the river and in the close life we lived off it. As in all sports, coaches are all important. We had no professional coaches. They were all old Jesus rowing men who would give us an enormous amount of time as well as wisdom. Derek Mays-Smith was our chief coach. He had a quite extraordinary ability to get the best out of a crew. I really got to appreciate his skill when, a couple of years later, I was rowing in London Rowing Club boat. Our Captain was Peter Bell from the 1939 Jesus crew. We had four Jesus men altogether. We had not responded well to coaching by an old Oxford blue but in the fortnight at Henley, Derek so transformed us that we reached the semi-final of the Grand. I wished he had been able to take us through the winter before. Our college boatman, Percy Bullock, was there all the time and he too taught us a great deal more about life than just rowing. 'If you can't do it easily, you can't do it all.' was one of Steve Fairbairn's many sayings which have a much wider application than just on the river. There is a friendship among our Jesus rowing men of many generations that spans the years and the diverse lives we have led.

Whenever we meet, we can slip effortlessly into our easy ways, however long the separation has been. Exactly fifty years after winning the Grand, the whole crew, except for one who had died, met together again at Henley. Some two hundred and fifty Jesus men and, nowadays, women, and their spouses joined in a sumptuous celebration dinner in the Stewards Enclosure on the Saturday night of Henley in 1997.

3

Arrival in Hong Kong

Thursday, 28 August 1950, was an overcast, hot, rainy, typical summer's day in Hong Kong as the P&O ship, *Canton*, anchored for immigration and customs procedures in Kowloon Bay. The atmosphere filled me with excitement. I had looked forward to this day for three years and was coming home to the place where I expected to spend my career.

Earning a living

As my time at university was drawing to a close, the awful realization dawned on me that I should soon have to earn a living. I had no vocation for any particular career and only the vaguest notion of the opportunities. The university had an appointments board so I called there. Being a scientist, I was first referred to the man who suggested careers for scientists. The possibilities did not sound attractive. I had been convinced that scientific research was not for me. More important, I came to realize that any of the jobs on offer would mean living in a big city. I much preferred the country. We drew a blank so I was referred to the man who dealt with arts students. This man was more realistic. He asked a number of simple questions that I could answer and said, 'You want to go abroad again — probably to China.' Indeed I did. His suggestion was Asiatic Petroleum Company, a part of Shell, who were looking for new graduates. This sounded much better. When I discussed this with my father, he said, 'If you are going East again, why not go into the government as a Cadet?' This was better still. I duly applied to the Colonial Office for a job in Hong Kong.

By the time of my final interview, I found myself in uniform. National Service was still compulsory. The navy was the service I preferred, but I could not see far enough to pass their eye tests. All of us who were graduating were assembled in a large lecture theatre to be addressed by highly bemedalled officers from the three services. As these distinguished men entered the theatre, they were heartily booed by the assembled throng. They took it in good part and went on to explain what sort of work we could choose. I was encouraged to learn that the navy was badly in need of school masters who did not need the eyesight of an eagle and who, furthermore, could join as officers without having first to spend six months in lower ranks as was the case with all the other possibilities.

As I sat in my smart new uniform before the panel of great men from the Colonial Empire, I was quizzed about my life so far. It was rather dull until one of them said, 'Were you in the Jesus crew that won the Grand at Henley recently?' They all looked much more cheerful when I admitted to this and the interview ended soon after.

The Royal Navy

Yes, I had been accepted but I should still have to do two years' National Service. This was more fun than I had expected. A crowd of new entrants assembled on HMS *Victory,* which was a large building in Portsmouth. On my first day in the navy, I was woken up by a steward bringing in a cup of tea. 'This is the life for me!' I thought.

We first had a Divisional Course for a month in Portsmouth where we learnt how to salute, how to drill, how not to say 'Good morning' to a senior officer for it was for him to decide whether it was good or not, how to fire a revolver from the hip, and many other mysteries of the Senior Service. We had a day at sea on a frigate and another in a submarine. We crewed in sailing races in whalers, my skipper being a grizzled Commissioned Gunner who had a rough tongue for idiots but was kindly to those who tried. We were a congenial crowd. One had to go off to get married when he found his girlfriend was pregnant — the consequence of an unusually active May Ball at Cambridge. One, who had read biology at Cambridge, turned out to be famous as being the brother of a film star.

At the end of this time, we were assigned to ships and shore establishments. Mine was to a Naval Apprentices training establishment at Rosyth in Scotland. Before I was due to go there, I did a little teaching at the gunnery school HMS *Excellent* — not gunnery, I hasten to add, but the simplest arithmetic and some reading to grown men my age who had managed to get through the education system without this knowledge but who had to pass a test called ET 1.

HMS *Caledonia*, as my land-based ship was called, was largely in temporary buildings on the bleak hillsides above the Firth of Forth. Teaching current affairs to boys only a year or two younger than me was fascinating. Their ignorance of affairs was staggering but they were bright. Teaching engineering drawing was more of a challenge as I only just managed to stay one lesson ahead of the class for the whole term.

I had not been at *Caledonia* long when I had a call from Rosyth dockyard. It was from one of the new graduates who had been on the course with me at Portsmouth and who was now serving on a destroyer. David Attenborough, for it was he who was destined to outshine his film star brother, invited me down to dinner on his ship. We had a most convivial evening, terminating in numerous glasses of Drambuie sold at duty-free prices — an evening I have often recalled as I watch his magnificent nature films.

Our work was in the mornings and the evenings, but the afternoons were mostly free. One afternoon, an elderly colleague carried me off to the Dunfermline Golf Club where I started to play golf. I acquired a mixed handful of old clubs and gradually replaced them, one at a time on each pay-day, with clubs from a matched set. It was some time before my elderly companion decided he could no longer give me a stroke at each hole.

The two years passed slowly but uneventfully and were completed at last. My appointment in the Colonial Service to Hong Kong was confirmed but I was not on my way yet.

Learning to govern colonies

Before setting out to govern colonies, Colonial Service recruits did an academic year's course at Oxford, Cambridge or London, called the Devonshire Course. In 1950, the Colonial Service was near its maximum strength. Although India had become the independent countries of India and Pakistan, the British Empire still stretched round the globe. The largest colonies were in Africa, with Nigeria the largest in area and population. In the east, Ceylon, Malaya, Sarawak and North Borneo were the most important.

The Malayan and the Hong Kong Cadets went to the London School of Economics for their Devonshire Courses. I was sorry not to get back to Cambridge where I wanted to continue my rowing career but found London Rowing Club an excellent substitute. Our academic work had very little to do with Hong Kong. There were only two of us going there. The law lectures led to exams that exempted us from similar exams on arrival in Hong Kong; Empire History was interestingly presented by a Canadian, but I found the anthropology and the history of colonial constitutional development pretty dreary. A week's course at Wye Agricultural College was fun but of no relevance to me. The most valuable part of the course was our language instruction in Cantonese which took up half our time in the second two terms. We were taught at the School of Oriental and African Studies by that excellent teacher Katharine Whitaker. I wish it had been a full-time course for that would have equipped us with a really good working knowledge of both the written and spoken language.

I do not think anyone managed to fail the course. On 28 July 1950, eight Malayan Cadets and I set sail from Southampton in First Class on the *Canton.* We entered a new world. England was still in the grip of wartime food rationing but there was none of this on the ship. The trip out was exciting. Port Said was the first stop where we barely had time to look in at the Simon Artz store before going through the Suez Canal. Adrian Alabaster, with whom I shared a cabin on the ship, and I climbed a hill in Aden at the crack of dawn. We had a splendid meal in the Taj Mahal Hotel in Bombay, went swimming at Breach Candy in Colombo and had lunch at the E&O in Penang where some of the MCS people got off. Others left at Singapore where we dined with an army friend, brother of my Captain of Boats at Cambridge.

My parents were back in Hong Kong where my father was building a church and school at Gascoigne Road in Kowloon. For the first week, I stayed with them in the Sailors and Soldiers Home in Wan Chai. This was a social centre with residential accommodation built in the 1930s by the Methodist Church for the armed services. The rooms were simple and clean with a ceiling fan. Air-conditioning had not yet arrived, so this was a good introduction to summer heat right down in the centre of urban Wan Chai. The trams woke me up in the morning, but I never did discover what contraption screeched slowly past at about 3 a.m., sounding like scraping out the tram tracks.

Cadet Officer Class II

On landing, I had been appointed a Cadet Officer Class II on probation. Cadet Officers were what we now call Administrative Officers. There were only two Classes of Cadet — forty of us were Class II while the top six were in Class I. This arrangement had enormous advantages. The powers that be were able to move the Class II Cadets around without worrying about affecting their pay — it was fixed on a nineteen-year salary scale with two 'efficiency bars'. This flexibility meant that a senior but not very bright man could be put in a post not requiring much imagination or drive, while a junior bright spark could be posted to a point of trouble without causing any offence — our pay was determined by our length of service, not by the work we did. It could not last. The long salary scale was the same as that of the other professional officers, but we had two large jumps in the middle which the doctors, engineers and so forth, did not have. A Salaries Commission put us all on exactly the same scales but had to invent a whole new batch of senior grades to match those of the professional services. This reduced the flexibility of our service as many of the Class II Cadet posts became Staff Grade posts equivalent to Assistant and Deputy Directors of the other departments. The plus point for us was that if you were a junior chap acting in one of the new posts, you got acting pay which you would never have had before. This was a colossal benefit. I was so scared of the enormous sums involved that the first time I got acting pay, I saved the lot and to this day still have a few of the shares I bought and have left alone since.

Assistant Secretary for Chinese Affairs

The first job I had was under the Secretary for Chinese Affairs. He was a very senior officer who sat *ex officio* on Executive and Legislative Councils and the Urban Council as well. As I entered his office, I was astonished to see a glass of whiskey water on his desk. I hope I hid my surprise. When I got to my own office, there was a similar glass on my desk.

What sort of a place had I landed in? As I took a sip, I found that the glass was warm and the drink was tea. The District Watchman at my door regarded it as his job to top up the glass whenever it dropped anywhere near half full. I soon got into the habit of drinking gallons of the stuff every day. This good acolyte was no mere messenger. He was one of the few remaining members of the fast-vanishing District Watch Force which had been set up in pre-war days to combat the illegal, but widespread, practice of families taking *mui tsai*. These young girls were supposed to be adopted into wealthy families but were often little more than domestic drudges and often badly abused. By my time, the police side of the work had been handed to the regular police but the force was not disbanded. Its members were kept on and assigned all manner of duties from doorman to messenger to measuring up the sizes of flats involved in legal cases. They did not speak English so my man was a continual source of local lore and language.

One of the senior officers was the Chinese Assistant Secretary for Chinese Affairs, Chung King Pui. He was a distinguished and venerable scholar steeped in Chinese traditions and with an encyclopedic knowledge of personalities in society, their families, feuds and friendships. A lesser part of his responsibilities was to determine a Chinese name for the newly arrived Cadets. I explained that my father had spent a long time in China and Hong Kong and indeed was resident in Hong Kong. When he arrived in China in 1914, he had soon realized that there was no Chinese surname remotely like Bray. He decided to choose a typical Chinese name Lai Pak Lim – so I had to have Lai as a surname. Chung King Pui therefore chose characters sounding like Denis, but also with the loftiest sentiments, so I was to be Lai Tun Yi. When my brother visited Hong Kong many years later, he was given the name Lai Tsang Yi, keeping both the surname and the generation name, Yi, and sounding vaguely like Jeremy. I have survived my time in Hong Kong happily enough with this name even though a great many people have no idea that Mr Lai is the same chap as Mr Bray — it has its advantages.

The post of Secretary for Chinese Affairs was set up in, I think, the 1920s, based on the office of Registrar-General, for the official concerned with the Chinese population. Now you might think that as 99 percent or more of the population was Chinese, the rest of the government was also concerned with the Chinese population as well, but this does not seem to have been the case. The Medical Department was set up to serve the expatriate civil servants, rather as the army medical services dealt with the army's needs. The Education Department was to run schools for expatriate children. It was only gradually, in pre-war years, that such services spread to the rest of the population. Nevertheless, it was realized that the Chinese population was important. A senior official, on a level with the Attorney-General and the Financial Secretary, was appointed to act as a channel of communication between the government and the Chinese population. I can remember being told of a long and bitter argument between one Secretary for Chinese Affairs, after the war, and the Colonial Secretariat on whether anyone other than the Secretary for Chinese Affairs should attempt to communicate with the Chinese population, the former sticking to his guns that only he understood how to communicate with the Chinese.

In spite of this rather unrealistic attitude, the Secretariat did have close relations with the general population of Hong Kong. The Secretariat for Chinese Affairs had spawned the Labour Department in pre-war days and the Social Welfare Department after the war. It was the place to which ordinary people went if they sought any form of assistance from the rather remote government.

Among these were people who were having difficulties at home and who would bring their troubles to us. The interpreters did their best to help. After these preliminaries they came to me, an English bachelor of twenty-four years, with rudimentary knowledge of their language, for helpful advice and arbitration on their family problems. People who had married according to Chinese custom, as most had, could not get divorced through the courts but had to divorce, pretty simply, also in accordance with Chinese custom. They could not do this in our office, so we often had to finish by explaining how they could go about arranging a divorce. I learnt a great deal about ordinary life here. I think the opportunity to unburden themselves in front of the *Dai Yan*, or 'Great Man', as they called me, did bring relief in some cases, and reconciliation in many.

I was still curious about all around me and even read the laws about the Secretary for Chinese Affairs. There I found that a body called the Secretary for Chinese Affairs Incorporated owned a great many properties denoted only by lot numbers. Nobody in the office knew what they were, where they were, or what we were supposed to do about them, if anything. I had to go and have a look. Most of the land seemed to be on Lantau Island to which I found I could get a lift either from the District Office or police launch. The District Office kindly let me have a demarcator who would know how to find the lots — a demarcator? These men were the database operators for the District Officers on land matters. All landholdings were recorded on maps drawn up originally in 1904–08.

By 1950, these plans were rather the worse for wear and required specialists to understand them. These were the demarcators, who I later got to know much better when I was a District Officer myself, and who could confidently say that the paddy-field we stood on really was lot number so-and-so in the demarcation district of so-and-so. The first property we visited turned out to be a temple. It seemed to be in good order and there was a temple-keeper. He was appointed by the village. Running the temple could generate a little income, so the job was tendered out. I also found that some of the lot numbers referred to paddy-fields which were cultivated. These, I was told, were let out also by tender and the income was used for the maintenance of the temple. The properties were scattered round Lantau at the principal villages — Mui Wo, Tai O, Tung Chung — and on the Soko Islands nearby. I wrote up a report about all this, with one or two fine photographs of old temples. Everything seemed to be running smoothly without any intervention by the Secretary for Chinese Affairs Incorporated. It is just as well that the report was simply filed and forgotten.

I also had to enquire into claims that a person convicted of a crime, incurring more than six months in gaol, was born in Hong Kong. He would be deported to China unless he could establish his claim to Hong Kong birth. Some could. Those who made such a claim appeared in front of me. Witnesses at the full moon feast, customarily held one month after the baby was born, and therefore likely to survive, could sometimes be found. Occasionally, a midwife was produced as a witness. Although nearly all birth registers had been found after the war, very few births were registered. I mischievously sent my own birth details forward to enquire if this criminal suspect was born in Hong Kong and was glad to find I had been. All the work of this junior Assistant Secretary for Chinese Affairs involved intimacy with classes of the population that none of my friends in the business world had ever heard of. It was fascinating. Although my posting was for only a few weeks, I think it gave me a feeling of sympathy for, if not complete understanding of, a much wider society than was known of by the expatriate community, official or not.

Language study

After a short time, I was released for full-time language study. It only lasted three months but was nevertheless a very useful period. I have always regretted that this study was cut short. How can anyone live in a place where you cannot speak to the ordinary people? The little Cantonese I had acquired in London was enough to build on. The advantage of having spoken Cantonese as my first language was that the peculiar use of tones in any Chinese language seemed to have stuck. I had no vocabulary but the tones were useful. 'Go into a shop and buy something' was the advice of a fluent Cantonese speaker. 'It doesn't matter what it is, or even if you don't buy anything. Just talk to them and try to find out what things are called. But avoid meal-times because you will find the whole family at the table in the shop.' Most of the shops, even in Central, were like this. Rather disorganized collections of wares, often of a rather narrow speciality, with the family living in the back somewhere but with no space for a dining-room. I was always impressed with the extensive knowledge of the shopkeepers in matters relating to their trade. In answer to my halting explanations, they would produce all manner of device that met some of my requirements but would not give up until they had found just the right gadget or tool or ball of string. Sometimes they would realize what it was that I wanted, but did not stock it. They simply directed me to a shop that sold nothing else for there was sure to be such a place nearby. What a difference from today's shop assistants who seem to know nothing about what they sell!

Invasion scare

My language study was cut short because there was a very real fear that Hong Kong was about to be invaded from China. The Korean War, which had started only a few months earlier, was going very badly. The United Nations were almost thrown out of Korea. Had this happened, Hong Kong was expected to be the next domino to fall. Our intelligence was that the Chinese had five divisions of troops on the border and two in reserve, though I did not get to know this until many years later. We had one division, complete with tanks and artillery, a naval presence and some Royal Air Force fighters. The hills were strung with barbed wire to deter infantry. The most junior of us had to take it in turn to sleep in the office of the Defence Secretary so as to be able to receive the call from the border saying that the invasion had started.

On Christmas Eve in 1950, a valley on the border was found to be full of men with torches flashing everywhere. It was thought this was the first thrust. The army was stood to; the troops were warned to be ready for action the next day. Fortunately, the activity turned out to be nothing more than kerosene smuggling on an unusually large scale. The Tai Po District Officer, in whose district the border lay, had to spend Christmas Day remanding the prisoners that had been caught. Outwardly, all was calm. The government's fears were kept a close secret. Fortunately, the threat was withdrawn and we were able to discontinue the duties in the Defence Secretary's office.

My job in this emergency was to prepare to be the personal assistant to the Colonial Secretary should the invasion become a reality. It lasted for the whole of a Saturday morning. The Establishment Officer, who dealt with all civil service staff matters, heard that I was doing nothing but read files as they went in and out of the Colonial Secretary's office. He got me downstairs to do some proper work. The Colonial Secretariat was the centre of the Hong Kong government, housed in a two-storey, pre-war building on the site of the present Main Wing of the Central Government Offices. Nowadays it would be a listed building, but then it was just gradually falling down. The rooms were huge, but only the top few bosses had a room to themselves with their own ceiling fan. None had air-conditioning. The rest of the offices were partitioned off into tiny cubicles, or people were put at tables in the corner of a large office.

There was the Colonial Secretary, the Financial Secretary, the Deputy Colonial Secretary, the Deputy Financial Secretary, the Defence Secretary, the Clerk of Councils, the Establishment Officer, and all the rest were Assistant Secretaries. I rejoiced in the title of Assistant Secretary 13. That was all that was holding up the government of Hong Kong.

I spent my time dealing with things that were too unimportant to be handled by anyone with experience. I only remember piles of files in which we were attempting to lay down consistent terms of service of all the grades in government, and another one in which I had to deduce how many dental chairs the dental service needed. The service only had about five chairs and no statistics of patients. Using my rather rusty mathematical and statistical methods, I produced an answer. As nobody understood my reasoning, they simply cut my total in half.

It was clear that when everyone was working flat out, I could not continue to be more or less a passenger. I heard that there was a vacancy in the Social Welfare Office which had recently been set up in the Secretariat for Chinese Affairs. This sounded like real work. I just hoped I would be considered. It was stunning news to be told to report to the old Fire Brigade Building on the site now occupied by the headquarters of the Hang Seng Bank. The building was then on the waterfront. It housed a fire station and the headquarters of the Fire Services on the Des Voeux Road side of the building. On the waterfront side was the entrance to the offices. The Commerce and Industry Department occupied the upper floors and the Secretary for Chinese Affairs had his office on the first floor. I was to take over as Chief Assistant Social Welfare Officer, in an independent office but still attached to the Secretariat for Chinese Affairs.

4

In at the Deep End

Social Welfare Office

Today, the Social Welfare Department in Hong Kong provides a massive array of social services of a quality second to none in Asia. It is staffed by hundreds of professionally trained social workers and extends its work to all corners of society. On reaching the age of seventy, it even pays my wife and me a non-means-tested pension of about $700 (less than £70) a month — which is commonly called 'fruit money'.

When I was posted to the Social Welfare Office in 1951, it had been set up in the office of the Secretary for Chinese Affairs only three years previously. We were a very different lot. The office was based on the Mui Tsai Inspectorate, which I described in the previous chapter. The Mui Tsai system had largely fallen into disuse after the war, but children in need of care were still found.

The Social Welfare Officer was the boss and a Cadet Class I. I was his Chief Assistant Social Welfare Officer, a Cadet Officer Class II, in effect an assistant head of department now at the ripe age of twenty-five. Ronald Holmes was the Class I Cadet. He had joined the government before the war and avoided capture by the Japanese during and after the battle for Hong Kong. He had a distinguished war record in the British Army Aid Group working in China. He gathered intelligence about Hong Kong, on one occasion even coming down as far as the hills behind Kai Tak to study the place personally. He was a most engaging and decisive man and I worked with him in several other contexts later on.

We had three very fine and dedicated professional social workers, Dorothy Lee, Daphne Ho and Diana Leung. These young ladies together with people in the voluntary agencies such as Kate Langford in the Family Welfare Service, and the Jesuits, Father Howatson and Father Ryan, accomplished wonders with very few resources in their work among men, women, and children living in the most appalling conditions. The first professionally trained probation officer had travelled out on the same ship with me. We maintained a liaison with non-government welfare organizations which sprang up to provide social services that the government could not find time or money for.

Kaifong Welfare Associations

Social services at this time were of the most primitive. There were not even enough places in schools for children of primary school age. Queues at public out-patient clinics involved an all-day wait for a two-minute consultation if you survived. This was an environment which cried out for charity and the good-hearted responded. The churches were in the forefront and secured considerable donations from abroad. But the local businessmen too, responded in a traditional Chinese way. Local leaders started to set up organizations to raise funds for welfare work. In our office, C. N. Li and his wife, who we have always called Mrs Li, were at the forefront of this work among both men and women. Called Kaifong Welfare Associations, groups of citizens in various localities got together to provide rudimentary welfare services such as free clinics and clubs for children who could not get into schools. The concept of the 'kaifong' or neighbourhood association is an old one in Chinese society. Men who had prospered gathered together and pooled their resources for the welfare of the poorest. Perhaps a quaint concept today when publicly financed services provide succour from cradle to grave, but in early postwar Hong Kong these associations did an immense amount of good work.

By their nature, the Kaifong Associations comprised leaders in their neighbourhoods. I once suggested to some of them that they should form a political party and stand for election to the Urban Council. This got reported in the Chinese press and I got a roasting from the Secretary for Chinese Affairs for playing with fire. 'If Kaifong Associations get involved with politics,' said the great man, 'they will be immediately taken over by the triads or the communists. Keep them on welfare.' This was perhaps an exaggeration, but it reflected the volatile political situation in Hong Kong in the days after the establishment of the People's Republic of China in 1949. Triads were straight criminal gangs with rituals claiming to have originated in uprisings in China. They operated in the underworld of crime and corruption but seldom made headlines.

The communists, on the other hand, were well-organized and hostile. They had several newspapers pumping our vitriolic anti-government propaganda, trade unions in all the major public utilities and schools where the young were fed a full diet of political rhetoric. Their schools were full for there was no place for the less able or influential in ordinary schools. The communists were a small, well-organized core, but refugees from the mainland had nothing to do with them. Circulation of their newspapers was minimal. Their trade unions were balanced by those organized by the Nationalists, or Kuomintang, who had fled to Taiwan but most workers wanted nothing that smacked of politics of any sort.

The desperately poor

We had a very wide remit in the Social Welfare Office but very little money or staff. There was no public assistance in any recognizable modern form, but there were very poor people who would starve without help. Actual starvation had been common in the very early postwar months when bodies would be found in the streets every morning. By 1951, there was no actual starvation. We provided cooked meals for about a thousand every day. For those who had somewhere they could cook, we provided 'dry rations'. For the even more desperate, we ran a relief camp — a place where we provided food and shelter. Most of the residents were disabled in some way. The man in charge had no social work training but was a fine thoughtful man of good heart, who managed his charges with compassion.

I had complete discretion on who should be admitted to our welfare camp. Only the most desperate could be accommodated, but there was a steady trickle of the most miserable forms of humanity. One day, a small blind boy was found wandering in the streets. There was a home for blind girls but none for blind boys. I immediately decided to admit the boy in spite of warnings that we should be swamped by blind boys from all over Hong Kong and south China. 'Fine,' I said, 'if we take in all the blind boys who come to us, at least we can provide food and shelter and perhaps proper provision will be produced for them.' In fact, we were not swamped at all, but we did gather together a band of young blind boys and were able to provide some rudimentary recreation and education for them. It was not long before this gap in social services was recognized and more suitable provision was made for them.

I mentioned the charitable organizations that were set up by the churches and others. At first, they relied entirely on their own efforts to raise funds. Gradually, the government got involved in giving them assistance. On this foundation was built the vast framework of subvented welfare services. The government provided the money, in greater or less degree, while the agencies operated the services. The system worked extremely well. It avoided the creation of a monstrous bureaucracy but the services were provided. The same system was adopted in education where again the government provided the finance and the schools were run by voluntary bodies. It has considerable advantages over a monolithic government-run organization.

Disabled refugees and killer diseases

It was during my time in the Social Welfare Office that we did help in setting up a refugee camp which became a centre of Nationalist sympathy until it was demolished in the late 1990s. It was the one exception we made in the way of special provision for refugees. As the retreating Nationalist armies reached Hong Kong, they brought with them hundreds of war-wounded and blind. These kept together and squatted on the hillsides at the west end of Hong Kong Island. They were a pathetic band characterized not by their warlike enmity to the communists, but by the very large numbers of wounded, crippled and blinded former soldiers. In any society these people deserved assistance. The government was not going to give special treatment to these people as refugees for there were thousands in similar straits. Jimmy Wakefield, my predecessor, did however get a group of leading citizens to form a committee to offer to build huts for them. A site was found in the then remote area of Junk Bay (Tseung Kwan O), to the east of the main. Here an ill-starred entrepreneur called Rennie had put a small share into a venture by Sir Paul Chater and Hormusjee Mody, one of the founders of Hong Kong University, for a flour mill in 1906. It failed and Rennie committed suicide by drowning in 1907. He did not hang himself, as tradition, encapsulated in the Chinese name for the place, has it. I learnt this detail from Kenneth Lan, a PhD student at the University of Hong Kong and son of David Lan, a former colleague and one of my successors as Secretary for Home Affairs. The mill was abandoned, but there remained a landing place and some flat land nearby. This site was allocated to the relief committee who built communal buildings and huts. The Social Welfare Office extended its free feeding to the camp inmates.

The camp was temporary. I was wondering what permanent arrangement we could make that would be caring for the wounded and disabled but not seen as a subsidy for former Nationalist soldiers. Just then, we had a visit from the Free China Relief Organization from Taiwan. Their leader called on me. I said that the Hong Kong government could not accept the indefinite obligation of feeding these people and hoped that his organization would shoulder the burden. He asked how long we could go on. Off the top of my head, I said, 'About six months.' The next day, the Nationalist press said the government was going to stop feeding the Rennie's Mill people in six months. It said something about the size of our administration at the time and the extent of responsibility devolved on youngsters like me at the age of twenty-five. There simply was not time to go round asking for authority. Once the papers had the story, I did seek approval to terminate the feeding for the able-bodied among the Rennie's Mill crowd. We were prepared to continue to feed the blind and disabled. This approval was soon given.

To finish the story of Rennie's Mill, as far as I was concerned, we decided to build a special institution for the disabled to which others in a similar condition could be admitted. The site was on Lantau Island at a place now called Chi Ma Wan. We had found this site, remote but accessible by sea, as a possible site for a camp for another contingency. This was to meet a threat that the Chinese had made to deport all the White Russians in China to Hong Kong. Of course, we resisted but we had no confidence that we could change their minds. In great secrecy, we made preparations to receive them. In fact, the Chinese relented and only deported Russians who had secured a final destination outside Hong Kong. The centre for the disabled was built. The government was on the point of moving the disabled from Rennie's Mill to Lantau when the Taiwanese took them all off. The centre was opened anyway. It did not have a long life as, being on a hilly site, it was really unsuitable for disabled people. The buildings were taken over by the Correctional Services Department who have run it as a detention centre of various sorts ever since.

The settlement at Rennie's Mill became a centre for Kuomintang, or Nationalist, sympathizers and was regularly covered in Nationalist flags on 10 October, when the Nationalists celebrated the anniversary of the

1911 revolution that overthrew the Qing dynasty. Only in 1998 were the last occupants of Rennie's Mill resettled in permanent accommodation. They won a legal case for compensation for being cleared from the land they were allowed to occupy as refugees in 1950. When they appealed against what they regarded as inadequate compensation, the Appeal Court ruled that they were not entitled to any compensation at all. They had got it by then and kept it.

It was while I was in the Social Welfare Office that I came across the killer diseases of tuberculosis and cancer. It was cancer that killed the man who ran our relief camp. I was staggered at the speed with which this disease could reduce such a fit, robust man to scarcely more than a skeleton in only a few weeks. The last time I saw him alive in hospital it was almost impossible to recognize him. The tuberculosis case was that of the infant son of a servant in my father-in-law's family. I had been able to get him into the Tung Wah Hospital, an ancient Chinese charitable hospital closely linked to the Secretariat for Chinese Affairs. My wife and I went to visit him. He was very near death and had been laid crosswise on a hospital bed with four other dying children. This was long before any vaccine had been found to immunize babies against the disease which spread like wildfire in the appallingly congested living conditions. It was by far the biggest killer in Hong Kong at the time.

Wedding day

It was also during my time in the Social Welfare Office that I met and married Marjorie Bottomley, the daughter of an architect in the Buildings Ordinance Office of the Public Works Department. She too had been born in Hong Kong. Whereas I had spent my early childhood in China, she had been brought up in Hong Kong. We nearly had our honeymoon terminated as a consequence of a squatter fire. This had taken place on the edge of the Kowloon Walled City and someone in Guangzhou had decided they could make a propaganda scoop by sending relief goods to their compatriot fire victims in Hong Kong. The train was to be greeted by a mass turnout of the trade unions. When it did not arrive, there were disturbances. Fortunately, we were on the island of Cheung Chau without papers or telephones and enjoying lazing on the beaches. It was not until we got back that we heard how busy my boss had been dealing with the crisis.

Squatters

Our emergency relief work also extended to another large section of the community which lived in squatter huts. In 1945, after the Second World War, Hong Kong was a devastated city with no working utilities or public transport. The total population was thought to be about six hundred thousand. When I arrived five years later, the population was guessed at about one and a half million. With a 300 percent increase in population in five years, in a war-devastated city, you can imagine housing was a bit of a problem. And it was on such a scale that no government could solve it. So in the usual Hong Kong way, it was solved by the people themselves.

They packed into the tenements in a way that makes today's caged accommodation look luxurious. Even though the demand for housing was so great, the demand for factory space was even greater. Thousands of factories or workshops were set up in tenement buildings. Although illegal, they were on such a scale that eviction, even if we had the resources for such tough measures, was impossible. Many years later, the factories had been pushed out of residential buildings, but by now the demand for industrial space was dropping. I asked the people concerned where the illegal conversion of factory space for residential use was taking place. Alas, Hong Kong had become so law-abiding that this sensible conversion was not taking place on a large scale — illegal conversion to office space was a lesser problem. Even with appalling overcrowding there was not enough room, so people camped down wherever they could in spite of notices saying that building squatter huts on unoccupied land was unlawful. Nobody knew how many squatters there were, but the figure of three hundred thousand was the most widely speculated.

The huts were built of wood, thin wood as it was cheaper, and covered with tarred paper roofs. They kept out the worst of the weather but went up in flames at the slightest provocation.

Remember this was just after the Communists had finally put an end to the civil war in China. Hong Kong was full of refugees, but so it had been in 1938, when the Japanese had got down to Guangdong. When things settled down then, the refugees returned to China. We hoped the same would happen now. There was a feeling that not too much should be done for refugees or we should be swamped by a further influx. In any case, we never admitted that we had any refugees in Hong Kong. This was thought to be offensive to the new Communist government and we did not want to bring the panoply of the United Nations Refugee Organization down on us. The refugee camps in Palestine seemed to us to be a model of stagnation and despair. Our squatter settlements were living societies where people worked and looked after themselves.

Fire was a constant danger. Something had to be done to provide some form of resettlement which would reduce this risk. The first resettlement scheme took the form of setting aside areas where those squatters who had to be cleared would be allowed to erect their huts in an orderly manner, with fire breaks and some fire prevention measures. The resettlement areas would be provided with paths, standpipes and communal latrines. Some site formation was done, but the house building was left to the squatters themselves. The resettlement method adopted was pretty inefficient and tested almost to destruction after a fire at Tung Tau Village, near Kowloon Walled City, in 1952. The Unofficial Members of Executive Council were rigorously opposed to any building of government housing because of this fear of further influxes. Unlike the case of previous influxes, it was becoming apparent that refugees were not returning to China even though things there seemed to be settling down.

This form of resettlement, relying on the squatters themselves to build their huts, went very slowly. The government would do a good deal to assist in site formation and the provision of infrastructure but would not actually build huts. It was not long before charitable bodies came forward to offer to build them. This was welcomed. The areas, which became known as 'cottage areas', sprang up in the places we had set aside for resettlement. Although the ventures were charitable, rent was charged in many cases. I remember in particular a scheme called the Hong Kong Settlers Housing Corporation, financed by wealthy citizens at the instigation of the government, which was allowed to make 6 percent on its investment which seemed to me scarcely to be charitable.

The Social Welfare Office had two jobs relating to squatters. First, we provided emergency relief after squatter fires and second, it fell to us to record the particulars of those squatters who would be eligible for resettlement. As a by-product of this screening, I did some analysis of the data with the help of a friend in the Commerce and Industry Department, Colin Wong. He had access to a Hollerith punched card machine — the latest thing in data analysis.

We did in fact produce the first crude demographic statistics of the postwar population of Hong Kong in 1952. We were a very peculiar population. The great majority were young men and women aged twenty-five to thirty-five and their babies. There were no elderly people: no teenagers. You had to be tough, young and single to be a refugee, but once arrived, no time was lost in producing babies.

Squatter fires

Squatter fires were commonplace. There was a routine. The Social Welfare Office got to know about them almost as soon as the Fire Brigade, for it was our job to prepare and distribute cooked food to the fire victims, to arrange for the reception and distribution of clothing and cash raised by charitable bodies. This was always a problem. The cash was raised by the Kaifong Welfare Associations and what they wanted to do was to get rid of it as soon as possible. We in the Social Welfare Office thought it would be better to use the money for new huts. We usually lost the argument. The money was spent on clothing and bedding or simply given out as cash.

Fires rendering three or four thousand people homeless were quite common. One at Fa Hui, in north Kowloon, burning down the homes of twenty thousand people overnight was pretty big. Immediately after that fire, the police opened the grandstands of their recreation ground for fire victims. At first, a good many went there. The numbers gradually diminished as people found relatives, but some two thousand remained. It was decided to build a temporary camp for two thousand people in the Army Recreation Ground across the road on Boundary Street. I had this job and did it in two weeks, laying on water and electricity in the bamboo and palm leaf structures we called matsheds. In order to limit the number of people eligible for this temporary camp, we closed the Police Recreation Ground at 3 a.m. one night and issued cards to those inside, giving them access to the new camp. We said this was a temporary camp. People gradually drifted away. A few were left at the end of the six-month period when the camp was closed.

Then came the Christmas Night Fire at Shek Kip Mei in 1953.

This conflagration was much more severe than anything we had seen. Shek Kip Mei was the largest squatter area by far. It might have contained up to one-third of all squatters. A fire here was a disaster we had all dreaded. I had left the Social Welfare Office by this time, but squatters were on my schedule as an Assistant Secretary in the Secretariat. I saw the blaze across the harbour from the car as my wife and I were driving down from the Peak after Christmas dinner with her parents. I decided to go over to see what I could do. All the great men were gathered near the fire site. I remember particularly the Commissioner of Police who had been so dissatisfied with the resettlement efforts. We all thought that something had to be done to provide housing and that, if this could be done now, then one-third of the problem would be solved.

I do not remember what time I got to bed, but the Governor had called a meeting at Government House at 6 a.m. on Boxing Day and so I went along. It was a bit of cheek as my only claim to be there was that I had recently built a temporary camp for fire victims. I was able to tell the august gathering that it would be impossible and futile to try to build temporary shelter for some sixty thousand people. The Governor, Sir Alexander Grantham, then turned to the Director of Public Works and asked him to make proposals for some permanent shelter. So the momentous step was taken for the government itself to build something for the fire victims.

Government housing — at last

The first two-storey Bowring Bungalows, named after Theodore Bowring — the Director of Public works — were up in a matter of days. Then came the six- and seven-storey Mark I Resettlement blocks and the beginnings of one of the largest and most extensive housing programmes the world has seen. The emphasis was on speed. These people were sleeping in the streets. Engineers, not architects, were given the task of clearing the fire site and producing fireproof shelter at the greatest possible speed. The resettlement programme of the 1950s was not a housing programme for the poor though nearly all the people who benefited were very poor. The aim was to house victims of squatter fires and to clear land for development. You could not apply for a resettlement flat. You were offered a resettlement room if your hut was burnt down, or if it was about to be pulled down. What you were offered was a concrete box allowing twenty-four square feet a head, in a seven-storey structure with no lifts, no windows but wooden shutters, no water, but access to communal kitchens and bathrooms. If this sounds dreadful, it was, but such was the alternative that people fought to get into the new blocks where you had your own place legally — and it would not burn down.

To provide emergency food for the numbers of people made homeless by the Shek Kip Mei fire stretched the Social Welfare Office to its limits. The distribution of cooked meals was a full-time, all-day operation which took place on two large playgrounds where the queues of fire victims stretched endlessly all day long as the huge tubs of cooked rice, vegetables and meat or fish were trucked from the kitchens. Cooking rice in a small pot is a skill that everyone had mastered. Today, the rigorous programme of high speed boiling followed by a long period of simmering at the lowest heat is all encapsulated in the electronic insides of automatic rice cookers. Trying to do the same thing in woks, some four feet across, using shovels for wooden spoons was a highly skilled job requiring considerable experience. The heat source was an ingenious burner invented by an engineer, by the name of Hughes, in the government dockyard at the time of the Fa Hui fire in 1953. This involved mixing diesel oil with a little water and dripping the mixture onto a hot plate. The water was instantly turned into steam, exploding the diesel into tiny droplets which burnt with a fierce heat. I was not involved directly in the relief operation after Shek Kip Mei, but I was pulled out of my quiet Secretariat job to organize the cooking and food distribution after a severe typhoon called Wanda, in 1962. So many people had been made homeless that we had to produce seventy-five thousand meals a day. We built makeshift kitchens on wasteland and looked for anyone who had experience in this sort of work. In the normal way, we never had to advertise for labour, but on this occasion we could not find enough men who had had the required experience, so we did advertise. A colleague, Jeremy Marriott, has ever since pulled my leg about using, in the advertisements, a vulgar phrase with a double meaning to get attention. I claimed innocence but we got our men, several having acquired the very experience we needed in the cookhouses of the prisons.

Colonial Secretariat

In the mysterious way, these things happen — I was moved after eighteen months in the Social Welfare Office to the Secretariat now with the grander title of Assistant Secretary 4. I took over from John Swain who did a spell in the government before going on to a brilliant career in the law. There were about five or six Assistant Secretaries, each given a schedule of subjects. In the morning, you would find a pile of files in your IN basket and tried to work out what to do next. One of my more congenial bosses, Kenneth Kinghorn, once said that he did not care how long I had to work on any file, but he wanted to see it in such a state that he would have to do no work on it at all.

Smuggling during the Korean War

My schedule included marine matters. This was at the time of the Korean War and the United Nations had imposed a trade embargo on practically all trade with China. Hong Kong is completely surrounded by China and the waters swarmed with fishing junks. The land border did have a chain link fence along it, but it was full of holes. Farmers crossed the border from China every day to till their fields in the British Colony. Some islands were almost in China, and on each side of the Hong Kong mainland, there was a bay whose far shore was China. Smuggling was a very profitable business. We had strict laws which were applied to those unlucky enough to be picked up by one of the very few police launches. Customs had none at this time. In addition to any penalty the courts might impose on those involved, the boats were confiscated. The owners could, and often did, petition for the return of the boats. These petitions were decided by the Governor sitting in his Executive Council. It was one of my jobs to prepare the papers for this body and recommend the decision. The appeal was prepared by a barrister so he put the best case on the matter. We found that an extraordinary number of fishing boats had stopped picking up boulders from the shore for ballast and were instead using such expensive weights as steel-reinforcing bars or galvanized iron pipes. Of course, this fooled nobody.

We found that permission was being given for the export of a great number of bicycles to the island of Ping Chau in Mirs Bay. This island in fact had no roads but was less than a mile from the Chinese coast of Mirs Bay. It lived by smuggling for it was no offence to transport materials within Hong Kong waters. Another centre was the Castle Peak area for this was no distance from the Chinese Island of Lin Tin and just across the bay from the Chinese mainland.

The Americans were our *bête noire* for they constantly imposed new rules on our trade. The life history of prawns and oysters had to be studied to demonstrate their respectable Hong Kong origin. Water chestnuts were a popular delicacy. Although they were not much grown in Hong Kong, they were freely available in the markets. The farmers even went to the length of importing the water chestnuts and burying them so that they could be dug up in the presence of the customs men to prove their Hong Kong origin.

That the Chinese authorities valued the services of those who smuggled the more valuable strategic goods has become clear in recent years. They have been rewarded by business concessions and prestige in their councils. After the Korean War, when exporting restrictions were relaxed, China's trade with Hong Kong was very much a one-way business. We imported most of our food and raw materials for our factories from China. Hong Kong exported practically nothing to China except money. This source of foreign currency was extremely valuable to China and, we thought, part of the reason British presence in Hong Kong continued to be tolerated. It was not until the opening up of China by Deng Xiaoping in the early 1980s that major two-way trade and investment between China and Hong Kong took place.

Letters to London

Our communications with London originated in the Colonial Secretariat. The most formal were despatches signed by the Governor. Most of the correspondence was in the form of Savingrams. Their style could be in the less formal one adopted in telegrams but were typed on very thin paper and went by airmail instead of the more expensive telegrams. Telegrams were much rarer. Of course the Colonial Office and, later the Foreign Office, could not possibly keep up with the events in Hong Kong. We really did operate with the 'high degree of autonomy' that is now enshrined in the Basic Law of Hong Kong. Certainly at my junior level we never gave a thought to what anyone in London wanted or thought of us.

One of my more memorable efforts at drafting was the report on the Shek Kip Mei Fire that we sent to London. I got all the bits from the departments involved and included a number of excellent photos that had been taken. We did not usually go to such trouble but I thought we had done a good job and that the people in the back offices of Whitehall should see a bit of Hong Kong life.

During this time, our old Secretariat building began to be replaced by the buildings that still constitute the Central Government Offices.

The East Wing was built first on the site of the mess of the Royal Hong Kong Defence Force Headquarters and we moved into the top two floors of this new palace. Air-conditioning, which had been the privilege of the top few, was laid on for all of us. I had a comfortable little room overlooking the Anglican Cathedral of St John's to the harbour. What a change from the plasterboard cubicle in the old Secretariat building. On the opening day, the Governor, Sir Alexander Grantham, said he was frightened by the thought of two thousand civil servants in one set of buildings. It did seem a monstrous number for the Secretariat and several complete departments that were originally housed in these buildings.

Cheung Chau again

Government quarters were very limited and many had to live in hotels. We had been lucky in being allowed to live in the flat of a Methodist minister while he went on home leave, but this came to an end. The prospect of living in an hotel with a small baby did not appeal to us. As the Methodist bungalow on Cheung Chau was empty at the time, we arranged to rent that. It was very small but bigger than some of the tiny flats. There were no water mains — supply being gathered from the roof or, if it did not rain, from a nearby stream. There was no electricity so lighting was by Aladdin Lamp and the fridge ran on kerosene. There was no phone. Groceries could be ordered from Asia Company by leaving the order book at the Dairy Farm shop near the pier for delivery the following day.

The snag was the commuting. The ferry used to take an hour and a quarter at that time so an early start was required for the run down to the pier. I did not mind that so much as the rather dreary trip home, often in the dark with very poor lighting on the ferry to illuminate the files I was working on.

What made it all worthwhile were the weekends. You could go home in daylight on a Saturday lunch-time and had the glories of the island. The bungalow had a magnificent view over the sea to Chinese islands and a delightful shaded verandah almost as spacious as the bungalow itself. There was a lively social scene on the island and we were popular with our friends from the big city who came to see us on Sundays.

5

District Office Tai Po

I had longed to be a District Officer but was a little disappointed to be sent there only a matter of months before I was due for my first long leave. This was to be for seven months after a four-year tour. I readily agreed to an extension of this tour for another four months. Who knew where I should be sent on return.

Terra incognita

In the 1950s, the New Territories were *terra incognita* for urban dwellers — and that included everyone of any seniority in the government. The Tai Po district, on the eastern side of the New Territories, ran from the Kowloon Hills to the border with China. The population was perhaps a hundred thousand. This was a farming community — rice being the predominant crop. Village life continued in very much the way that it had done for generations. Few villages had access to roads; none had electricity, running water, sewage, or refuse collection services. You had to go through an operator to make a phone call from town, and pay on a per-call basis. Where communal services were found, they had been put in by the people themselves.

Democracy was up and thriving, for the Hong Kong government did little in the villages. There were even remnants of crude local taxation systems. In Tai Po, Yuen Long, Sheung Shui and probably other centres, there was a sort of sales tax on all goods sold in the market. This was levied for the use of the Public Weighing Scales which had to be used for all major purchases so that buyer and seller could be satisfied as to the weights exchanged. The operation was put out to tender by the elders annually. Funds from the Public Weighing Scales financed schools, clinics and local public works. On Lantau Island there were a couple of stream crossings where the villagers levied a toll for public purposes. There was also what could be regarded as a wealth tax. Rich men were expected to contribute substantial sums for village facilities. Social pressure was such that no law was necessary. On Cheung Chau Island where there was a population not far short of ten thousand, there was no running water, no sewage system and electricity cost the earth from a private company. The villagers managed a market and dealt with all street and rainwater drainage. There were good little businesses in shipping fresh water from Lantau Island and the farmers saw to the disposal of night-soil. They had a police station, schools and a charitable hospital. In discussing the supply of water to Lamma Island, the Director of Water Supplies said it was not a requirement of his job to supply every little centre of population with a main water supply. 'In that case,' I said, 'you should be called the Director of *Some* Water Supplies.'

The only manifestation of government in the more remote rural areas was the occasional police village patrol, the village school and the registration of all the land title. Education had always been important. All villages had a little school. It was one of the successes of government policy that school buildings, and the salary of the schoolmaster, were paid out of general taxation. In this respect, the country kids were better off than their urban counterparts for there were nothing like enough schools in town, even at primary level.

Local public works

The Tai Po district can be thought of as comprising a capital letter 'C' adjoining a mountain range to the left. The hollow of the 'C' is a large sea inlet called Tolo Harbour. On the north side is the Sha Tau Kok peninsula and on the south, the Sai Kung peninsula. There were dozens of villages in these areas without any road access or any form of public service. Today, both peninsulas have networks of roads and it takes only an hour or two to tour the lot. At that time, the only way to get round was to walk or go by boat. The areas seemed much bigger when you had to put aside a whole day to visit a village or two.

I was fascinated by these huge areas on the map that nobody in the office seemed to know anything about, so I went on tour to see what was there. This involved long walks, rides on sampans and sleeping in the village schools. At each village, I asked about everything I could think of — crop expectations, ravages by wild pig, and so forth, but talk always reverted to the need for what we would now call 'infrastructure' — a rather grand name for a well, or a footbridge, or a pier, or an irrigation dam, or concrete on a village path.

District Officers had a vote called 'Local Public Works' from which they could draw money to buy cement for public works that the villagers undertook themselves. Each District Officer had $13,333 (a bit over £800) a year to spend. As the requests for infrastructure works could be assisted through these Local Public Works funds, I made a note of them. When the staff totted up the total requirements, they amounted to twenty years' funds. This was absurd. Even when I cut the list down to really essential works, the total came to two and a half years' funds — five thousand bags of cement when the annual allocation was for two thousand bags.

We all lived in pretty closed circles then so that any social gathering was often a continuation of discussion of our problems. It was at one of these parties that Norman Wright, the splendid Agricultural Officer, asked if I had asked Horace Kadoorie to help. It had never occurred to me that I could approach the great man who was one of our prominent industrialists and was doing so much to set up poor farmers all over the New Territories. Norman raised it with Horace and the next thing I knew, both of them had come to my office to ask about the problem. In a very businesslike way, Horace asked exactly what I needed. Fortunately, I was able to say 5,253 bags of cement, or some such figure. The Kadoories owned a cement factory. 'Done,' said he. 'You can have the cement if you can collect it from the cement company.' Of course, I had no transport for such a large consignment but the Kowloon-Canton Railway ran through the district. With a little persuasion, the KCR kindly agreed to lay on a special cement train to bring the bags to station sidings from which the villagers could collect it.

Not having told the District Commissioner what I was up to, I was a bit worried about his reaction. Fortunately he approved, which was just as well.

This turned out to be the beginning of a tremendous expansion in the Local Public Works scheme. It was not long before the Kadoorie

Agricultural Aid Association started its own works. To this day, you will see the letters 'KAAA' in the cement of paths, bridges, wells and piers throughout the old rural areas. Not to be outdone, we put DOTP on the few works we could do. Eventually, the government money was boosted from $40,000 a year for the whole New Territories to over a million — just to show that we too could match the charity of the Kadoorie family.

Domestic and agricultural water

These works transformed village life. One of the most significant for the women was the construction of simple water supplies. Many of the villages were in the hills and they were there because there was a plentiful supply of water for their rice paddy-fields. With a supply of cement, aggregate and pipes, the villagers constructed a simple intake on the nearest stream and piped water to a standpipe on the threshing floor in front of the village. For the women who had had to carry water from the nearest stream to the *kongs*, or water jars, in the houses, the elimination of this daily chore was an immense blessing.

Irrigation was another area that the villagers were prepared to spend effort on because rice can only grow in running water. Supply systems to the paddy-fields in our hill villages were very simple but more complicated in the Yuen Long plain. In our case, the irrigation works were just an earth-and-stone dam on the stream from which an earth channel was dug to the fields. They all leaked like sieves. The works we assisted in were the replacement of the earth and stone dam in the stream with a concrete one and a cement lining for the irrigation channel. These channels had usually been there for years so their alignment and gradients were already determined. The tricky bit was the division of the waters between that allowed to continue to flow over the dam and the amount to be diverted. We had no scientific or engineering expertise, but I found it was usually possible for the villagers to negotiate a split. They would first agree the approximate areas of paddy-field served downstream and along the channel. We then arranged for the level of the dam overflow and the channel intake to be the same. The widths were made in proportion to the areas of fields served. This tended to be in favour of the downstream fields. The dams all leaked underneath, though perhaps not so much as the original earth dams.

The other main group of works were the improvements to communications. A few of the paths in the New Territories had been built hundreds of years ago and consisted of broad paths paved with slabs of local stone. Most were much worse and had no paving at all. You could usually make them out but they were rough-going. Cement for paths was in great demand, but there was need for so much more that I took a rather jaundiced view of the desire for such luxuries. Only the experience of walking on some of the newly paved paths convinced me of the enormous improvement such simple works could achieve. They also made it possible to use bicycles for village transport of men and materials. In the hill country, streams usually had to be forded but in torrential summer downpours this could be dangerous, especially for school children. Traditional footbridges involved the construction of piers in the stream on which massive slabs of stone were set. There were very few of these. With the use of concrete and steel reinforcing, construction was much simpler and this became the fashion. Coastal villages had no piers so these were also in great demand for there was no other access. Before the pier was built, you had to wade out to the sampan — at least not always if you were the District Officer (DO). I remember my wife being most indignant at one village where I was carried out on the back of a villager while she was required to wade through the mud.

There was one set of major works I was never able to rehabilitate. These were massive earth walls, as wide as a road, fronted with stones, which were constructed across the mouths of the valleys at the seashore. There were nine of them, all except one in the Sha Tau Kok peninsula. As far as I could make out, they were built about the end of the eighteenth century. The whole coastal region had been cleared of inhabitants much earlier as a piracy suppression measure. As the villagers came back, they chose these valleys which were wide plains, practically at sea level, for their rice fields. They protected them with these massive sea walls which also enabled the villagers to reclaim a good deal of marginal land for rice. A gap with sluice-gates let the water out at low tide and the gates shut out the high tides. The 1937 typhoon, which did such damage all over Hong Kong, also damaged these sea walls and no proper repairs had been done at the time I was a DO. The cost of repairs was prohibitive. We did, however, use the shelter of one wall at Luk Keng to provide a large, and profitable, fish-pond — financed by the Kadoorie Agricultural Aid Association and run by the village.

Village communications

Most of the villages in the Sha Tau Kok peninsula were accessible by paths to the market town of Sha Tau Kok, though a sampan trip was easier for some. When the New Territories boundary was fixed in 1898, it divided the agricultural area serving the market town in two — half in China and half in the British Empire. The boundary actually went down the main street of the market town though it was not demarcated by anything more than a solitary boundary stone. The 'Ten Villages' continued to operate as they had always done until 1949 when the Chinese People's Government was set up. Even after the arrival of the Communists, the market town continued to be used by villagers on both sides. The border street occasionally became the scene of little demonstrations, one of which was unwittingly generated by a visit two of us made with the police inspector. The Police Superintendent was not pleased.

Villages in the northern part of the Sai Kung peninsula that fell in my district did not even have footpath connection to the rest of the district. They had to travel by junk. It struck me that a ferry plying in Tolo Harbour would not only be popular but also profitable. Tolo Harbour was cut off from the main Hong Kong harbour by some thirty miles of sometimes very rough sea, so it had never been considered for a franchised ferry service. I approached the Hongkong and Yaumati Ferry Company, which ran ferries all over the harbour and to the outlying islands to the south and west of Hong Kong island. I did not get an enthusiastic response. Now it happened that a friend of mine worked in the company that ran the Star Ferries which had the monopoly of the shortest and most profitable cross-harbour route. He complained to me that the government always went to the Yaumati Ferry Company when they wanted new ferry routes and never offered them to the Star Ferry Company. I immediately said I should be delighted if the Star Ferry Company would run a ferry in Tolo Harbour. The proposal was raised at a board meeting and immediately turned down.

News of the Star Ferry Board's discussions leaked out. Such was the rivalry between the two companies that the Chairman of the Yaumati Company sat up. No way was Star Ferry going to usurp his predominant position in the ferry network of the New Territories. He asked the District Commissioner if he could arrange for a tour of Tolo Harbour. We had a delightful old naval liberty boat as the District Office launch, so we took him on a tour of the waters of Tolo Harbour. We sailed in slow dignity past all the villages on the coast and out to the well-populated fisherman's island of Tap Mun at the mouth of the inlet. It was a glorious early spring day, not yet too hot to fear the sun. The villages were at their best for the spring rice crop had just been planted out. The bright green of the paddy-fields and the more sombre green of the new growth on the hills set off the white walls and black roofs of the villages with a background of brilliant blue skies and the occasional fluffy cloud.

The great man was moved by what he saw. The company had an old small ferry that was not big enough for his busy routes, so he sent it round and from that day there has been a twice-a-day sailing from the pier that used to adjoin the railway station near to Tai Po town. I do not think it ever made any money, but it was an immense boon for the villagers.

Judicial functions

I was glad that I arrived in the District Office just after the first professional magistrate had been appointed. I did not have to sit in court to deal with criminal cases as my predecessors did. We did not have much serious crime, but villagers would not put lights on their bicycles at night. District Officers were, however, still Land Officers and as such had to sit in Land Courts to judge disputes involving land valued up to the quite high figure of $10,000. We could also convene Small Debts Courts to hear cases involving sums up to $5,000. Although these figures were comparable with the jurisdiction of District Courts, they were unchanged from pre-war days when they must have seemed very substantial. I did not in fact have to sit in court as often as my colleague in Yuen Long where they seemed to be much more litigious. I cannot remember any small debt case of interest, but I did have a curious land case. This related to the management of some ancestral property close to the border with China, owned by a clan in China but managed by the registered manager living in Hong Kong. The plaintiffs came across to my office to argue that the manager was failing in his duty to use the income from the land for communal purposes and had neglected the proper observance of ceremonies of dedication to the ancestors. The poverty of these peasants compared to the same people in the New Territories was striking. Their clothes were freshly washed but patched and worn. Their demeanour was candid but they had a grievance. Our Land Courts were pretty informal places. We usually tried to arbitrate between the parties and were often able to reach a settlement without having to resort to formal proceedings in court. Sometimes this was impossible. The court also had to be convened if a formal decision was to be recorded as a judgement. Here the Land Officer, who was me, had to explain that nothing that had been said during the informal negotiations in the office could be taken into account. The parties had to make their case out from scratch. While discussions in the office involved Cantonese on both sides, in court we had to use English and interpreters. As the case was for the removal of a manager of clan property, and his replacement, it had to go to court. The evidence was clear even though I tried to empty my mind of all that had gone before. The villagers from China were right. The manager in Hong Kong had been pocketing the money for years. I duly appointed a new manager resident in China. How all this was reconciled with the communist doctrines of communal ownership and abolition of superstitious practices I did not try to enquire.

People would also come with problems that needed law but not my judgement. One such involved the Buildings Ordinance, a huge volume of legislation controlling every aspect of design and construction of buildings. The New Territories were considered to have so few buildings needing such complicated law that the Ordinance did not apply to the New Territories at all. Building plans involving reinforced concrete were submitted to the District Officers and we forwarded them to town for scrutiny by the Buildings Ordinance people. We passed on their reply. It was in our capacity as Land Officers that only we had power to approve the plans, but we were merely post offices. There were very few postwar buildings in Tai Po, but tenants of one such building came to complain that the landlord was putting their rents up. There was no inflation in those days so that prices tended to stay stable for a long time. I said to the tenants that as their building was a postwar building, there was no statutory control of rents and the landlord could charge whatever he could get. They still left with a sense of injustice. I could not help feeling some sympathy for them. Shortly after, they came to show me the summons they had received to appear at the District Court in Kowloon. Looking at this carefully, I saw that the definition of a postwar building exempt from rent control was defined as one for which the Occupation Certificate issued under the Buildings Ordinance was dated after some date in 1945. I told them to say to the Judge, 'As the Buildings Ordinance does not apply to the New Territories, no such Occupation Certificate has been issued and so rents are controlled at pre-war levels.' They learnt the formula off by heart. The next I heard was the District Commissioner telling me of a lunch with the District Judge when he said he had had a most peculiar case from Tai Po. Defendants had argued that no buildings in the New Territories were exempt from rent control because the Buildings Ordinance did not apply. He had had to find in favour of the defendants. 'What is more,' the Judge said, 'these were simple people and were not even legally represented.' I kept mum. The landlord in question was not happy. At a land auction, he asked whether buildings to be built on the land I was about to sell would be exempt from rent control or not. 'That is a matter you had better seek legal advice on,' I replied. The law was soon amended.

Disasters

We also had our share of disaster. A squatter fire in Tai Po Market burnt down a few huts. These fires were not uncommon, but I went to inspect the scene. The huts had been crammed together, laced with wire-netting keeping animals in pens. Quite unusually, there had been casualties among some who could not escape. The corpse of a young woman, burnt black, had not been removed when I arrived. Another glimpse of death occurred one Sunday afternoon. I was at home when the police rang to say there had been a tragedy at a nearby stream, popular with picnickers. Again I went down. The picnickers had been scattered all over the streambed when a sudden rush of water cascaded down washing them away. I helped to pull some of the bodies out of the stream bed before rescue work stopped with the onset of further rain. Some seventeen young people lost their lives. The villagers were devastated. They erected a simple monument at the site which is still there. These were not disasters on an international scale but brought me face to face with sudden death striking in the midst of ordinary life.

Foreign devils in dragon boats

We worked hard but we also had fun. I had rowed at Cambridge so when the Dragon Boat Festival approached, I began to wonder if I could beg a place on one of the fishermen's boats. Chatting after dinner with Jack

Cater, who was running the Fish Marketing Organization, we wondered what the chances were. One of the company said, 'Why not raise a crew yourself and row in the races?' This conversation took place after dinner. Jack thought we could borrow a sampan, so before we broke up, we had drawn up a list of people to be tackled. The idea was so popular that we had to raise a second crew. We called ourselves by the very irreverent names of *Fan Kwai* for a mainly police and army crew, and the *Kwai Lo* for the civilian team — two common abbreviations for *fan kwai lo* or 'foreign devils'. Tai Po did not have proper dragon boats at that time. The races were rowed in Hoklo fishing sampans. These were stripped of fishing gear and accommodated a crew of fourteen — six oarsmen, or paddlers, on each side, a coxswain and a gong-banger. We practised a good deal and I began to get the hang of this novel style of paddling. The trick was to twist the paddle just before the end of the stroke so that it feathered and flew out of the water for the next stroke. The rates of striking made any boat race crew look like picnickers. Steering these craft with a long oar over the stern was not a thing novices could do, so we engaged a fisherman for the job. When the great day arrived, we were astonished to see the massive crowds which had gathered to see foreign devils rowing dragon boats. We were left at the start by the fishermen but put in a spurt and were gaining rapidly. It became clear that we were not so much going to overhaul the fishermen as collide with them. Our coxswain boldly put his oar hard over to avoid this embarrassment and the effect was dramatic. The boat heeled over sharply and all six men on the outside of the turn fell off. That meant that the boat tipped over the other way and the other six all fell off. The sampan filled with water and would have sunk if the water had not been so shallow. Our gong-banger was a splendid Italian Catholic priest, Father Poletti, with a fine beard. As his seat sank below the waves, his beard floated up, but he uttered not a word until the boat grounded — which was just as well as we found he could not swim.

I should say a little more about Father Poletti. He had already spent a lifetime in South China, not far over the border, among the Hakka. He continued his mission throughout the Japanese occupation but found he was thrown out by the Communists after 1949. He then set up his church in Luen Wo Market, just outside Fan Ling Village. He and his large black motorbike on which he whizzed along our roads, beard flying in the wind, were familiar to everyone in the area. His mynah bird, in response to his command to say its prayers, would cry out 'Ave Maria' in a loud Italianate voice. Every day he would go down to the railway crossing at the border to meet any refugees that happened to be crossing — at that time, a great many Catholic and other missionaries were being pushed out of China. On one occasion he met my wife's brother who, with a couple of other young lads, had drifted into China in their boat some six weeks earlier. One of Father Poletti's brother's daughters came to call the other day, bringing news of the Poletti family we had visited on the shores of Lake Como.

Austin Coates has written a charming whimsical account of the life of a District Officer in the 1950s in his delightful book *Myself a Mandarin*. Austin had the Southern District when I was in Tai Po. His stories could have been only slightly embellished, if at all, for they rang true to me on the other side of the New Territories. I cannot resist adding one of my own.

The Tai Po slaughterhouse

District Officers were supposed to be all-powerful in their districts but apart from the absurdity of this suggestion, when I had a staff of eighteen to do all the land administration as well as everything else, you had to realize that New Territories villages were self-governing. The elders settled disputes, undertook public works, financed school building, ran clinics and generally saw to the orderly lives of those under their care. No DO could move without the support of the villagers and to challenge anybody of opinion was idiotic.

I found myself in a just such a confrontation brought on by the enthusiasm of the public health doctor. Pork is the favourite meat and every market town had a few butchers. It was available fresh every morning in the markets. Many other sorts of meat were eaten including dog meat. This was illegal, but the well-to-do seemed to be able to enjoy a dog meat dinner without interruption. Our health officer was appalled at the way pig-slaughtering was done in the market towns. The butchers did their own slaughtering in their backyards at five in the morning and the meat was on sale when the carcasses were still warm. There was no meat inspection or regulation of the slaughtering process.

Well, this could not go on! By laws were enacted which said that all slaughtering had to be done in licensed slaughterhouses and that all slaughtering outside licensed slaughterhouses would be prosecuted. The snag was that there was no licensed slaughterhouse and the government had no intention of building one. The hope was that someone else would.

Quite a lot of publicity was given to the new legal requirements and encouragement was given to anyone willing to build a slaughterhouse. Eventually, a bright businessman said he would build a slaughterhouse in Tai Po if he could have some land. A site happened to be available because it had been used for the local village refuse incinerator. The incinerator could not cope so refuse was taken a little way out of town and simply dumped in a new refuse dump. There was no tendering for the slaughterhouse site as it was a 'temporary structure' and the permit was issued, much to the relief of the health officer. Although the early publicity implied that many licences would be issued, it turned out that as there were insufficient meat inspectors, only one licence was contemplated for the Tai Po district. The businessman had spotted a nice little monopoly to be enforced by the government.

When work on the building actually started, the butchers became alarmed. Who was this businessman that was to be given a monopoly to slaughter all the pigs in the district? There were no restrictions on his charges. They would die rather than use the new slaughterhouse.

It was at this stage that I was brought into the dispute. Clearly, the government had made a bad mistake. There had been no consultation with the butchers. They were not going to use the new slaughterhouse. They got so worked up that they asked for a permit to build their own. How could I refuse? And what about the butchers of Sheung Shui, of Fan Ling, Ta Ku Ling, Sha Tau Kok and Sha Tin? They were not going to go to Tai Po for their slaughtering.

I could think of no solution so I invited the chairmen of the five Rural Committees to the office. I put the problem to them and we had some discussion. In the end, Ng Chung Chi, the doyen from Sha Tin, said, 'Let us think about this. We shall come back to you.' I felt a load lifted off my mind. If these men said that they would think about the problem, I felt sure they would think of a solution.

Their plan was simple. They would buy out the businessman and let the butchers have shares in the new slaughterhouse. The butchers seemed to go along with this except that the people from outside Tai Po were still not keen that the slaughterhouse should be called the Tai Po Slaughterhouse. I said that the name was meant to cover the whole district, not just the town. Before the war, there had only been two District Officers — North and South. The slaughterhouse was for the whole district, not just the town. We would call it the *Tai Po Pak Yeuk* (or North District) Slaughterhouse to emphasize the territorial reach of its services, thus reviving the pre-war use of the term *Yeuk* for the district.

So it was all settled — at least this is what I thought until I was at a wedding party forty years later. Chatting about the incident to one of the principal leaders, he said, 'Did you know how we fixed it in the end?' The businessman realized he was on to a good thing and was under no obligation to sell to the Rural Committee chairmen or the butchers. He held out and wouldn't budge. The Sheung Shui people then put it about that the government had agreed that they would also build a slaughterhouse. The butchers would use only theirs. 'What is more,' said my friend, 'we let it be known that the government had agreed that we could also slaughter dogs for the table.' That fixed the businessman, for it was clear that dog slaughter would not be allowed at Tai Po.

It was Cheung Yan Lung who told me the story. He had been an energetic young man when I was in Tai Po and was a great help in all sorts of problems. Together with Liu Yan Sum they built schools, including a secondary school, for the children of Sheung Shui. Liu was of the original Sheung Shui clan and Cheung had been brought up in Shek Wu Hui next door. I mentioned Ng Chung Chi from Sha Tin. He was a calm, unflappable Buddhist, vegetarian and teetotal, and generally regarded as the doyen of the rural leaders in my district. He was to play a significant part in the problems of the Thirteenth Term Heung Yee Kuk that I shall tell you about later. Pang Fu Wah from the old Pang clan of Fan Ling was the man of that village. All these men, even the rather retiring Chan Yau Choi from Ta Kwu Ling, without any formal official position, managed the affairs of their villages with very little help from officialdom. I have always thought that such men of worth were never properly recognized for the part they played in maintaining the peaceful life of the villages, particularly when hot heads might well have started trouble.

The passing of the rural scene

Life in the villages, even with such improvements as we were able to make, was tough. It was miles over rough paths to the nearest town, the villages were too small to support shops or any form of entertainment. Reading Reginald Thompson's account of that other territory leased to Britain for ninety-nine years in 1898, Wei Hai Wei in north China, you cannot help noticing the similarity with the old New Territories. Thousands of miles away, the social pattern was almost identical. It must have been the same all over China as recently as the 1930s.

That rural scene is no more. Even when I was in the District Office, we began to see the exodus of the New Territories villagers. For generations young men had gone abroad to earn a living either at sea or as part of the Chinese diaspora in south-east Asia. In old age, and at Chinese New Year, many came back to the villages. This was different. These young men were now going to the Chinese restaurants in London, Liverpool and elsewhere in England. Being born in a British territory, they were — until 1969 — able to enter the United Kingdom freely. Although not going in such numbers as the West Indians or Pakistanis, they did form little settlements in the larger English cities. At first, it was only the young men who went. Those whose births had not been registered had to get the Village Representative to make a statutory declaration before me to verify their birth in British territory. That is how I came to realize that some new shift was occurring. Others left the villages for better work in the urban areas until the villages themselves became the homes of women, children and old men by the 1970s. In 1980 I was in London, doing a Chinese New Year television programme of greeting for Hong Kong. Seeing an old lady in traditional Chinese Hakka dress in a supermarket in Soho, I asked her what village she came from. It was one in Sha Tin. 'Do you go back for Chinese New Year?' I asked. She laughed, 'There is nobody there,' she said, 'they are all here.'

By the 1980s, all the more remote villages had been abandoned completely. Left to themselves, the hills are no longer stripped of undergrowth for fuel. Trees are no longer chopped down for firewood. The hillsides are not burnt for the ashes to wash down as fertilizer. The jungle is taking over. In areas which were almost bald hillside, we now have thick forest and substantial trees.

6

Towns in the Country

In the early 1950s, town building in the rural New Territories was fraught with difficulties. The government took the view that it would only allow limited development in certain towns and do the minimum to provide infrastructure. Even in towns like Tsuen Wan, Tai Po and Yuen Long, there was only a very restricted plan within which development could take place. To put up a block of flats, you first had to acquire the paddy-fields encompassing the building lot together with half of the surrounding road and lanes. The government gave no assistance in this process. The developers were on their own in dealing with the landowners who might be individuals, but who often were clans or *tongs*. The process was excruciatingly slow. Very little development took place under this policy, nor was there very great pressure for it in most of the New Territories.

Permits for temporary structures

The advent of the new government in China and the subsequent flood of refugees brought new pressures to bear. The town of Tsuen Wan was close to the principal urban areas. Slow progress was being made in providing for the new industrial enterprise brought down by the Shanghai factory owners. There was no town plan to guide development. Tsuen Wan was administered by a District Officer. He was frustrated at every turn by urban land officials when trying to sell land for new factories. He could, however, issue temporary structure permits without permission from anyone. This he did and some quite considerable textile factories sprang up round the town. Workers came from the old urban areas and built their own squatter huts nearby.

Many of these new enterprises were quite small but they needed finance. Their land was not worth anything. If the factory was not in a squatter hut, it was only on a temporary permit. They did, however, have expensive equipment so the factories' head offices in town were able to arrange loans secured against their equipment.

Pierre Mardulyn, the manager of the Belgian Bank, was the first to set up a branch in Tsuen Wan. At first it lost money until the local manager, Yung Wah Kan, saw the pent-up demand for consumer finance. Individual loans, such as hire purchase, were small but such was the paucity of financial facilities that the aggregate was sufficient to turn loss into profit.

Further out in the New Territories, there was less progress and only a little less pressure. A pre-war initiative was agreement to a development called On Lok Tsuen, near Fan Ling where the owner of a substantial property was allowed to divide it up into individual lots for development. The streets were, according to the lease, to be built by the landowner with the only sanction being re-entry of the whole lot. A number of large family houses were built on the land, but no streets were built nor was drainage ever installed. Based on this experience, a postwar development nearby, by Pang Fu Wah, was authorized at Luen Wo Hui. Again, the government took no responsibility for the streets, drains, the market, or the common areas, leaving these to the original developer. The small market town did get built and streets were laid out. They were poorly maintained and again the only sanction was re-entry of the whole lot. In the case of Sha Tin, the District Officer, Brian Wilson, simply issued temporary structure permits for the market town by the station with the developer providing the streets and drainage. There was also one legal factory authorized in the middle of the paddy-fields. This textile factory came to be called Barrow's folly, by the city administrators, after John Barrow, the first postwar District Commissioner. He was an excellent District Commissioner but did not always see eye to eye with the government.

The first town plan

There was an ironic imperative for the first proper town plan in the New Territories — an imperative not in the interests of the people of Tsuen Wan but to accommodate interests of the urban areas. A large new reservoir was being constructed in the western New Territories, for the old ones were inadequate even with restrictions on water supply in the winter. The pipelines to the urban areas had to pass through Tsuen Wan, but the place was such a mess of old villages, temporary structure factories and squatter huts that only by drawing up a town plan could the line for the pipelines be determined. This led to the first resumption of land for urban development in Tsuen Wan and the first proper town plan in the New Territories.

The arrangements for the acquisition of agricultural land for development were outrageously unfair. The statutory requirements for land resumption in the Crown Lands Resumption Ordinance gave the government powers to resume land for public purposes and required that owners should receive compensation for the full market value for their land. This sounds fine, but what is the market value of a lease for agricultural land? One might think that all you needed to do was to examine prices at which land changed hands. Not so easy. There was a section in the Ordinance, Section 12(c), which limited compensation to the value of land used only for the purposes for which the lease was issued. No allowance was made for the speculative value of the land nor even adjustments to take account of the government's policies in land administration. The courts, on assessing land values, would contemplate only the value of land in use in accordance with the lease conditions. The compensation was derisory when compared with the price you actually had to pay if you wanted to buy land. The villagers felt so strongly that, had we persisted, we should have had serious riots on our hands. The government was seizing land which had been in the hands of the farmers for generations. They were not city dwellers. They had no way of earning a living in the town. They were simple sons of the soil and would resist all efforts to seize their land. There was no answer to these simplistic sentimental arguments, yet the facts of population increase and lack of land in the urban areas demanded development in the New Territories. You might think that the easiest way out would be to repeal Section 12(c) of the Resumption Ordinance so that the courts could simply have regard to market transactions when assessing the value of land. I did in fact suggest this many years later when I was District Commissioner, but lawyers and estate surveyors alike rejected it out of hand.

Fire and reconstruction

The lack of encouragement for orderly development meant that where there was demand, there was disorderly development of the squatter type. Such was the market town of Shek Wu Hui adjoining the old village of Sheung Shui. Both village and squatter town thrived on cross-border trade, for the border with China was only a few miles away. The best I could do here was to issue permits for some 'temporary' housing for an extension to the town. In 1955 the whole place burnt down. Lawful land tenure was still the Block Crown Lease for paddy-fields, whose boundaries were now obliterated. Clearly, reconstruction of the squatter town should not be allowed. The elders and the government were one on this. But how could lots be allocated on the basis of the new town plan in a fair and reasonable manner? Government policy was that all land for permanent development had to be disposed of by public auction, but the villagers were determined that city slickers would not be allowed in on their land.

The elders came up with the idea that all the agricultural land should be resumed by the Crown. The area resumed was larger than the area of building land to be sold, because land had to be used for the new streets. The ratio of agricultural land to building land turned out to be 5:2. It was therefore proposed that the auctions of the new lots should be restricted to holders of entitlement deriving from the ownership of agricultural land in the burnt-out area. Owners would be allowed to bid for two-fifths of the area of their agricultural land resumed. After some argument, the government agreed. These closed auctions then proceeded in several stages. As nobody had exactly the entitlement for a building lot, a good deal of negotiating and trading in entitlements had to take place beforehand. These discussions in fact led to the villagers deciding among themselves exactly who should bid for which lot. At the auctions, only one bid was made for each lot which went at the upset, or minimum, price — about two-thirds the estimated market value. All went well until the very last lot which involved the most protracted and heated negotiations before the auction when, again, only one bid was made.

That Cheung Yan Lung and Liu Yan Sum and their colleagues managed to secure agreement on such contentious issues showed how much weight their prestige carried.

This little scheme was a great success. Later on when we came to do serious urban development, we found that the ratio of agricultural land surrendered to building land available for development was still roughly 5:2 so that this ratio became embedded in development lore for many years.

New land for old

All over the world, agricultural land in the environs of an expanding city acquires what the economists called 'unearned increment' in value. The landowner needed to do nothing to reap untold riches from the increased value of his land. In the New Territories, the government had simply nationalized all the land by an ordinance in 1909 and granted leases to all the owners of their land. In order to maintain some control over development of this land, the grants of what was now Crown Land were made by a lease expiring three days before the end of the New Territories lease itself on 30 June 1997. After the initial surveys of the land in 1904, and the enactment of the ordinance declaring all to be Crown Land, a Block Crown Lease was drawn up. It would have been impossible to get every leaseholder to sign an individual lease for his few square feet of land, so a single Block Crown Lease was made out to cover the whole area. None of this seems to have caused much uneasiness for nobody seemed to lose anything. A Crown Rent was charged for the land, but it was less than old land taxes and, with inflation, came to be purely nominal. Land Courts were set up to settle many longstanding arguments over ownership and their judgements were generally regarded as fair.

The Block Crown Lease did, however, restrict the use of every lot to that which prevailed in 1904. If you wanted to build a house on an agricultural lot, you had to get permission and this permission was only granted at a price. Our policy in Hong Kong was an extreme form of socialism. The government expected to get the whole unearned increment and the landowner not a dollar. A really ludicrous situation developed some years later when a very left-wing MP for Liverpool, many of whose constituents were formerly New Territories farmers, was got at by the New Territories people. In England he would rant at the iniquity of unearned increment going to wealthy landlords, but in Hong Kong he was persuaded to protest at the 'unfair' policy of the government robbing the landlords for the good of the people. The Hong Kong government was being more extreme in seizing this unearned increment than any UK government had ever dared to try. He was not a very bright MP who did not enjoy the best of reputations for sobriety.

In 1960 we did not spend much time on doctrinal arguments about unearned increment, but we did need to get the farming landowners on our side. The Shek Wu Hui scheme, and the device used for hurried resumption of land for the first water pipeline from China, were the clues. We would accept the surrender of the land in exchange for a promissory note saying that when the infrastructure for the town had been built, we would grant the landowners building land in the ratio of 5:2 on payment of the difference in values of the land in the two uses. An important provision was that both agricultural land and building land would be valued as at the time of the surrender, not the time of grant of the new land. There were two benefits for the agricultural landowners: they got the new land by private treaty and land granted in, say 1968, for land resumed in 1960 would be valued at 1960 prices not 1968 prices and so would the value of the land granted. A further essential feature of the scheme was that the entitlements could be assigned or sold if the original landowner wanted to do so. The promissory letters were called Letters B, Letters A having been issued for the resumption of land for the water pipeline from China.

Letters B of course came to be documents of great value as the scheme matured. As the new town programme blossomed, so did a tremendous market in the Letters B. It all worked very well. The sons of the soil happily parted with their land for these new promissory notes which commanded such a good price in the market and we heard no more about the sacred rights passed down from generation to generation. Rural landowners soon found that they could get a realistic price for the land they were surrendering. Developers found that there were brokers who would assemble blocks of Letters B which they could use to get land by private treaty.

The scheme involved private treaty grants of land with no competition among possible bidders. At first, this did not matter for land was granted fairly quickly in the neighbourhood of the agricultural land surrendered. There was adequate demand but no real pressure. This could not last. When somebody got the grant of a fine site on the newly built road from Sha Tin to the Lion Rock Tunnel, on the road to Kowloon, without any form of tendering, the Financial Secretary started asking questions. By this time I was District Commissioner, so I devised a scheme by which auctions could be held in which bids by holders of older Letters B counted for more than those of holders of recently issued ones. This proved to be too complicated, but a simplified scheme in which land went to the bidder with the oldest Letters B was devised and it seemed to satisfy everybody.

The scheme was modified again and again and is now defunct. As an interesting footnote, I was fascinated to learn how the policy was adapted. It was found that, because of the enormous volume of public housing in the new towns, the ratio of 5:2 was no longer practical. It had to be reduced but the ratio itself had become almost sacred. It was decided that the ratio should be retained, but only for half the agricultural land surrendered — that is 5:1 for the whole lot but expressed as 5:2 for half the agricultural land surrendered and cash for the rest.

These devices for enabling development to take place without upsetting the legal doctrines of leased Crown Land may sound devious, but some urgency was needed to provide for increasing population and wealth. Even on reflection many years later, I do not believe better arrangements acceptable to the general population could have been devised. Land was made available for infrastructure and development as fast as it could be used and the landowners were satisfied with the compensation that they received. Both landowners and the government were left well-off.

7

The Big City

My time in Tai Po was drawing to a close at the end of 1954 for we had four-year tours followed by a long leave in England. I was asked to stay a little longer so that the man I had relieved in the office could complete his leave and take over from me. I did not mind a bit. The District Officer lived in a fine little bungalow called The Lookout. The government had bought this from the estate of a judge who had been executed by the Japanese during the war. It had no water mains but water was supplied from an intake on a stream which ran strongly all the year round. This not only supplied the house, the overflow went to a swimming pool in the garden. The view from the spacious lawn over Tolo Harbour, with scattered stake-nets for fishing, to the Pat Sin mountain range was spectacular. The job was great fun and as a young man with his wife of only two years and a baby daughter, we were very happy. I did not want to budge at all. But leave came at the end of 1954 and we travelled home on the old P&O ship *Carthage*.

When we returned to Hong Kong, I was very excited to find that I was returning to the District Office. Just as I was settling into a full four-year tour as District Officer of Tai Po, I was wrenched out of the New Territories back to town in the Urban Services Department. There was something of a crisis in the Urban Council and Urban Services Department which Ronald Holmes was asked to sort out. We had worked well together in the Social Welfare Office and he asked for me to be posted to him as Assistant Director of Urban Services.

Urban services

Urban Services — what a depressing sort of name, yet what else could you call a department which dealt with refuse, the dead, parks, food, hawkers, and became the custodian for such newfangled facilities as public car parks and swimming pools? We really had everything and I found myself as Assistant Director of the department at the age of thirty.

The new facilities were a test of initiative. The government had decided to build a public car park in the city centre by the Star Ferry pier and charge for its use — a novel concept in 1956. Nobody in Hong Kong had any idea how to run such a facility or which department should do it. It was an urban service, wasn't it? Give it to the Urban Services Department. As it was being built, we invented the rules and operational details as we went along, bearing in mind that anyone using the car park would be pretty mad at having to pay for parking at all. Then we had to think out a way of running the first public swimming pool which was being built in Victoria Park on the reclamation of a typhoon shelter. This was more complicated for we had to work out how to look after the swimmers' clothes as well as run the filtration plant and arrange for school swimming sports. It was a splendid pool, built to Olympic standards, and still gives great pleasure.

Gin Drinkers Bay

My first real challenge was the problem of Gin Drinkers Bay. This quiet inlet had earned its name from the launch parties that used to frequent it before the war. Now it presented quite a different picture. It was the refuse dump for the whole city. The working conditions were so bad that, desperate as people were for work, the men on the dump started to go slow as a form of silent protest. This put us in a tough position. The simple mathematics of refuse disposal meant that we could not face delays at the dump. The department owned eighteen refuse barges which carried the urban refuse to the dump. A day's refuse required six barges so we had six loading, six unloading yesterday's refuse and six usually under repair. Come what may the six barges had to be unloaded every day, or the stuff would pile up in the streets. The dump, which was in the sea, was protected on only one side by a sea wall running out from a promontory to an island. The barges were moored alongside this wall and the refuse was simply dumped into the sea on the other side. There was no road connection with the town. Lorries took the men to the nearest access point and they then walked to the dump. Once there it was a simple matter for a man to avoid work by reporting sick without losing a day's pay. The supervisor had no choice but to send him to the doctor back in town, a journey taking several hours. The least he got was one day's sick leave. As more and more men reported sick, the unloading process took longer and longer. It could not stop until it was completed later and later at night. The men got paid the same, however long they worked. It was clear to me that the situation could only get worse.

So I went out to see the place for myself. It was appalling. The stench was almost unbearable for there was no attempt to cover the refuse up. In the hut where the overseer worked, they were literally sweeping up a pile of flies six inches high. These were just those that insecticide in the hut had brought down. I went down onto the dump itself. I was warned that it was half-floating and I should look out for holes. The refuse in the barges had to be carried out by hand, basket by basket, to the face of the dump. I went down onto the dump and was soon surrounded by a small crowd of workers. They were not angry or rebellious — just weary and finding the going tough. They pulled up an old abandoned rattan armchair for me and we talked about their working conditions. Without any authority, I put a few simple proposals to them. I suggested that there should be a standard working day which should start from the time they arrived at the dump, and that there should be overtime for work in excess of this. They pointed out that there was no standardization of the volume of refuse, its nature, or the distance it had to be carried. I recognized the problem and said we should have to work out a scheme. They said that the nearest place where they could get a meal at lunchtime took more than half an hour to walk to and that there were no cooking facilities on the site. Back at the office, I was surprised how easily I was able to persuade the old hands that some changes were sensible. All agreed that we should give them a free cooked lunch for it was quite impossible for them to get fed any other way. As to the standard day's work, we decided that we could not fix a time in hours. If we fixed on, say eight hours, and paid overtime for hours worked in excess of this, they would dawdle all day and ensure they got plenty of overtime. Instead, we decided that the overseer would make a judgement on the spot as to how much, and what sort of, refuse there was and how far it had to be carried. He would express his conclusions in terms of a reasonable day's work for a number of men. If the men finished early, they could go home but still get a full day's pay. If there was more than could be handled in a reasonable day's work, they would be told how much overtime the day's work would involve and again the men could go home when the job was done.

The scheme was full of loopholes, but there was no time to argue. Once introduced, the scene was transformed. Men stopped being sick and would finish the day's stint at three or four in the afternoon, instead of ten or eleven at night. Extra loads got overtime pay but not very much more in hours worked. The free lunches were welcomed as was the new rule that their working day started from the time they got on the lorries in town, not the time they got to the dump. Other little improvements were introduced but it was still a fiendish job.

There was a constant turnover of labour. This gave me an idea when a priest, Denham Crarey, who was doing good work among discharged prisoners asked me if I could find work for his people. He swore they would do anything. 'Even work on the refuse dump?' I asked. 'Sure, they are tough and will do anything.' We always checked with the police for criminal records before employing anyone and they were amazed. My police contact asked where we were getting our people — murderers, burglars, and thugs of all sorts. I explained and he washed his hands of the security clearance if Denham vouched for them. Well, they nearly all turned up. Some even worked for a whole day, but the rest pushed off after the free lunch without even waiting for their pay.

Slaughterhouses again

I found that there was an ancient plan to replace the old pre-war slaughterhouses with modern abattoirs. It had got stuck and nobody seemed to know what to do next. An architect had been brought out ten years previously specially for the job. He was now the Chief Government Architect, but there was still no new abattoir.

I went to see the slaughterhouse on Hong Kong Island. I should imagine the scene would fit well into Dante's *Inferno*, though I must admit I have never read it. The whole place was swilling in blood. The men had on the briefest of shorts which they had been compelled to wear after some Urban Councillors found that they had been wearing nothing at all when working. The pigs were more or less running loose but were soon held down and stunned electrically by our staff — this was an innovation as the butchers had been in the habit of cutting the pigs' throats without any preliminary. The men of the Blood and Hair contractor cut the pigs' throats while they were unconscious but with their hearts beating to pump out the blood for collection in basins, and leave better meat for the butcher. The carcass was then dumped into scalding tanks to make it easier to remove the hair. There was this separate contract for the blood, which had a market value as did the pigs' bristles, but everything else belonged to the butcher who had bought the animal. The butcher then dressed the carcass on the concrete table tops, loading the offal and meat onto his lorries. The wholesale trade took place in live animals in lairages adjoining the slaughterhouse. Here the butchers would examine the animals meticulously and estimate their dressed out weight, an estimate requiring much skill and experience for it was on this that he made his offer and his profit. The offal would also be his to sell.

I found that the trouble with the plans for the new abattoir was that the butchers wanted nothing to do with the new scheme. My experience with the Tai Po slaughterhouse gave me a good deal of respect for the power of butchers with their long knives. In the new abattoirs, the wholesale trade would no longer be in animals but in carcasses which would first be chilled, the better to preserve the meat. The butchers could no longer get the offal of their pigs and cattle but would have to buy these separately. Furthermore, it was proposed that the two slaughterhouses, one in Kowloon and one on the Island, should be replaced by a single abattoir on the Island. The butchers would have none of this. I found they had never been consulted about any of the plans.

All the pigs came by rail from China, so I was first able to show the government that transporting all the Kowloon pigs across the harbour, and all the carcasses back would be very expensive. In any case, the population of Kowloon had now grown to exceed that of the Island so there was a need for two abattoirs, not one. Getting agreement to abandon the proposed change in wholesaling methods was more difficult. The new abattoirs were to be run on modern lines. After the initial stunning, the animals would be suspended on a moving track while our staff, not the butchers' as hitherto, dressed the carcasses which were intended to be delivered to the chill store where the wholesale trade was to take place. All the hard-won skill of the butchers in estimating the weight and value of the meat from an inspection of live animals would be of no use. They wanted the meat in the markets still quivering and could not accept the delay in the process involved in purchasing chilled carcasses. I not only had to deal with the public health people, but also the consultants for the abattoirs who had never designed a method to match up the offal of individual pigs and cattle with the carcasses after the slaughter and dressing of the animals. They were puzzled enough with the enormous throughput we required, which was larger than anywhere except Chicago. I spent hours poring over the plans, often at home, and for years after our daughter, then four years old, would not touch pork — rather like the effect of that wonderful film *Babe*.

I decided to call a meeting of the principal butchers to discuss the plans. I was warned against this by the health inspectors who had been used to doing things their own way. The problems the butchers anticipated were real enough. We in the Urban Services Department were in no position to dictate the methods of the wholesale trade. The customs were deep-seated and the butchers were strenuously opposed to change. They were happy to see new, more hygienic methods introduced at the abattoirs but would not change the way in which they conducted the wholesale trade. This must still continue to be carried out in the lairages before slaughter. There was nothing for it: we had to back down and design the abattoirs to suit the traditional ways. This I agreed to and the consultants were briefed accordingly. We actually saved money on the chill stores which would no longer be required.

I was posted away from the department before I could see the results of my work, but the two abattoirs were built — one in Cheung Sha Wan and one in Kennedy Town.

Hawkers

Much more interesting and difficult was the question of the control of hawkers. I admired these people. Practically, the whole of the retail trade in vegetables was conducted by them, yet nearly all of them were operating unlawfully. Meat, fish, cloth and a whole multitude of merchandise was also handled by hawkers. No policy that had been attempted by the Urban Council had brought order to this vibrant activity which clogged up so many of the streets and market areas for much of the day. The police did not have the manpower to control them but occasionally made raids to gather in multitudes of hawkers who were lightly fined and returned to their streets.

This was crazy. I prowled round the whole town looking at conglomerations of hawkers one by one, trying to see what we could do better.

I found that there were two natural limits to the activities of the hawkers. They did not operate all day and they did not operate everywhere. What was it that limited their activities in space and time? It soon became clear that it was their customers who imposed these limits. They wanted to shop every day, perhaps twice a day. They wanted vegetables to be sold near places where other food was sold. The key was the markets which were the only lawful outlets for the sale of what was called 'food for man', a quaint term from the by-laws used to cover only meat, fish and poultry. Although these commodities were sold by some hawkers, the fines were severe so sales were mainly confined to the markets. This meant that hawkers were also attracted to the environs of markets. Second, they only operated when housewives wanted to buy — the main time being early in the day, with some business in the afternoons, but none at night.

I went round the streets looking at the trade, area by area, and wrote a report for the Urban Council. The basis of the report was that hawkers provided an essential service in the absence of alternative retail outlets. The downside caused by congestion, lack of order and legality could be eliminated by proper daily control of the size of individual operations, by setting aside sufficient areas for all who wanted to operate, and by clearing everything away at night. We could accommodate all who wanted to trade because we could go on allocating pitches in the streets further and further away from the markets until nobody wanted them. Control would, however, require a considerable force of men to keep order and the police were not interested.

We did some experiments to show what improvements could be achieved. We picked some really crowded areas. One such was Yuen Chau Street in Sham Shui Po. This was no longer a street in the ordinary sense of the word. Down the centre was a substantial row of buildings, housing the shops of the so-called hawkers. We found an Urban Council by-law that said licensed fixed pitch hawkers could only trade from stalls approved by the Council, so we planned to give the hawkers two weeks to produce the stalls under pain of losing their licences. The Urban Council was prepared to see this through, though with some misgiving. When the notices were duly issued, nothing happened. We made a stall and put it on display at an adjoining playground. After several days, a man came up with a stall made like the model and it was approved. One or two more came but then a man came with one painted apple green instead of dark green. It was the right size and design but the wrong colour. He was turned down. I must say I was a bit uneasy when this happened, but it was in fact the decision that carried the day. The carpenters of Sham Shui Po now knew exactly what was required and the stalls were turned out in great numbers.

But still the street was cluttered with masses of stalls and huts. A few had moved but the bulk stayed put. We went round saying we really meant business and the Urban Council stood firm. On the last day, the deadline for the cessation of business was 10 p.m. There was a huge police presence and the department assembled enough trucks to cart away everything in the street. We found nothing but rubbish for this was all that was left as the hawkers had removed all their goods. From then on, the street took on an entirely new appearance. By day, the hawkers traded from their new small stalls three feet by four feet. By 10 p.m., these were cleared away and the street cleaned. The improved environment in fact improved business, but it needed substantial staff resources to keep up standards. We found the staff from the beaches as this was winter and the beach guards did not have much to do on the beaches.

Better day-to-day control of the hawkers required the presence of men on the ground. The police had better things to do. I therefore proposed a Hawker Control Force to be a disciplined, uniformed body under command of a police superintendent. This was before there were any traffic wardens or any uniformed staff of any sort except the police on the streets. The work of the new force would be excruciatingly boring and wide open to corruption, so I said their morale and discipline had to be of a high order or the whole scheme would flop. In the way these things happen, I was transferred back to the New Territories before the Hawker Control Force was established. It achieved some improvements, but it proved too difficult to motivate the men and in the end it was disbanded.

Unlicensed hawkers are still a problem but not on anything like the scale of the 1950s and 1960s. Oddly enough, the most successful hawker operations seemed to be those operated entirely without government intervention of any sort. I refer to the so-called 'poor man's night clubs' that used to spring up from time to time. One such operated on the Central reclamation near the Rumsey Street Car Park. This area was used for parking and for marshalling vehicles for the vehicle ferries by day, but at dusk the vehicles vanished and a thriving cooked food bazaar sprang up, complete with kitchens and lighting supplied from their own generators. By morning they had gone and the cars were back. There was no government intervention of any sort and the whole operation was entirely illegal.

In later years, I often wondered if we could have been more successful if we had involved the hawkers themselves more in our thinking. We did talk to them but we never devolved any part of control to them. It was said that the triads would take over, but it seemed to me that whoever it was that regulated the hawkers operated more on the lines of a club than a terror organization. In the nature of small businesses like these, some would prosper and some go under, pitches would change hands, all without any control by the government for it operated under such restrictive rules that procedures took forever. If they could manage what was really quite an orderly trade without government assistance on the Rumsey Street reclamation, would they not have co-operated in a system which gave them security in exchange for control by a body elected from among themselves?

Market rents

I mentioned markets as being the attracting hub for hawker operations. The Urban Services Department ran dozens of these markets all over Hong Kong where stallholders dealt in meat, fish and poultry — vegetables being the preserve of hawkers on the streets. In these markets, individual stalls were rented to the operators. If any became vacant they were auctioned, but there would usually be a claimant who was a relative or natural successor who would take over. Rents were not revised in any systematic way so that one could find one stall rented at pre-war prices while the one next door was rented at a much higher figure fixed by a recent auction. How could a logical system be brought to the thousands of stalls rented in the dozens of markets? And how could the stallholders be persuaded that the new rents were fair?

The only way out was not for us in the department to think up some new rent formula but to consult the stallholders themselves. The method I proposed was to assemble all the holders of meat stalls in one market and ask them which was the most valuable stall in the place. Oddly enough, this did not prove particularly difficult for they all knew the layout of the market and the habits of customers. The most valuable stall was then given a hundred points. From this starting point, all the other stalls were graded in point value measured relative to the most valuable. No rents were mentioned — just points which would one day be related to rents.

Next, a meeting was held with the fish traders and the same process followed. Of course, there was a good deal of discussion, but it did prove possible to come go agreement on the point value of each stall.

When all the stalls in the market had been graded with the most valuable in each commodity at one hundred points, a representative group of all the stallholders was asked to grade all the most valuable stalls in each commodity against one hundred points for the best meat stall. This was more difficult, but surprisingly decisions were reached without rancour.

When the process had been completed for all the markets individually, there came the task of grading the markets against each other with the most valuable stall in Central Market valued at one hundred points, and the final step of determining what the rental value of a point was. Thousands of stallholders had an interest in this, but I was determined that the grading should be done by the stallholders themselves so that the result would be accepted generally by all concerned. It says a good deal for the common sense of the traders and the patience of the departmental staff that a result was achieved at all, but it was. It formed the basis of revised rents which, in some cases, involved considerable increases. Everyone knew what everyone else was paying and all had made some contribution towards the final outcome.

Fish jumpers

Then there were the fish jumpers.

Fresh water fish are in great demand in restaurants. Practically, all were imported down the Pearl River from China. The fish were shipped live and landed at the two wholesale markets at Kennedy Town and Sham Shui Po. Market stallholders would then buy their stocks from the wholesalers. Unfortunately, there was often competition among the wholesalers for the fish brought down in the boats, either for the best fish or, in times of scarcity, for any fish at all. Prices were fixed by the state-owned importers while the wholesalers secured their supplies by physically seizing them. The wholesalers hit on the bright idea of hiring athletic young swimmers who would leap into the harbour with a net strapped round their middle, scramble aboard the boats as they neared the sea wall, and scoop up the best fish they could get. The scarcer the fish, the greater the number of fish jumpers that were hired by the wholesalers.

Harmless enough you might think. The coxswains of the boats took no notice of the scramble among the fish jumpers and so, sure enough, one poor lad was caught in the propellers and drowned. The police had racked their brains to find an offence that was being committed. It was not unlawful to swim in the harbour and the owners of the fish transports did not object. Some jumpers were arrested on some trumped-up charge. The fines were trifling and clearly were not going to put an end to the practice.

The number of wholesalers was not very large so we called them to a meeting and put it to them that this was a pretty silly way of rationing a scarce commodity. Could they not devise an auction system so that it would no longer be necessary to hire fish jumpers? The wholesalers were not particularly concerned, but they saw that we were seriously worried and wished to put an end to a dangerous practice which resulted in casualties. They did hoist the problem aboard and suggested they go away to think about it.

The solution they proposed was to prepare a priority list of all the wholesalers which would be valid for only one day. The next day the man at the top would go to the bottom while number two went to the top. When fish were scarce, they would be rationed to each wholesaler but the man at the top got first pick. There would be no competitive bidding.

This sounded fine in theory but would it work? We were assured it would and fixed on a day when the new system would be introduced. We put out a good deal of publicity and arranged a considerable police presence at the waterfront, though nobody was sure what they could do if the fish jumpers persisted. I went down to the Sham Shui Po dock and watched the boat come in with considerable trepidation. The fish jumpers were lounging round too. Closer and closer the boat came, but not a man jumped into the sea. The boat tied up. The fish were unloaded, raced up to the wholesale market and put on sale. It was incredible but who was complaining?

The answer was the jumpers after fish who said we had done them out of a job. They now had no means of earning a living. I saw some of the most affected and said that if they really did not know where they could get a job, I would offer them one as a workman in the refuse dump. Some took the offer but none lasted long.

Why were the wholesalers so co-operative? The import of freshwater fish from China at that time was in the hands of a Chinese state monopoly. The sale of marine fish landed by the Hong Kong fishing fleet was in the hands of a Hong Kong government monopoly, the Fish Marketing Organization. This had been introduced in the face of prolonged and fierce opposition of the wholesalers in the earliest postwar years. The China state firm had got it into their heads that when I talked about auctioning, I meant a new government monopoly. They were not going to have this at any cost. So they thought it better to co-operate in a less violent system of rationing to please the government, rather than not do so.

Disposal of the dead: The 1956 riots

The department also had charge of the disposal of the dead — people that is. We ran the cemeteries and the mortuaries. This was a weird and wonderful world. The cemeteries in town were full, but it always seemed possible to find a nook or cranny for some special person. The men in charge were competent and did not need me to tell them what to do. I was, however, shocked out of my complacency when some serious riots broke out in October 1956.

The trouble started in a housing estate where there were many supporters of the old Nationalist government, now in Taiwan. They plastered the buildings with the flags of the Kuomintang on the occasion of the Double Tenth, the anniversary of the 1911 revolution which deposed the Qing dynasty in China. The Communist government in Beijing did not celebrate this occasion: only their own National Day on 1 October, marking the day in 1949 when they installed the Chinese People's Government. There was a sort of annual competition in the early days of October every year when the Communist flags came out on 1 October and the Nationalist ones, in far greater numbers, on 10 October. Emotions ran high and there was always the danger of scuffles turning into outbreaks of violence.

In the Li Cheng Uk Housing Estate, the Nationalist flags were even more prolific than usual. The government was somewhat concerned at the ensuing mess but aware of the importance attached to the flags by the people in the estate. An officer in the estate decided to take some of the offending flags down. He was immediately surrounded by a hostile crowd and the police had to intervene. The trouble spread and led to general rioting in the Sham Shui Po area. It was so bad that the refuse collection staff were too scared to work that night. The trouble did not end with the night but continued and spread during the following days. Confrontations with the police led to open street battles. The army was called in at Tsuen Wan. The wife of the Swiss Consul was burnt alive in her taxi. The police had to open fire because tear gas was not dispersing the crowds.

The situation was getting very confused. Sporadic outbreaks of violence seemed to be occurring all over town. A curfew was imposed in some areas at night. What was worrying the Defence Secretary was that he could get no authoritative figure of the number of people killed. Some communications turned the army slang of 'bods', referring simply to people, into 'bodies', suggesting horrific numbers of casualties. The Defence Secretary rang me as it was the job of our department to deal with the dead. I undertook to give him a reliable and verified figure and keep it up to date.

Even in that confused situation, dead bodies were not left lying around. They were taken to the mortuaries where the doctors wrote down the cause of death. I went to both mortuaries to study the doctors' reports. Nothing could be learnt by me from the rows of cadavers lying on the slabs. The doctors' descriptions were very difficult to follow — nothing so simple as 'shot dead' — but written in obscure medical terms. Quite apart from casualties from the riots, people were dying in the ordinary way from all sorts of causes, including murder and accidents as well as just old age. I found it very difficult to work out from the reports just which had been riot casualties and which had not. It took a long time but I came up with a figure which greatly relieved the Defence Secretary. On his cross-examination, I insisted that if a man had not been found in our mortuaries, he was not dead.

In the fervour of the rioting, we began to get rumours of plans by the nationalists for great funerals for the fallen martyrs. This would have been very dangerous for the emotions of the crowds would be at fever pitch and ready for fresh trouble. I decided simply to order the immediate burial in the public cemeteries in the New Territories of all those in the mortuaries. If relatives came forward, they were to be treated sympathetically. They were to be told that immediate temporary burial had had to be undertaken. When things quieted down, we would identify the burial site and, if they wished, we would exhume the coffin for them to conduct their own ceremonies at the cemetery.

An enquiry after the event found that fifty-six people had been killed in the rioting. This had involved far more than mere patriotic excitement of nationalist supporters. The triads had taken the opportunity to show their strength and were the principal cause of the prolonged disturbances. It was still possible at that time to deport to China bad characters, described as such by the police, without any very great scrutiny. A huge clear out of the triads took place in the immediate aftermath of the riots. They never recovered from the damage done to their organization afterwards.

The Urban Council

All these matters were the responsibility of the Urban Council, but I do not remember spending very much time in meetings with them. I suspect that the Chairman, who was also the Director of Urban Services, Ronald Holmes, did most of the negotiating with the Council. We had such redoubtable characters as members of the Reform Club group of Brook Bernacchi, Alison Bell and Raymond Lee, the Civic Association led by Hilton Cheong Leen, and Sonny Sales who was so active that he was almost a party himself. Y. K. Kan, who I saw much more of later, was a sober, though often critical, voice in the bedlam. Of course, all our proposals had to be endorsed by the Council but I do not remember any hostility to any of them.

My time in the Urban Services Department had been nothing if not varied and, sometimes harrowing. We had elderly health inspectors from pre-war days whose methods I did not always find easy but whose help and wisdom were generously given and who were surprisingly supportive to this new young man with funny ideas. I am still friends with some of their children, now either retired or people of great importance themselves. The younger Chinese health inspectors were tremendous enthusiasts. They would kick new ideas around with enthusiasm and worked with great determination to make them work.

8

The Heung Yee Kuk and
Reservoirs

Return to the New Territories

I was now well into my second tour and was resigned to spending the
rest of it in the Urban services Department. It was not to be. A crisis in
the New Territories had led the Governor to post Ronald Holmes, my
boss in Urban Services, to be District Commissioner. In the New
Territories, an election of the Executive Committee of the Heung Yee
Kuk had been fiddled by an unscrupulous bunch of elders, and the new
bunch had picked a quarrel with the government. As usual, the people in
town had no idea of what was going on, but it was thought that a change
of face might do some good.

Ken Barnett was a most unusual man. A highly gifted linguist, he
had learnt his Chinese before the war in Canton (Guangzhou) where all
newly arrived Cadets spent two years on language study. During this
time, he not only learnt to speak Cantonese but also to read and write
and gain a deep knowledge of the Chinese classics. His war record in the
Hong Kong Volunteers was exemplary. As a prisoner of war, he was
tortured by the Japanese but he also, as a pastime, taught at least one
future Cadet his excellent Cantonese. He was a logical and scholarly man
but not really suited to the hurly-burly of the day-to-day politics of
administration. He was a fascinating conversationalist — if you had time
to listen. When he was District Commissioner and I was District Officer
of Tai Po, he called one Saturday just before lunch and sat down with a
beer and a bowl of peanuts, as I did. A few hours later, after declining

several times my wife's invitation to stay to lunch, he reluctantly decided to leave. The extraordinary thing was that I do not ever recall him telling the same story twice.

Ken was posted to undertake the first postwar census of Hong Kong's population. Here found his *métier*. There was no Census and Statistics Department then. He had to start from scratch to set up the organization and conduct an astonishing and meticulous piece of work which laid the foundation for the very high quality of Hong Kong's official statistics since.

I was sorry to lose Ronald Holmes as my director in the Urban Services Department, but it was not long before he had me posted to the New Territories to be his deputy. This was tremendous news.

What made it even more exciting was that Ronnie had very recently secured one of the plum houses on the Peak. He did not want to give it up to live in the official residence out in distant Tai Po. In view of the exceptional nature of his sudden appointment, the Governor allowed him to stay and I was required to take up residence there instead. What bliss. Island House was built in 1906 on a little island connected to the main road by a small causeway. Sitting on the small lawn to the east of the house, you had a splendid view over the waters of Tolo Harbour to the hills behind Three Fathoms Cove. When the moon was full, it rose directly in front, with its path of light on the sea stretching to the shore not fifty feet below. On a very clear moonlit night, you could see the mountains of the Tai Pang peninsula in China on the far side of Mirs Bay. The foreground was occupied by the Tai Po fishing fleet, a collection of sea-going junks and their attendant sampans. Fishermen then lived all their lives afloat and spoke a language that was unintelligible to the landsmen. They were not the quietest of neighbours but they did, for the most part, sleep when we did. At the back of the house was the main lawn and a tennis court formed by flattening the top of the island. The surrounding slopes were thickly wooded for many exotic trees had been planted by my predecessors. The stables, at sea level, had been converted into a garage so that on return home you had a fine health-giving climb up to the house.

No longer a Cadet Class II, I found that I had landed in one of the new senior posts that attracted acting pay. The sums were so enormous that I realized that if I got used to living in such style, I would never be able to survive on my basic pay. I saved the lot. I have never felt poor, but this was the only time in my career that I was able to save at all.

Although living in Tai Po, my office was in Kowloon. My children went to school there too. The best way to get to town was by train and many a scramble we had to catch it. Between us and the station was a level crossing. We reckoned that if we were held up by the train at the level crossing, we could just make it. Other friends would hear the sound and fury or our tearing down the hill to the station and dawdle about so that we could. It was a friendly station and it was not unknown for the man with the flag to stop the train when it was about to start. When we were in Island House, the trains were drawn by diesel electric engines. When we were at the Lookout, in 1954, we still had steam trains.

Political organization in the New Territories

There was not much time to enjoy our new luxuries. I had to dive into the crisis that had caused this sudden transformation in my affairs. Ken Barnett had withdrawn government recognition from the Heung Yee Kuk. This had not caused a ripple in town, but in the New Territories the enormity of his action shook the whole countryside. It was tantamount to a declaration of war between the government and the people.

The New Territories were the home of a long-settled population when the lease was signed in 1898. The Hong Kong government left the political and social system intact and it continued largely unchanged until after the Second World War. Village government was informal but effective. It was based on the elders of the village who emerged or were elected in a variety of ways. The Heung Yee Kuk had been established in 1926 as a result of one of the periodic squabbles between the New Territories landowners and the government. The Kuk had a loose sort of constitution based on the system of Village Representatives (VR), a system which we had formalized after the war. Village Representatives usually emerged by some form of consensus. In Tai Po, our people were much less quarrelsome than those in Yuen Long on the more prosperous western side of the New Territories. When a representative died, a replacement would be nominated by consensus. We would post a notice in the village calling for objections, if any, and in our case there were none. A VR once in was usually there for life, or until senility took its toll. In Yuen Long, they always seemed to need elections. These were good democratic jamborees in which all the male heads of households had a vote.

The Village Representatives from neighbouring villages would meet from time to time and a system of Rural Committees was beginning to be established. When I arrived in the District Office at Tai Po, Rural Committees had recently been set up for Sha Tin and Sai Kung North.

Sha Tau Kok had their Rural Committee which was formed from the rump of a much older organization of the Ten Villages based on the market town and fishing village of Sha Tau Kok itself. This area had been cut in half by the new border between the New Territories and China — not that it made much difference before the advent of the Communist government in 1949. The boundary between the New Territories and China was marked by a series of boundary stones, one of which was right in the middle of the main street of Sha Tau Kok.

Tai Po itself did not have a Rural Committee but did have an organization called the Tsat Yeuk, or Seven Districts. This body had been set up by the seven villages of, I think, Tai Po Mei, Cheung Shue Tan, Tai Po Kau, Tai Po Shui Wai, Lam Tsuen, Wo Hop Shek and Fan Ling. The object of the organization was to take advantage of the new railway station built to suit the line of the tracks but a mile from the then market town and fishing centre of Tai Po Old Market. Not surprisingly, the elders of the old market stood aloof from this new market on the other side of the river. So did Tai Po Tau, the home of part of the Yuen Long Tang clan. Although two of the villages in the Tsat Yeuk were well outside the environs of Tai Po, we treated the body as a Rural Committee for the time being.

When I arrived as District Officer in 1954, the District Commissioner, Eddie Teesdale, urged me to complete the coverage of the district by setting up one more Rural Committee to include the villages of Sheung Shui, Fan Ling and Ta Kwu Ling. This looked pretty hopeless. Sheung Shui and Fan Ling were right beside each other and were both of great antiquity. Perhaps it was their proximity that led to considerable rivalry between them so that neither would agree to join with the other. Ta Kwu Ling was part of another agricultural area that straddled the 1898 border of the New Territories. Its market town was Shenzhen which was firmly in China, adjoining the railway crossing at Lo Wu. A good deal of the land in Ta Kwu Ling was still owned by villagers on the Chinese side of the border who would come across daily to farm it. The Ta Kwu Ling people wanted no union with either Sheung Shui or Fan Ling. I did not try very hard to get them all together because it was obvious that it was a hopeless task, so I agreed that we should have three Rural Committees and helped them draft their constitutions.

The inaugurations of these bodies were splendid affairs. We wanted to give some dignity to them so it did not seem proper for the District Commissioner, who was then Ken Barnett, to walk across the paddy-fields to the ancestral temple at Ta Kwu Ling, dressed formally in his

Colonial Service uniform. 'Why not a chair?' I asked. They loved it and so did Ken. By this time, the only chairs around were designed for carrying demure little New Territories brides to their weddings. Ken was a man of ample proportions and had great difficulty in getting in and out of the chair. Later, my wife overheard the chair coolies say, 'Must have weighed at least two hundred catties.'

This structure of Village Representatives and Rural Committees was never meant to cover the whole population of the New Territories. Even in the 1950s, there were thousands of immigrant farmers from China who were outside the system. They were involved almost exclusively in vegetable growing and in fact produced about two-thirds of the vegetables consumed in Hong Kong. Their interests were largely looked after by the Vegetable Marketing Organization and the Marketing Co-operatives which maintained even closer ties to them than we did in the District Office with the traditional villagers.

The Village Representatives, Rural Committees and Heung Yee Kuk were designed for the indigenous villagers and have never effectively been expanded to cover other residents. The Village Heads, as is a literal translation of the Chinese name, are still heads of villages even if the villagers do not live in the villages or even if they have emigrated. There is a case for the continuation of the system so long as the limited coverage of the representative status is recognized as all villagers owe a loyalty to the village. In many cases, the whole village corporately owns substantial tracts of land.

Election coup for the Heung Yee Kuk

Although the Heung Yee Kuk constitution was not written down, it worked reasonably well. The Kuk faithfully reflected the views of the old established villages. In 1957, an unscrupulous bunch decided to stage a coup by conducting an election for the chairman and committee by a method that could yield only one result. All the names of all the Village Representatives, about a thousand of them, were printed on huge ballot papers. The VRs were to mark their choices for Executive Committee. Of course nobody knew everybody. How could the VR from the far end of Lan Tau Island know who was the best man in Sha Tau Kok? The villagers were helped in their choice by the coup leaders who gave them a list of the people to be elected. Ken Barnett saw what a farce this election was but he failed to prevent it. The election went ahead and the Thirteenth Term Committee of the Heung Yee Kuk was installed. The District Commissioner then withdrew government recognition from the Kuk. This was the situation when the new Commissioner and I were posted to our jobs.

Just to make things more complicated, construction of the northern catchwaters for the new reservoir being built at Tai Lam Chung had been brought to a standstill by villagers who were threatening the contractor's men with violence.

Hong Kong has an average annual rainfall of 2,000 mm, but it nearly all falls between May and October. The winter months are very dry so the water supply depended on having enough reservoirs to store the summer rains against winter shortage when the supply hours of mains water were often curtailed. This new reservoir would double the existing storage capacity so it was pretty important. To make the most of its capacity, a system of catchwaters, that is drainage channels, was strung out along the hills to gather water which did not drain directly into the reservoir. These ran along the whole length of the hills from Tai Mo Shan to Lam Tei cutting off all the water needed for agriculture in the Kam Tin, Pat Heung and Shap Pat Heung valleys below, that is practically the whole of the northern plains. The villagers, having found that protests to the District Officer were in vain, took the law into their hands and frightened the contractor's men off the site.

Tai Lam Chung catchwaters

The Tai Lam Chung and Heung Yee Kuk disputes involved many of the same personalities and the two disputes fed on each other.

The first thing was to find out what on earth the waterworks engineers were thinking of. Water was always scarce in these valleys in the winter. I had to do some research on water and agriculture. I found that to grow rice, the paddy-fields had to have running water. During the summer months, the direct rainfall on the fields is enough, on average, to supply all the water needed. For winter vegetables the fields needed every drop from the streams. The water engineers saw no problem. They only wanted water flowing off the hills from the summer deluges. The villagers could have the whole of the dry weather flow. It was scarcely worth collecting for the reservoir. They offered to construct a small intake on every stream just above the catchwater and put in a pipe big enough to carry the whole of the dry weather flow across the catchwater and down to the fields. The intake had no tap so the waterworks only got water that could not squeeze through the pipe in the summer rains. We had to tramp over the hills looking at the intercepting pipes and satisfy the villagers that the waterworks would only take water when there was more than enough for their cultivation. In addition, two small irrigation reservoirs were built on the northern slopes to store water for irrigation in the winter.

Of course, such a hot dispute could not be settled so easily. The catchwater would cut through the ridges behind several of the villages. These were the dragon's back of villages and the catchwater would destroy their *fung shui*. 'Right,' said the engineers, 'we shall tunnel past the villages so that the hillside will remain unscarred.' It saved them money and mollified the villagers. To ensure that all would continue to be well with the villagers, a *dun fu* ceremony was paid for at each village to pacify the deities. The Rural Committee chairman told me some years later that not all the money had actually gone in ceremonies but the spare cash had been spent on village public works. As everybody knew exactly what the government had paid out, I do not think much went astray. The last two major reservoirs to be built in Hong Kong did not rely on catchwaters dug along the hillsides. Instead, they depended on a network of tunnels that passed beneath the streams. From this network, branch tunnels reached up to the streams and swallowed the lot. Goodness knows what the Yuen Long villagers would have made of such a system.

The five principles

But the Kuk problem had not been solved though tempers had cooled somewhat. Again, the good sense of the elders came to the rescue. I did not try to draft a constitution for them. It was still rather disreputable to be seen to be involved with detailed discussions with the government. Instead, I suggested certain principles that could be incorporated in a formal constitution. These became known as 'The Five Principles'. They were released, as a proposal from the signatories, when I had got sufficient supporting signatures for them from among the most respected elders from all over the New Territories. Five men stuck out and it was impossible to persuade them. They had engineered the original coup and were not giving up. The dispute raged on, but I sensed we were winning.

In working out just what withdrawal of recognition meant, the appalling realization dawned on us that the Rural Committees were all unlawful societies, like the triads. They had not registered under the Societies Ordinance. Neither had the Kuk itself. It was a delicate matter, in the atmosphere of the dispute with the Thirteenth Term Kuk to try to get the Rural Committees to apply for registration under the Societies Ordinance. After some considerable persuasion, they did, one by one, apply for registration but only after being assured that they would immediately be exempted from the provisions of the Ordinance. That is their status now — societies exempted from the Societies Ordinance, not creations of the government. The government cannot tell them what to do.

As to the Kuk itself, I offered those on our side a formal legal constitution for the Kuk in the form of an Ordinance, or law of Hong Kong, which we were able to discuss in a reasonable way. This had the advantage of not requiring the formal agreement of the quarrelling elders for it would be enacted by the legislature — we just needed them to refrain from opposition, a much easier way of saving face. A place was found for the Village Representatives and the Rural Committees in the new ordinance. I thought all the wise men were included but was reminded that the Justices of the Peace, of which there were only a few, had been left out. One was the last surviving Qing dynasty mandarin, the elderly Li Chung Chong, who had qualified in the Civil Service Examinations. Although in his dotage, he was still of considerable influence, so we included a special place for the New Territories Justices of the Peace on the Kuk's Executive Committee.

The ordinance was fine, but what about the only physical asset of the Kuk, its office in Tai Po Market? All the registered owners of the land were long dead and it was not clear who it belonged to. The Thirteenth Term people had taken it over, but their claim was doubtful. The Gordian knot was cut by including in the ordinance a provision that the land would be resumed by the Crown and granted to the new body set up by the ordinance. The District Officer of Tai Po mounted a dawn raid on the Kuk premises the moment the new law came into force so that there would not be any unseemly fracas at the site itself.

Throughout this dispute, we had to proceed very cautiously. We could not make a move until we were sure of substantial support in the countryside. Government lobbying for support is no new thing: we lobbied like mad. Nobody in town had the least idea of what was going on though we did try, by way of lengthy reports, to enlighten them. A little public gesture of support for the government was made when all the New

Territories Justices prepared, on a vellum parchment, an illuminated loyal address which they were able to present to the Duke of Edinburgh who happened to be visiting Hong Kong at the time. I doubt whether anyone in the Legislative Council had any idea of what they were making a law about. The Colonial Secretary's speech talked about the desirability of an organization to give advice on New Territories affairs, but it was really a lot of hot air. The purpose of the ordinance was to bring peace to the factions who were tired of fighting each other but could not quite bring themselves to reconciliation. The bill went through on the nod.

During both of these disputes, I have to say that it was the wise elders who, in the end, brought peace to what was a very disturbing situation. I spent many anxious hours talking to these rural leaders, all involved in one side or another of the disputes. At first, they were so worked up that it was impossible to conduct discussions at all except individually and secretly. The two sides could be loosely described as pro-government and anti-government, but allegiances were not at all clearly defined and shifted. Tempers in the Tai Lam Chung villages were so hot that I felt quite uneasy on my first visit to the village nearest to the reservoir. In the case of the Heung Yee Kuk, many old enmities came out of the woodwork.

Ng Chung Chi, on the Tai Po side, and Chan Yat Sun, on the Yuen Long side, came to be the leaders who first recognized the futility of the quarrel and tried to mend fences. Between them and their supporters, they managed to cool things down to the extent that they were able to get backing for the Five Principles. My old friend of Tai Po days, Pang Fu Wah from Fan Ling, though now somewhat less friendly, was one of the coup leaders. I did not really know Tang Kin San, who was elected Chairman of the Thirteenth Term Heung Yee Kuk. The men I remember most clearly as being of such help in the case of the catchwaters are Tang Nai Man, from the ancient Tang clan at Ping Shan, and Tai Kuen. There were several others whose faces are still clear before me though their names have slipped away.

Reservoirs and village removals

I have mentioned the requirement for vast fresh water storage reservoirs to keep a constant water supply during the dry winter months. Until the de-industrialization of Hong Kong in the early 1980s, the demand for water grew at a steady 6 percent a year, year after year. Everyone knew about the state of the reservoirs, how low they were getting in the spring, how they were filling up in the summer, what was the state of the reservoirs at the end of September when the rains stopped. A report on the state of water supplies was made every week to the Executive Council and in fact only discontinued long after we had secured most of our supplies from China. During my time, four major reservoirs were built in the New Territories. Each of them required the displacement of old established villages and the setting up of a new home for the villagers. I was not a District Officer for any of them and the District Commissioner personally dealt with the policy problems they raised. Nevertheless, I could not avoid being involved when in the departmental headquarters.

All the villages to be displaced for the first postwar reservoir at Tai Lam Chung were ancient, well-established farming villages, so it was thought that rural agricultural resettlement would suit them. A site was found for them but the villagers did not like it. In fact, they did not want to farm at all. They saw this as an opportunity to move to the bright lights and asked for resettlement in Tsuen Wan. The upshot was that the villagers were settled in a new village, laid out in a square, in the new town of Tsuen Wan. Fields were replaced by shops and flats as a means of earning a living.

The second postwar reservoir was at Shek Pik on Lantau Island. Not only was the island itself remote from the urban areas, but the reservoir was to be at its south-western extremity. There was not a single road on the island which is twice as big as Hong Kong Island itself. Villagers scarcely ever left their village for this would involve hours of walking over the mountains to Tai O or Silver Mine Bay from which ferries sailed for Hong Kong Island. Both ferry terminals would take the best part of a day for most villagers to reach. The first problem was the discovery that, without bothering to tell anyone, the whole village at Shek Pik had been moved after some disaster had convinced the villagers that the site on which they were surveyed in 1904 had very bad *fung shui*. Technically, they were squatters on Crown Land and not entitled to any compensation. The District Officer was James Hayes who regularized everything by holding a series of Land Courts, deciding who owned which house and which fields so that they could be properly compensated. Some were resettled in a new village nearby, but most again opted for resettlement in Tsuen Wan.

James has included an excellent description of the trials and tribulations of moving the villages in his book *Friends and Teachers*. My recollections were of a harassed James turning up from time to time for long talks with Ronnie Holmes. No sooner was the last outstanding problem solved than yet another complication was discovered.

First visit to Sai Kung

My first visit to Sai Kung district — the area on the south side of the peninsula forming the lower part of the big letter 'C' round Tolo Harbour. The north side was in my district when I was in the Tai Po District Office. Ken Barnett, the District Commissioner, had decided to make a visit to both my district and to the south, which, at that time included Sai Kung. We did a tour round my district one day and spent the night on the District Office launch in Long Harbour. After more visits, the next morning we walked over the hills to Pak Tam Chung. Today, the whole area is a tourist attraction and all is a country park. At that time, it was remote and mysterious. The district had a distinguished history of communist resistance to the Japanese during the war and nobody was sure whether there were not still armed bandits about. I was somewhat alarmed on my first visit to the northern villages as I walked down to Chek Kang from the hills, to hear small arms fire. I kept on walking and was relieved to find that the noise was the letting off of firecrackers to greet the first District Officer they had seen since the war.

The bridge at Pak Tam Chung

The occasion for the visit to the Sai Kung district by the District Commissioner was to attend the formal opening of a new school and a bridge built by the District Officer, Austin Coates, over the river that gave the village its name. He had spent the whole of his Local Public Works money for the year on two projects in the district — this bridge and a causeway linking the island of Yim Yin Tsai to the adjacent island of Kau Sai. It was an extravagance, but only by visiting these remote but populous villages did the reason become obvious. The river could be forded in the winter, but in the summer rains it was a torrent that nobody attempted to cross. The school without the bridge would only have half its pupils. That little bridge is still there though everybody now uses the main road through the valley over to Long Harbour.

After the ceremonies, we returned to Sai Kung on a police launch which was a large Admiralty steam tug which had been given to the police after the war. There was no road beyond Sai Kung town and even the town only had a one-way twisting and precipitous jeep track.

Getting roads from waterworks

We now started to get what we could out of the Water Works Department for the general development of areas where the new reservoirs were to be built. In the case of Shek Pik we got a two-lane road from Silver Mine Bay to Shek Pik, albeit a dangerous road with a great many blind corners. It was the first road on Lantau and the subject of a novel by Austin Coates. The crisis in the story was the protest by suicide of the village head's daughter by drowning in the new reservoir. The book came out as we were in the middle of negotiations on village removal. Fortunately, it was only in English: we hoped nobody would tell the villagers about it. A narrower road was built over the centre of Lantau Island to Tung Chung on the north because one had to be built to a tunnel intake there. This is still the only road between north and south Lantau. There was more of a battle to get a decent road to Tai O, the principal town at the western extremity of Lantau Island. The engineers had to build a road over the mountain from Shek Pik nearly to Tai O to another water intake, but refused to make it more than a jeep track. In the end, we compromised by agreeing that the initial work should be for formation for a two-lane road but that only one lane would be surfaced.

Each reservoir was more ambitious than the last and they all seemed to double the total storage capacity of the whole system. The third postwar one was at Plover Cove, a large inlet off Tolo Harbour. This was the first time anyone had tried to build a dam in the sea to wall off a bay so that the salt water could be pumped out and be replaced by fresh water. The direct catchment was substantial but was supplemented by the construction of large tunnels to major streams miles away. Again, the villages on the shore had to be evacuated. This time, there was no argument about rural resettlement. All the villagers were resettled in flats in Tai Po Market, again with the income from flats and shops replacing that from fields.

There was no difficulty in getting a new road from Tai Po to the dam site out of this scheme. The road incidentally passed over the largest of the old village sea walls, built in the eighteenth century, which was finally incorporated in works that would be maintained forever after. We resisted an intake at Sam Ah with its road from Plover Cove to Double Haven on the grounds that there was practically no population there and that the area should be kept in its pristine state for conservation and recreation.

The last and largest reservoir was built not with one dam in the sea, but two across either end of a shallow channel between the mainland and High Island. Again resettlement was to town, this time to Sai Kung.

This work generated a whole network of roads throughout the Sai Kung peninsula to Three Fathoms Cove and over to Long Harbour and Jones' Cove. While the villagers benefited from the road network, development has been held at bay in what is now almost entirely country park.

I got myself into a bit of trouble over this project. I was by now District Commissioner and on a sailing trip over Chinese New Year. We called at the principal village on High Island, Leung Shuen Wan. They said they were having great difficulty with their water supplies from the local streams and asked for help to improve them. As the biggest reservoir in Asia was in the process of construction just over the hill, I felt I could easily promise them supplies from that source. You have no idea what consternation this caused in the Water Works! Yes, it was true that a huge reservoir costing hundreds of millions would be just over the hill from the village, but they had no intention of laying a pipeline for the villagers. It was built in the end, but only after a long struggle.

The engineering achievements of these massive works, the network of tunnels and pipelines, the filtration plants are worth a story on their own. That it was possible to complete them without any discontent, not to say fracas, with the hundreds of villagers whose homes and way of life had to be destroyed, is a remarkable testimony to the patience and care of the District Officers concerned.

The reservoir that wasn't

I was not one of these District Officers though at one time it looked as if I was about to be one. When I got back from leave after my second tour in 1959, I was posted not to headquarters but to a hot little new district of Sai Kung, where it was proposed that a new reservoir was to be built. The proposal was to wall off a major inlet called Hebe Haven and turn it into a fresh water reservoir. Unlike Tai Lam Chung and Shek Pik, this was a heavily populated area with several major villages on the shores of the bay. I began to talk to the villagers about resettlement, but before I got very far, it was decided that no reservoir would be built there after all. Plover Cove was favoured instead.

Great sighs of relief, but it left me with a tiny district and not much to do. Fortunately, the district included the southern half of the Sai Kung peninsula whose northern half I had got to know from Tai Po, so it was a wonderful excuse to visit all the villages on the other side of the hills. The district had no major towns and only two roads. One was a good two-lane pre-war road down the length of the Clear Water Bay peninsula to a gun emplacement for the defence of the eastern approaches to Hong Kong. In early postwar years, a permit was required for access to this road as nearly the whole length of it was used as an ammunition store, the munitions being stored in little huts at intervals on alternate sides of the road. The main road to Sai Kung town was a jeep track rejoicing in the name of Hiram's Highway. It was built by the army in the very early postwar years as a reward for the resistance by the Sai Kung people during the Japanese occupation. The road derives its name from the Commando Lieutenant, Hiram Potts, who was in charge of its building in early postwar days. He and his commandos laboured alongside people of the district to construct a perilous jeep track down from the Clear Water Bay road. Traffic could only move one way, and if you missed the timing, you had to wait forty minutes for the next window of opportunity. The widened road was only opened for two-way traffic just before Chinese New Year in 1960 — and it is twenty feet higher than it needs to be where it runs along the shore of Hebe Haven, so as to avoid its submersion in the rising waters of the reservoir that wasn't.

The district included Junk Bay which became the site of one of those short-lived industries that came and went at that time in Hong Kong. This was ship-breaking. This is a dangerous and badly paid industry. It needs little investment and can only survive on the meanest wages, which were then paid in Hong Kong. Our ship-breakers were able to pay less than the Japanese so the industry had moved to Hong Kong. Several very large plots of land and seabed were sold for this industry to move it from the main harbour. There was a steel mill in Junk Bay to turn the ships into steel-reinforcing bars. New mills were envisaged as adjuncts to the breaking process. Before any progress could be made on the new mills, the bottom dropped out of the ship-breaking business which shifted to Taiwan whose wages were even less than ours. The industry has now left Taiwan and is to be found at Bombay.

The Sai Kung interlude was an enjoyable one. We still lived in Island House because the man who had taken over as Deputy District Commissioner was a bachelor and was glad to give it up. I did not have so many late evenings in the job and was instead able to enjoy sculling in Tolo Harbour. I had bought a sculling boat from an old rowing friend in England and kept it in the garage at Island House. The waters of Tolo Harbour were wonderful rowing waters. It was possible to row in a straight line for seven miles from the house, knowing there were no other boats competing for space. Three outings a week and some at the weekends melted the weight off me. What with the sculling and the hill walks, I was fitter than I had been since leaving England — or ever since. The fishermen on the large mechanized fishing junks thought this little boat a great joke. I could just keep ahead of them even when they revved up their engines to full throttle and cheered like mad. I also had the boat when the Dragon Boat Festival arrived. I found the new proper dragon boats, which had replaced the Hoklo sampans, more of a challenge when practising off Island House. On the day of the races themselves, I rowed behind them but found that, because the racecourse was in very shallow water, there was a drag which reduced the dragon boats to a crawl however hard they rowed. My boat, drawing only a few inches, was not affected and I found I could scarcely go slowly enough to keep behind them.

This idyll in Sai Kung was not to last. Stern work beckoned in town.

9

People Moving

With the cancellation of the Hebe Haven Reservoir, I realized that there was very little left of the Sai Kung District Officer job, so it was not an entire surprise to be transferred back to the Secretariat. It sounded like an ordinary Assistant Secretary's job, but I was told of a new initiative. There was a good deal of dissatisfaction with the state of public transport, so it was decided to establish a new high-powered committee to investigate and advise. I was to be the Secretary of the Committee.

The Advisory Committee on Public Transport

It became a fascinating job. Nobody really had any idea of who travelled when or where, or what future requirements would be. In fact, nobody knew anything about transport as a subject. The police licensed the vehicles, the Public Works Department built the roads, and the Economics Branch of the Secretariat drew up the bus and ferry franchises. Nobody tried to bring the strands together as a subject called 'Transport'. This sort of situation kept on arising. The solution was to put one of us in the job to work it all out. Starting from scratch, I had a very interesting and stimulating time looking into long-term and day-to-day problems of all manner of transport.

In the process, I got myself into a promotion post as a Staff Grade C and became the first Commissioner of Transport. As Commissioner and as the Secretariat man in charge of transport policy, I was happily able to steer the Commissioner's sensible recommendations through the policy hurdles without difficulty. In my successor's time, the Commissioner was shifted into a new Transport Department. In due course, a Secretary for Transport was instituted so that the Commissioner could no longer approve his own departmental recommendations.

There had been a Traffic Advisory Committee, but it was stuffed with the public transport operators and was thought to be too partial to their wishes. This had been disbanded some time earlier. The new committee was to be confined to the issue of public transport and called the Advisory Committee on Public Transport. Chris Robertson, the CEO of Shell in Hong Kong, was appointed Chairman.

At a time when public transport operations in other countries were largely run by state companies, ours in Hong Kong were all run by private enterprise, except the railway to China. This carried only a few commuters to town and a minuscule passenger traffic to China. It was the big bus, ferry and tram operators that we were after.

It was obvious from letters to the newspapers that people were getting fed up with the bus services and nobody seemed to be worrying about them. As we had no other guidance, we started with the letters to the paper. It was then considered bad form for senior government officials to react to letters to the newspapers. We took a different view. From the outset, we made it a point to answer every letter we saw. It was my job to draft them, but the chairman signed. Often we could not say much for we did not know much, but we learnt quickly from our investigations into the substance of the matters raised.

An Advisory Committee to the government was, you might think, a pretty tame response to a bad situation. The chairman moved in much more influential circles than I did and lost no opportunity to champion our cause. Double-decker buses were common in Kowloon but rare on Hong Kong Island. When the boss of the Hong Kong Island bus company boasted, at a cocktail party, that he had introduced two double-decker buses on the Island, my chairman boomed out, 'But why haven't you got two hundred double-decker buses?'

Through his forthright public statements and the letters to the papers, the chairman began to get a good public image and much public support, so that when the committee 'advised', it was not easy to reject the advice. His ultimate weapon was resignation but this could only be a viable threat if he, and his committee, had widespread public support. This is what we went for. In addition to his letters to the paper, we put out regular reports and the chairman never declined an opportunity to speak. When the first chairman resigned on leaving Shell, his successor was Y. K. Kan, a tough and coherent member of the Legislative Council, who was in an even more influential position to champion our causes.

Nobody ever admits that their public transport system is good, but ours had pretty obvious symptoms showing that it was bad. The buses had no proper doors at the entrances. They had sliding railings which were manned by tough guys who pulled them shut when the bus was full, or more than full. They often had to use feet to repel boarders. There were no queues at bus stops — you fought your way on. At terminuses of services which were really totally inadequate, queues did form because the crowds were so great. We clocked waiting times of up to three hours. Only some sort of order could make the position tolerable and the people themselves formed and regulated the queues. Buses seemed to be full all day long. Rush hour started at about seven in the morning and went on until ten at night. Some experts said this was because of the funny working hours of our people. Because there were never any slack hours, the bus companies were very profitable. Years later, when people had more choice of when they could hope to travel, we found that Hong Kong people, like everyone else, really preferred to travel at the beginning and at the end of a normal working day. We developed less unusual rush hours. Empty buses were seen at off-peak hours.

Having said all that, I do not believe the public transport situation was as bad as it could have been. There was never a demand for bicycles in Hong Kong. When there really is no public transport, this is what people use, as we found years later when it was possible to learn more of what was going on in China. We saw the same thing in Kowloon in the early hours of the morning. There were no buses or taxis around at 3 a.m. Instead, tandem bicycles would emerge and cruise the streets. You jumped on the back seat, put your feet up on a footrest, and your driver pedalled you home. Goods carrying bicycles were used a little, but we never became a bicycle-riding community of the sort found in many other less prosperous Asian cities. All of Kowloon and the thickly populated parts of Hong Kong Island were flat and there were plenty of roads. The absence of bicycles suggested that people preferred to struggle with the bus system.

Taxes on public transport: Subsidies for car parking

As I studied the subject, I came to realize that our financial incentives were all wrong. In terms of the cost of accommodation, we were subsidizing car parking in the government multi-storey car parks in Central. At the same time, the bus franchise legislation imposed a sales tax of 25 percent on every bus ticket sold in Kowloon. It was described as a royalty of 20 percent of gross takings for the franchise. The formula was different on Hong Kong Island and for the ferries, but the tax was there. Public transport users were not only generating generous profits for shareholders but also paying substantial taxes to the government. No wonder there was nothing left for investment. It so happened that the large profits of the electricity generator and distributor on the mainland, China Light and Power, had also been noticed by the Financial Secretary. China Light had no franchise, anybody could set up a power station, but of course China Light had, in practice, established a monopoly. The upshot was that the government drew up a Scheme of Control which limited the profits going to shareholders and required that any excess should go into a fund for development. I saw the Financial Secretary, John Cowperthwaite, and asked if we could do the same with buses. He saw no real objection but asked how we could proceed, now that we had such a powerful advisory committee. I spelled this out to our new chairman, Y. K. Kan, who had established a reputation for taking on the establishment in the Urban Council. He agreed to make the proposal and asked me to draft for him. There then followed a curious situation in which I drafted a speech for him in the debate on the budget and then the reply from the Financial Secretary. For good measure, the chairman suggested that the loss in revenue from the franchises should be made up by increased taxation on petrol which was not used by diesel engine buses or taxis. I need hardly say what message emerged from this exchange in the Legislative Council.

Y. K. Kan was particularly good at taking on causes he thought of, or which I suggested. He acted like a minister and I was his civil servant, never appearing in public but doing the drafting and digging. Without any constitutional reform, we had in effect passed responsibility for public transport policy to this man and his advisory committee. The public went to them rather than the government. This was not the norm in Hong Kong where we had no ministers. It was the senior officials who announced and defended public policy. The situation is the same today. There are no ministers. There is no government party. Policy is made in the Executive Council acting as a single body. The Legislative Council enacts legislation and holds debates in which the civil servants, who are now not members of the Council, defend government policy. The difference then was that Y. K. Kan was a leader with ideas and not afraid to champion them. Without any constitutional authority, he established himself as a *de facto* minister for transport. Nor was transport the only field in which he took the lead, as we shall see.

When we started looking at public transport in general, we found an astonishing picture — rather, we could not get a picture at all. Nobody had any statistics of public transport travel, nobody knew where people wanted to travel. Nobody could make any believable forecasts of future travel demand. Our first initiative was therefore to commission a survey of public transport. We wanted consultants to find out where people travelled — no, the bus companies did not know — and devise a means of forecasting future demands.

Public transport survey

This was not the first traffic survey in Hong Kong. This had been done in 1958 by the British government's Road Research Laboratory for the promoters of the cross-harbour bridge or tunnel. It was a very workmanlike document. We decided to ask the same team to do a public transport survey for us. This involved putting together a model of travel generation related to such things as population, economic activity and so forth, and making forecasts based on more readily accessed forecasts of these parameters.

These forecasts led to more realistic planning for road building and began to tell us that road transport would not be enough to satisfy demand in the long term. In 1963, a Public Works Department Assistant Director and I toured several European cities to look at every form of public transport we could find. Several cities, Zurich and Hamburg, for instance, were putting faith in modern trams. We looked at a mono-rail in Germany; we got material on a French system that ran on rubber-tyred wheels. Nobody was building underground mass transport systems.

Our surveys led us to realize that even a major expansion of the road system and bus services would not be enough to carry people to work and play. A mass transport system for Hong Kong would be required. It was not long before it became clear that only a conventional steel wheel on steel rail train system, largely underground, could hope to carry the volume of traffic. When the consultants arrived, we were appalled at the extent of the devastation the construction process would cause. Could not the trains go along the coastline in reclamations or under the sea? 'No,' said our experts, 'the only way a mass transport system can pay is to choose the busiest parts of town and put the stations there.' It is obvious really, but it did mean that we should be faced with construction chaos on a scale that we had never seen — and we had just spent years completely reconstructing the whole length of Nathan Road, the transport spine of urban Kowloon.

I left the transport scene before the planning of the new system had gone very far. We had not thought about what we should call the system but kept using the term 'mass transport' in all our papers. The consultants did a doodle of a logo on one of the early drawings of a train. Nobody really approved the name or logo, but today the Mass Transit Railway and its logo are found all over town.

Taxis

While all this planning and thinking long term was going on, we had more mundane tasks ahead.

As bus services fell so far short of demand, entrepreneurs found many ways of providing illegally what was not provided legally — as has happened so often in Hong Kong before. Illegal taxis were found everywhere. They were called *pak pai*, or white plates, because their licence plates were white with black lettering, as in the case of private cars, which they were. Goods vehicles had white lettering on black plates and taxis were painted red and had red licence plates. The police would prosecute the illegal taxis but they fought a losing battle. There just were not enough taxis or buses, but who said there were not enough? It was the police who consulted taxi operators from time to time and would issue a new tranche of licences more or less when taxi operators thought they were needed. It was also the general view that only operators of taxi fleets could be relied on to maintain their vehicles properly and engage responsible drivers. New licences went only to owners of twenty taxis or more. I had just returned from a short course in London when this problem surfaced, and I had learnt something about the London taxi industry. There they were very tough on the requirements of the vehicles and on the geographical knowledge of taxi-drivers, but they imposed no overall limit on the number of taxis and had no objection to people owning a single taxi. Our police were open-minded and quite happy to depart from custom, so we decided to look at the problems *ab initio.*

Because taxi licences were so scarce, they commanded a high price. You could not sell them legally, but means were found to transfer operations with the payment of a hefty premium for the licence. I suggested that instead of the taxi operators getting the premium, we should put new licences out to tender for a premium and allow the owners to buy and sell licences freely. The taxi operators did not like this, but we got approval to go ahead. The first issue involved something like a 50 percent increase in the number of taxis. Tenderers had to tender for blocks of, I think, five licences as we could not get agreement to single operators yet. The first tender brought in $25 million, over £1.5 million. It was a huge sum then. When I bumped into the Financial Secretary, I expected some appreciation but, with a smile, he grumbled that I had made his budget surplus even bigger than he wanted.

Our object had not been to make money. We intended, and said we intended, to go on issuing licences until the premium dropped low enough to take off all numerical limits to the number of licences. In subsequent years, it was never possible to issue enough licences to prevent the inexorable rise in their value. Financing these licences became a new esoteric part of banking operations. We might have been wiser to eliminate the limit in numbers of taxis at the start and impose a colossal annual licensing fee. These fees could be adjusted from year to year to regulate the numbers in the traffic makeup. In later years, I sat in the Executive Council where we approved rises in taxi fares on the basis of increasing costs of operation. I never saw any attempt by the transport authorities to produce accounts which reflected the cost of servicing the premium, though this must have been substantial. If fares had been kept down, the premium would have been squeezed, since drivers had other means of earning a livelihood. I am afraid though that the premium is now such a large financial asset, neither the banks nor the taxi operators can afford to see it decline in value.

As usual, the picture in the New Territories was completely different. There just weren't any taxis at all. The only legal taxis were the red taxis of the urban areas who never entered the New Territories unless they were taking somebody home. The equivalent service in the New Territories was provided illegally either in lorries or *pak pai.* The law was so openly flouted, and for such good reason, that a new licence was devised for a vehicle called the 'dual-purpose vehicle' which could carry goods and was allowed to carry people accompanying their goods. The 'goods' soon became purely nominal so that these dual-purpose vehicles provided a cross between a bus and a taxi service and were the predecessors of the mini-buses that are so useful today.

There was clearly a demand for a taxi service that operated for journeys in the New Territories, but how could they be kept there and not disappear into the big city? We devised a new taxi licence which allowed operation only in the New Territories. They would be painted green and not allowed into town. Their fares were lower than town taxis so the premia tendered for them was less. We did think of allowing certain urban routes for them but decided the temptation to operate in town would be too great.

The cross-harbour tunnel

While I was in the transport field, another major issue was coming to a head — the cross-harbour tunnel. With the population almost evenly divided on each side of the harbour, and each amounting to around two million, one might have thought that everybody would be in favour of a bridge or a tunnel which would replace the car ferries. It did not happen often, but I do remember clocking up two hours waiting for a car ferry. Nobody expected to be able to drive straight on to a ferry. It is difficult today to recall the emotions, hostility and prejudices generated by the proposal to build the first cross-harbour tunnel.

There were vested interests in the establishment. Jardines owned the Star Ferry. Yaumati Ferry was owned by the Lau family. None of them would join in nor would Swires. The prevailing thought seemed to be that letting the Kowloon hoards swarm on to the Island, especially on race days, would be terrible. Who, I was asked, would run the buses to and fro in the tunnel between the areas where the two major bus companies operated? The protagonists were rather way-out people — Ken Watson, something of a maverick on the Legislative Council and those up-and-coming new entrepreneurs, Duggie Clague and John Marden who were challenging the old established *hongs*.

I was handed the three volumes of the Secretariat file in 1963 and tried to make sense of the government position. This seemed to be that while the government had no basic objection to a tunnel or bridge, it was not going to build one nor would it put a cent into it. Land for the ends of a bridge had been set aside. The promoters would be charged for all the land required for the approaches. A royalty of 7 percent of takings was spun out of the air by the Financial Secretary.

The first comprehensive transport study for a road crossing of the harbour had been paid for by the promoters in 1958. It showed that not only would the tunnel or bridge pay on the basis of a $2.50 car toll but that, to be sure of avoiding congestion, it should be of six lanes. The vehicular ferries at the time were charging $2.00 for a small car and $3.00 for a large one with an additional 20¢ for people in the car. There was plenty of time in the ferry queues for ferry company people solemnly to write out tickets in duplicate for every vehicle. The bridge was the slightly cheaper option but had to be ruled out because its towers would interfere with aircraft manoeuvres involved in emergency landings at Kai Tak airport.

The tunnel promoters were spending money without any acknowledgement or obligation from the government. I thought the government should get off its fence and say whether it wanted the tunnel or not. If it did, it should give some form of undertaking that the tunnel could go ahead if the promoters would comply with some basic conditions. As no formal company of the promoters had yet been set up, there was nobody we could do a deal with. It seemed to me that a Resolution passed by the Legislative Council would be sufficiently binding and give sufficient reassurance for the promoters to go ahead. The resolution, which set out the basic conditions for a franchise, was passed with one vote against. Only the one company came to ask for the franchise.

All seemed to be going well when my leave came due in 1963. When I got back, I was appalled to discover that the government was asking such a high price for the land for the approaches, and that the tunnel company was only going to build a single tube of two lanes. I can still remember the figures. A two-tube tunnel would cost $128 million, a single one $64 million. The government wanted $64 million for the land approaches.

The attitude in the government seemed to be that this was a private venture and if the tunnel was bunged up on opening day, that was no fault of the government. I could not understand how my engineering friends could go along with this even though they knew perfectly well that the forecasts foretold a disaster.

I decided to tackle the problem at source — the cost of land. The man in Crown Lands, Darcy Musson, explained his reasoning to me. It seemed difficult to challenge. Land worth $64 million would not be available for development. If the government wanted $64 million for the land, only one tube could be paid for. I am not sure how it came into my mind, but I said to Darcy, 'They do not want to develop the land occupied by the tunnel approaches. They only want to pass over it. Can you give them a wayleave and retain development rights for the Crown?' This proved perfectly acceptable to him for an annual fee of $75,000. And so it was. The tunnel was built in two tubes providing four lanes.

This ill-fated venture had another stroke of bad luck. In 1967, just as the promoters were finalizing arrangements to borrow money from the UK's Export Credit Guarantees Department (ECGD) at a concessionary rate, riots broke out in Hong Kong in support of the Cultural Revolution in China. The ECGD withdrew. The risks were unacceptable. Undaunted, Duggie Clague went to France to see if he could borrow there. He could. It would be more expensive but acceptable. The tunnel company was on the point of signing up when the British Prime Minister, Harold Wilson, heard that those nefarious Frenchmen under de Gaulle were about to finance the most prestigious infrastructure project ever built in his British Colony. Instructions were instantly issued to ECGD not to be so silly and get on with lending the necessary money. The same riots gave Hong Kong financiers cold feet. Only Duggie's determination kept the scheme alive. Jake Saunders at the Hongkong Bank showed the bank's support by taking a $20 million shareholding, but promoters were still short. The Hong Kong government was the only hope. The Financial Secretary was prepared to pull the plug on the project. He asked the Colonial Secretary if he thought it would be damaging to Hong Kong if the project were to fail at this critical juncture in our affairs. The Acting Colonial Secretary, who happened to be Ronald Holmes, decided that the damage to the standing of the territory would be serious. The government should take a 25 percent share. This not only provided finance, but was also a demonstration of the government's confidence in its own future at a time when many feared that the Chinese were on the point of taking over this last colonial outpost on its territory.

I had again been transferred to the New Territories by the time the tunnel was built, but I was an Official Member of the Legislative Council and so got a copy of the Executive Council papers. The paper on tunnel charges said that these had been set at $2.50 for a car in the original Legislative Council Resolution, but that if the tunnel opened on this basis, the vehicle ferries would immediately go out of business. If there was any trouble in the tunnel, Hong Kong would have no means of transport for cross-harbour traffic. The tunnel toll should therefore be doubled to $5.00

practically on its opening day. In the original Executive Council paper on the granting of the franchise, I had done a very elaborate discounted cash flow calculation to arrive at the tunnel toll — I think it was the first application of discounted cash flow used in the government. Yet, here was the charge being doubled simply for fear that the vehicle ferries would immediately go out of business. There was no discussion of the excessive profits the company would earn. I wrote to the newly appointed Financial Secretary, Philip Haddon-Cave, saying I was astonished at this omission and the lack of any fresh consideration of the royalty of 7 percent. He never answered — and I was too busy with more discussions with the Heung Yee Kuk to spend more time on it. That may explain how the tunnel operated profitably for its full thirty-year franchise period, through a period of great inflation, on a $5 toll and even with a $5 tax in later years.

The grand opening by the Governor in August 1972 took place in the centre of the tunnel itself. It was sweltering hot. I said to my daughter, 'Let's walk to Hong Kong. We shall never get the chance again.' And so we did. The tunnel was an immediate success. In addition to the tunnel itself, an entirely new road system had been built on both sides of the harbour feeding the tunnel. Journeys that used to take hours could now be completed in a few minutes. One casualty was the helicopter service from central Hong Kong to Kai Tak Airport on the mainland. The journey by vehicle ferry had become so unpredictable that the wealthy were prepared to spend a substantial sum to make sure they got to the plane on time. I do not suppose the owner of the helicopter company really minded. He was Duggie Clague.

Fortunately, I was on the Executive Council when the Secretary for Transport wanted to double the toll again to reduce congestion in the tunnel and, of course, the Tunnel Company was happy with the idea. Congestion at the tunnel had become horrendous. There was no financial justification for an increased toll for the company, but there was a good argument on transport grounds to jack up the toll to cut the traffic. It was in the Executive Council meeting discussing this increase that I suggested that instead of doubling the toll, the government could impose a tax of $5 which would ease congestion without interfering with the financial arrangements of the Tunnel Company. The paper was withdrawn and the new tax was introduced. The franchise reached the end of its thirty-year span in September 1999 when the tunnel reverted to ownership of the government. The Financial Secretary decided that the tax would be abolished but that the tunnel toll would be increased to $20 for a car to cut usage again. Taxpayers will get a nice windfall.

Star Ferry fares

A much less happy affair was the fracas over the increase of five cents in the first-class fare on the Star Ferries in 1966. For twenty years since the war, there had been no real inflation in Hong Kong. Transport charges had been unchanged and so had many government fees and charges. This was about to change with the advent of the ogre of inflation which was sweeping the world. The first increase was in the low water charges. The government proposals caused great public disquiet. Emotions ran high. The original intentions had to be modified. Public fury was largely assuaged by the allowance of free water up to an amount which was sufficient for daily use by a family. This is still the case today.

The first hint of a change in transport charges was the proposal to increase Star Ferry fares. In the days before there were any cross-harbour tunnels, the cross-harbour ferries were a vital part of the transport system and were very cheap — ten cents for second class and twenty cents for first class. The Star Ferry route was the most important and shortest link between Hong Kong Island and Kowloon. Ferry fares had been unchanged since the end of the war. The mere suggestion of a fare rise was greeted with horror. The service was very heavily used by commuters to Central, especially at rush hours.

The problem was thrown to the Advisory Committee on Public Transport for advice. One of the staunchest critics of the transport companies was the redoubtable Elsie Elliot. I recommended that she should be appointed to the committee so that its recommendations would have a better chance of being accepted by the public. The matter was studied at great length and it was clear that something had to be done to raise revenue in the light of increasing costs. I forget just what recommendation we made but it was for some form of fare increase which was not accepted by the Executive Council. They cut the proposal. An increase of five cents was to come in but only on first-class fares. Second-class fares would remain unchanged at ten cents.

Demonstrations had been mounted for several days. There was a hunger striker at the Star Ferry piers in Kowloon. The announcement of the decision led to the demonstrations turning into riots in Tsim Sha Tsui. The Chief Justice was appointed to conduct an enquiry into the causes of the riots. Elsie Elliot believed that the police were out to pin responsibility on her though it seemed pretty unlikely. She certainly had been vocal in public against the fare rise though she had signed the report of the Advisory Committee. She had considerable public support. The Chief Justice's report found nobody responsible but consigned Elsie Elliot 'to the bar of public opinion' — a phrase I never did really understand.

Hong Kong was not the only place to get into trouble over public transport fares at the end of a twenty-year period of practically zero inflation. There was just as much trouble in London when the $2\frac{1}{2}$d bus fare was to be doubled. In our case, I believe myself that the problems over water charges and the Star Ferry fares were also symptoms of deep-seated ineffective communication between the government and the people — a problem that came into sharper focus during the troubles stemming from the overflow of the Cultural Revolution into Hong Kong in the following year. The next chapter is about this.

Road pricing

When on leave from the transport work in 1966 and 1967, I found that Britain was considering the introduction of electronic road pricing. The economic arguments were sound, but the political difficulties formidable. I had read this up in my economics studies and found that the technology was now available. Through my brother, who was a member of Parliament, I suggested that Britain might like to assist or sponsor the introduction of road pricing in Hong Kong on an experimental basis and as a major development project. We had, then, about a hundred thousand vehicles and our roads formed a closed system as there was no cross border traffic. We also had an administration that could provide the engineering and running of the system and a public that could fiddle it if that was possible. I thought we might introduce this, first in the proposed cross-harbour tunnel and for charging for roadside parking, before moving to tackling congestion. The minister my brother consulted, Barbara Castle, turned us down. Even so when I got back to Hong Kong, I did tackle our economics chief. 'Has anyone else done it?' he asked. 'No, but Hong Kong could be a world first.' I was not encouraged. Perhaps it was just as well that I was posted away from transport to deal with the crisis of the 1967 disturbances.

10

Cultural Revolution

In May 1967 I was on leave in England when I began to read about strikes and demonstrations in Hong Kong. Just as I was just about to go on a sponsored visit to America in June, I got a message to return direct to Hong Kong. Thank goodness I did not get the directive earlier. I was just going to sit the final exams for an economics degree for which I had been studying on and off for three and a half years. For the last six months I had been at it from nine in the morning to midnight, six and a half days a week, so I was most relieved that this effort was not to be wasted.

When I got back to Hong Kong, I found the place in turmoil. I was due to go back as Commissioner for Transport but found instead that I was to be the second in command to Jack Cater who had been appointed Deputy Colonial Secretary (Special Duties). He was in charge of a small unit that had been set up in the Secretariat to deal with all matters relating to the troubles that we were going through.

Sir Jack Cater

I had first met Jack in London before I came out to Hong Kong when I was on the course for new recruits. Jack had joined the Hong Kong government in the British Military Administration, after distinguished service in the Royal Air Force. He is a man of great vision and determination. This was demonstrated in the very early postwar days when he and Dr Herklots and Father Ryan set up the fish and vegetable marketing organizations. Herklots was an academic botanist who produced a definitive account of Hong Kong plants but also knew the difficulties faced by vegetable farmers. Father Ryan was a teacher at Wah Yan School but also writer on music for the *South China Morning Post* and a tireless welfare worker. The ideas had been formulated during the war in the prison camps and were completely out of line with the view that the government believed wholeheartedly in business being run by private enterprise. These men knew of the hard lives of the fishermen who lived all their lives afloat from childhood until death. They were perpetually in debt to the wholesalers who were landsmen. The idea was formulated for the government to set up a fish marketing monopoly to take the place of the *laans*, as the wholesalers were called. In the heat of the early days of the resumption of government after the war, the scheme received the blessing of the Governor. The fishermen had a very tough time at the hands of the *laans*, but the organization was set up and still flourishes today, now in the hands of the fishermen themselves. A similar organization was set up as a monopoly for the wholesaling of vegetables grown in the New Territories. Jack was one of only two junior administrators to be made an MBE before reaching the top posts. When the government was faced with the 1967 disturbances, the Governor, Sir David Trench, picked him out for the novel post of an additional Deputy Colonial Secretary to mastermind government reaction to the disturbances. Again, it was drive and vision that enabled Jack to command the support of all the people involved — the police, the military, the intelligence community, the many departments on the fringes, the members of Executive and Legislative Councils and the general public.

Overflow of the Cultural Revolution

This was one of the most testing times suffered in Hong Kong. We were getting the overflow of the Cultural Revolution in China. I will not try to give an account of that extraordinary period of Chinese history for much has been written about it. In Hong Kong, we learnt about events from the papers but also from travellers into Guangdong Province. A sort of hysteria was sweeping through China. Thousands of ordinary people were being denounced as counter-revolutionary. The least they suffered was public humiliation. Many were killed. Factions fought each other in the streets. In Hong Kong, hard core supporters of the Communists in China thought they should emulate their fellow countrymen and start an uprising against the Hong Kong government. The first strike was at a factory whose owners the workers denounced. It led to disturbances outside the building which were put down without difficulty. There then followed a series of demonstrations, mainly in Central. The gates of Government House were plastered with posters of quotes from the Thoughts of Chairman Mao and so had a sort of inviolability. A procession formed to march up the main road to Government House but was turned back by the police. The demonstrators then besmirched themselves with red ink to make it look as if they had been brutally attacked. Loudspeakers were mounted on the roof of the Bank of China. Slogans and songs blasted out from them. The government responded with an even greater noise of Cantonese opera from the roof of the Information Services Department across the road. It was not long before both desisted.

While some of this may sound comic, there was a deadly campaign being waged by the hard-line communists in Hong Kong. In Macau, they had forced the Governor to go into China and make abject apology for the wrongs of the Portuguese government. Of course, our Governor would not dream of doing any such thing.

Had someone, in 1966, asked, 'If all the communist papers denounced the government, all the communist trade unions went on strike, the Foreign Ministry in Beijing issued the crudest vituperation about the wickedness of the Hong Kong government, then what would happen next?' I think most would have answered that this was only the preliminary to a Chinese takeover of Hong Kong which would be supported, or at least not resisted by the general population who would be too scared to do anything else.

In 1967, all these things happened. The government was lambasted in the most extreme language by the communist press in Beijing and in Hong Kong. The most senior political figures in Beijing used extraordinary language of abuse of the Hong Kong government and its governor. Our position was difficult. Although the troubles were an obvious reaction to the official encouragement of the Cultural Revolution in China, we had to make it clear that in dealing with the protesters, we were not acting against the Chinese government, or against the communists as such or against the Cultural Revolution. Our actions were directed simply at the preservation of law and order. Those arrested were prosecuted in the courts for offences against public order and, if found guilty, were sentenced as criminals.

Ostentatious support for the government

Public reaction was the reverse of what might have been expected. The steadfast action of the police in resisting the rioters, acting not against the Chinese government or its leaders, but maintaining civil order, won universal support from a public that was becoming terrified. Most of them had fled the Communist revolution in China and wanted to stay under British protection. More than $3 million was donated overnight to a Police Welfare Fund. Public declarations of support for the Hong Kong government began to appear. The first such declaration was made by the Hong Kong University Students Union. It was the start of an avalanche of similar declarations from hundreds of organizations who advertised their support in the papers.

The tactics of the communist agitators took many forms. Bombs were made up from gunpowder extracted from firecrackers. A commentator on Commercial Radio, Lam Bun, who ridiculed the communist propaganda was burnt alive in his taxi. The communist press threatened a further campaign of assassination and carried photos of the next targets. Students in a communist-controlled secondary school prepared bombs in their laboratory. The whole port was said to be on strike though in fact cargoes were being handled normally.

For a couple of days, there was no delivery of pigs from China by train. This was serious as it was always possible for China to cut off the food and water supplies on which we depended. We searched the region for alternative supplies of pigs, but none could supply the volume of animals we needed. The summer rains had failed and the reservoirs were nearly dry. We had been getting water from China for some years, but the agreement was that none would be supplied in the very wet months of the summer. The agreement did say though that if we needed additional supplies during this period, we were entitled to ask for it and our request would be considered. A request was made through the normal channels. There was no answer.

Border trouble

There was trouble at the border too. One night, gangs from the Chinese side swarmed over and surrounded a border post. The Gurkha Commander and the District Officer went to negotiate. They were not allowed to leave. A tense situation developed. Both the Gurkha Commander and District Officer and a handful of Gurkhas, who had been disarmed, were held inside the police post. This was surrounded by the mob armed with knives and bludgeons, while the mob itself was, in turn, surrounded by Gurkha soldiers ready to put them all to flight. The stand-off continued all night during which an attempt was made to negotiate a quiet end to the incident. The mob was worked up into a hysterical state and would have gladly taken on the Gurkhas even knowing they had no chance of survival. After a night of on-and-off negotiations, it was agreed that if the District Officer and Gurkha Commander signed an apology, the mob would withdraw and return the arms they had taken from the soldiers in the early stages of the confrontation. Not many criticized the two officers who had signed under duress. Had they not done so, there would have been a short but fierce action resulting in many being killed.

In another incident, a police inspector went down to the border to try to deal with an argument that had developed over the handling of trucks bringing pigs across from China. The Chinese captured the inspector and carried him off to China. Protests to Beijing led to negotiations between the District Commissioner and Chinese officials at the border, but no formula was found for the return of the inspector. In the end, he escaped and got over the border. To this day, there is dispute as to whether things had been made easy for him to escape and walk for some distance through heavily patrolled country to the border. His cap and some other items of uniform were returned to the Hong Kong negotiators afterwards, accompanied by contemptuous derision from the communists.

Raids on union premises

In town, a steady campaign of rioting was being mounted. Mobs would emerge from union premises or communist shops yelling slogans and waving the little red books of Mao thought. Although we were pretty sure that preparations for these forays was undertaken in easily identified communist buildings, we refrained from entering them for quite a long time. In the end, the public became impatient with our reserve. The decision was therefore taken to raid the union premises and communist shops and announced in a stirring speech by Ronald Holmes, who was Acting Colonial Secretary, when he affirmed that the government would 'seize and retain the initiative' in dealing with the troubles. These raids resulted in colossal hauls of knives and other weapons though not much in the way of firearms. The raids got massive publicity especially when one shop building was raided by police landing from helicopters on the roof. The organized forays ceased.

Perhaps the most alarming incident took place one Saturday morning when armed militia came over the border at Sha Tau Kok. They shot up the police post, killing a number of Hong Kong policemen. There was no knowing whether this was a local initiative or the beginning of a proper invasion. A response in strength was clearly beyond a police action. Were we to send in the army and possibly start a war with China? In 1949 when the People's Liberation Army came down to the Hong Kong border, they were confronted not by the British army but by the Hong Kong police. Ever since then the border had been manned by the police, not the army, which occupied positions slightly further back. A decision to send in the army to retake the police post at Sha Tau Kok required approval in London over a weekend. It took the whole day to get it, during which time the Gurkhas were formed up just short of the border. When approval eventually arrived, the militia were found to have retreated. From that time, the army took over control of the border until shortly before the handover of Hong Kong to China when the police returned.

Ban on firecrackers

Bomb attacks in the streets became a real worry. Packages bearing warnings for compatriots to keep away were attached to some real and some fake bombs. Children could not read this and some were killed. A police inspector had his leg blasted off by one such bomb. For a while, until we got proper bomb disposal squads organized, these bombs did some serious damage. The bombs were simple home-made devices using gunpowder extracted from firecrackers. As they persisted, the government took a step it had never felt strong enough to take before. All firecrackers were banned. People were told to hand in any they had to police stations. For years the government had wished to ban the indiscriminate discharge of firecrackers because of the casualties that were caused at Chinese New Year. Letting off firecrackers was a traditional means of celebrating weddings, grand openings and especially at Chinese New Year when there was a free-for-all for a few days. Now public support for a ban could be counted on. For a night or two, everybody let off any firecrackers they had so that it was a bit like Chinese New Year. The police were pretty relaxed about this for, as one said, 'At least those will not be used in bombs.'

Throughout the disturbances, we took great pains to emphasize that we were not acting against communism or the Chinese government but only against people who were breaking the law in Hong Kong. The authorities in Beijing did, however, protest at the detention of a man from the New China News Agency who was arrested at the head of one of the street riots. They put pressure on the British embassy for his release which was resisted. Threatening mobs appeared outside the embassy building. The pressure for the release of the New China News Agency man increased for he was really a diplomat. The governor would not agree to a release for he was being held simply for breaking the law. He had no diplomatic immunity and had been found guilty and sentenced to gaol. The culmination of this incident led to the burning down of the British embassy in Beijing and the detention of a British reporter for Reuters.

We were kept busy for nobody knew where the next attack would occur. We put ourselves in the shoes of the agitators to see what mischief we could devise and then prepared counter-measures. For a short time the government took powers to detain, without trial, people who were suspected of causing trouble but against whom there was insufficient evidence that would stand up in court. A maximum of about fifty people were held for some weeks.

Sir Y. K. Kan

I have made several references to Sir Y. K. Kan. I should say a little more about a remarkable man who has served Hong Kong so well over decades. We first found ourselves tackling hawker problems together, in the 1950s, when he was a young solicitor newly appointed to the Urban Council. I worked most closely with him in the Advisory Committee on Public Transport in the mid-1960s.

Y. K. Kan was what we used to call an Unofficial Member of Councils; that is, he was a man in private business, a solicitor and banker in his case, who was appointed by the Governor to various government bodies. First, it was the Urban Council, then the Legislative Council and then the Executive Council, in which he finally served as the Senior Unofficial Member. This was a position of great responsibility. The holder did not simply turn up on Tuesday mornings to a meeting and then go home. Quite apart from other bodies on which he would sit, he would be consulted frequently by the Governor on any matter of importance, particularly on matters which were arousing controversy. He would also be of considerable influence in the community, due partly to his personal standing and partly his position on Councils.

During the 1967 disturbances, Y. K. played a significant part in securing support in the community for the government, and was vilified by the communists for his pains. His photograph was printed in the communist press as the next target for assassination after the murder of Lam Bun. A bomb was put outside his house. On police advice, I tried to persuade him to accept a firearm for protection but he declined.

Nor were his public activities confined to counsel in meetings. I have seen him in action cajoling intransigent public transport operators and coaxing people with a grievance. He would be asked by Murray MacLehose, who was his last Governor, to intervene in disputes of great notoriety — for instance, when he ended a strike by slaughterhouse butchers which had halted all meat production for days. Again, the police were once on the point of going on strike. They were consumed by resentment at the mayhem that the Independent Commission Against Corruption was causing in the syndicated corruption that permeated the force at the time. Y. K. was asked to intervene. He gave them an account of a police strike he had seen in Guangzhou and how, when law enforcement was withdrawn, the police themselves were the first to be butchered. The strike never happened.

Leaders of this calibre are rare.

The passing of the frenzy

As time passed, it seemed to us that there was a lack of determination to follow through the action of the agitators. The train loads of pigs were soon restored. We learnt that the stoppage was due to chaos in China disrupting rail services, not a plan to deprive Hong Kong of its food. Although no reply was received to our request for extra water during the summer months, the water supply was resumed on 1 October in accordance with the agreement. No further assassinations took place after the first incident. Although it was rumoured that the Bank of China building was a veritable arsenal of firearms, none were issued to the mobs. The rioters had no guns. Good ways of upsetting the system were not followed through. It gradually became clear that the agitation in Hong Kong was not being supported by the powers in Beijing. By August, the communist unions seemed to be definitely toning down their hostility.

If this chapter is confusing, it is nothing to the state of affairs at the time. We never knew what would hit us from day to day. I find it difficult to give a coherent account of a very confusing time. At the time, I was living in quarters at the New Territories border of Kowloon and working in the Secretariat on Hong Kong Island. I concluded the fastest way to cross the harbour was to use a motor bike and so bought a 90 cc Suzuki. This not only enabled me to move through the traffic with expedition but, as motor bikes were sent on to the vehicle ferries first, I had no waiting there. Even so I had to leave home soon after seven in the morning and got back very late. The day started with a reading of the overnight intelligence reports, if there was no urgent meeting to attend. Throughout the day, we were kept in touch with events from POLMIL, the headquarters of the joint police and military organization that was in charge of security. We then had to react, usually with a seat of the pants reaction for there was no plan to follow. Even lines of communication sometimes got confused. On one occasion, the Governor was having a meeting with the top military and civilian security chiefs when the Tai Po District Officer came through direct to me about a developing incident on the border. I got through to the Colonial Secretary who suggested a change of tactics. Fortunately, a rather ham-fisted plan was aborted. Using the formal line of communication, the message would not have got through for another twenty-four hours — about that length of time too late.

During all this time, the need to ensure public support for each step of the escalation of our actions was paramount. Some thought we were too slow in reacting to provocation, but we would rather suffer this criticism than be accused of brutality or using unreasonable force. In general, we did not move until we were urged to act. This was a delicate balance to strike. Had we been rougher, or had we not scrupulously observed legal niceties, we could have easily lost public support with untold consequences. This was a testing time. I believe we came through it with credit. The police force was named the Royal Hong Kong Police Force in acknowledgement of the key role they had played.

11

City District Officers

Lack of communication

During the 1967 troubles, we did a good deal of thinking about communications between the government and the people. 1966 had been a bad year. We had experienced considerable hostility to the raising of water charges. We had had the Star Ferry riots over a five-cent rise in their first-class fares. Although the primary cause of the 1967 riots was the overflow of the Cultural Revolution, the 1966 problems suggested a serious lack of communication between the government and ordinary people in town. In the New Territories, there were the District Officers who were accessible. They had a brief to maintain close communication with local leaders and generally with the life of their districts. The widespread disturbances of 1967 in town were not repeated in the New Territories. There was no equivalent to the District Officer in town. All senior officials were located in a few offices in the business centre on Hong Kong Island. None were to be found in other urban centres. Jack Cater and David Trench, the Governor, were determined to change this.

Town learning from the country

The plan was to take a leaf out of the District Officer book in the New Territories and set up a similar organization in the urban areas, in order to transform communication between the government and the people. It was my job, in the few intervals of action during the 1967 troubles, to get this City District Officer Scheme off the ground. Any policy must start with approval by the Executive Council so I simply started to draft an Executive Council paper. Normally, this would be preceded by numerous meetings, minutes, interdepartmental discussions, perhaps even the appointment of a committee. I thought it simpler just to start drafting. We were in a hurry. Of course, I had to get my draft paper cleared by a few people, but everyone was so busy with the disturbances and their ramifications that nobody wasted much time on examining my paper in great detail. There was generally sympathy with the idea and I encountered no opposition. Eventually the draft was completed, but the Governor mauled it about. Governors do not usually spend much time amending draft Executive Council papers but this was an exception. David Trench had been keen on the idea for some time so he had considerable input. I was delighted, for it showed he was really interested. The paper went through the Executive Council without difficulty and the senior posts were approved by the Finance Committee on 24 January 1968. By then, it was possible to disband the Special Duties organization in the Secretariat. The Secretariat for Chinese Affairs had been the traditional link with the population so the new scheme was to be housed there. I was appointed a Deputy Secretary for Chinese Affairs to implement it.

It was a great pleasure to find myself again working for Ronald Holmes, under whom I had worked in the Social Welfare Office, the Urban Services Department and in the New Territories. He was, by now, the Secretary for Chinese Affairs. During the 1967 troubles, I had also come into contact with him, for he had acted as Colonial Secretary for some time, and was deeply involved with our activities in the Special Duties group. His leadership made it easy to launch a new scheme, feeling our way but working at speed in untried ways.

From the first, we had an excellent press. Our aim was to reach the people so that they could access the government in their districts. At that time, the only senior people in the urban districts were the Divisional Police Superintendents. The City District Officers (CDOs) were to be a local manifestation of the government, accessible for complaints and enquiries and a source of information on government policies. The CDOs were also actively to get to know society in the districts and understand their own particular problems.

Some said we should give CDOs some services to run but I resisted this. I believed that if we once went down that road, we should be given trivial work or work that nobody else wanted to do. The object of the scheme was not to do something that someone else was already doing, but to do something that nobody was doing at all. So we had no powers over other departments. For convenience, we followed the police Divisional boundaries and so had ten CDOs — to do anything else would take time and time we did not have.

Each District Office was set up in a small rented shop in the busiest part of the district. And we made the place look like a small local shop. We had a counter and took over the Public Enquiry Service which had already been established in the Secretariat for Chinese Affairs. We had a shop window with displays about public services. During the 1967 disturbances, many shops had installed steel shutters over their shop windows and pulled them down at night. A few were beginning to leave them up. Our shop windows had no steel shutters down and we left the lights on all night. People were encouraged to drop in.

The key to success

The key to the success of the City District Officer scheme was the quality of the men appointed as CDOs. George Rowe, the Establishment Officer, a genial and kindly man saw this and quite ruthlessly picked out some of the best men in the service for these appointments. There were also two City District Commissioners, Stuart Webb-Johnson in Kowloon and James Hayes on the Island. Both had been very successful District Officers in the New Territories and knew what we were after. There were no girls among the first CDOs for there were so few of sufficient seniority in the service, but it was not long before girls started to be appointed. No new grades of staff were invented for the supporting staff who were all Executive Officers operating in field rather far away from their desks. Most of the District Officers have gone on to greater things though Hong Kong suffered a great loss in the premature death of David Lai. He surely would have been the first Chinese Chief Secretary had he survived.

People contacts

City District Officers immediately set about making contact with the social groups in the districts. Important people in the districts began to call on them. One very perceptive CDO, David Lai in Mongkok, reported with glee that the *taam cheung*, or senior non-commissioned police detective, called on him before he called on the *taam cheung*. The significance of this was that these *taam cheungs* were widely believed to be hand in glove with organizers of vice and corruption and not men to be trifled with. David also wrote a report on illegal gambling which was found all over town and very largely ignored. It could have only survived on the back of widespread syndicated corruption in the police. Such was found to be the case when the Independent Commission Against Corruption was set up in 1974.

In these days when all departments go to much greater trouble to keep in touch with their customers, many of our initiatives would look commonplace. Things were different then. Perhaps an extreme example was the attitude of the Treasury. When I suggested they might have more than one centre on the Island and one in Kowloon for the collection of taxes and charges, the response was, 'People have to pay taxes, don't they?' The distancing from the public looks extraordinary now. In the police stations, the inspector on duty sat at a large desk set up behind a lofty barrier looking down on anyone unfortunate enough to want help. He had to shout to be heard. Even departments meant to alleviate social problems, like the Social Welfare Department, had nobody in the districts who could handle more than a narrow range of their services at junior level.

Letters in Chinese

Another barrier to communication was that all official correspondence was conducted only in English. No translations of official letters were enclosed. Meetings of the Legislative Council were in English only with no facilities for interpretation. The same applied in the Urban Council. At less exalted levels verbal contacts had to be in Cantonese, but the general rule was that English only should be used. All our discussions with the public were in Cantonese and we used written Chinese when we wrote letters.

Our object was to break down these barriers. There is a Chinese saying, 'When alive do not enter the mandarin's door; when dead never enter the gates of hell.' I had a copy of the characters for the first half of this saying pasted up behind my desk. There are four characters. I had a large cross in red ink put through the character for 'not'. It raised a few chuckles but the message was clear.

The name of the Secretariat for Chinese Affairs was causing confusion for many thought this was the department which dealt with relations with China. It was not the Chinese in China but the Chinese in Hong Kong that the organization was set up for. We changed the name to Secretariat for Home Affairs. Elsewhere, the Home Secretary or Minister for the Interior dealt with police and immigration matters, but in Hong Kong these were the responsibility of the Secretary for Security. Our new name soon caught on though in Chinese we retained a few characters of the old long name which made a distinguished title.

Getting reaction in departments

The CDO's job was to look out for trouble but also be readily accessible. There was a very short line of communication to the Governor as the Secretary for Home Affairs attended his weekly meetings on Friday mornings. If we found some aspect of government policy or action was causing irritation or distress, we tackled the departments direct. We had no executive powers, but we did have some very able and persuasive District Officers. Without executive powers, there was no limit to the subjects we could raise or the people we could see. Because we had a good press, and some very bright people, departments were pretty civil with us and we were seldom shown the door. We were very pleased with our little triumphs. Whoever heard of the police changing a one-way traffic system just because the people in the area did not like it?

Perhaps a more typical example was the question of compensation on the clearance of some shops and workshops. By the late 1960s, there was a well-worn system of compensating and resettling squatters who had to be cleared to make way for development. Trouble arose because in amongst the squatters in a Kowloon City clearance, there were a few ancient legal village buildings. The squatters were given resettlement compensation as a favour, but owners of the legal buildings were legally entitled to compensation under the Crown Lands Resumption Ordinance. The trouble was that the legal compensation was worth less than the *ex gratia* compensation so that the lawfully operating citizens stood to get less than the unlawful squatters. The situation was ridiculous but the departments stuck to their guns. The CDO brought up the case and we escalated to Government House in a trice. Orders were given to arrange realistic compensation for owners of the lawful buildings being cleared.

Such confrontations were not common as it was usually possible to smooth things out at a senior departmental level. Everybody knew that our job was to look out for the ordinary citizen and nobody wanted trouble that they could avoid. But we were also advocates of government policy. All new announcements were available in the District Offices. When we found policies too complicated, we arranged for departmental heads to come to talk to the people.

One result of having very bright District Officers was that our in-house meetings were lively. Nothing was taken for granted. Tradition was, if anything, a handicap. Competition started to emerge between districts which, in turn, began to generate local social cohesion. At Chinese New Year, one CDO decided to get his people to string coloured lights between the lamp posts along his patch of Nathan Road, the major artery in Kowloon. His neighbour, not to be outdone, got his people to string bigger and better lights — and the next, until Nathan Road as it passed from Tsim Sha Tsui to Yau Ma Tei and to Mongkok was a blaze of coloured lights paid for by the citizens of the districts.

District Committees

There was no formal body of citizens which represented the residents of districts. There was no mechanism for conducting elections. There was not even an electoral roll. We did not wait for the authorities to set up formal arrangements for it was obvious that this would take years. Instead, we set up our own District Committees by asking leaders of the various groups and organizations in the district to informal meetings. If they had established a reputation or emerged as leaders, that was good enough for us. We wanted to contact men and, even in those days, women who carried weight. We invited senior officers from departments to come along when they had messages they wanted to convey, or when some aspect of their operations was causing trouble. This was hard work for the departments. Few subjects were confined to a single district, but our colleagues in other departments gallantly turned up month after month.

The tenth CDO was appointed and ensconced in his office on 24 January 1969, exactly one year after the funds were approved by the Finance Committee. The scheme was a success because we had good people and our aim was always to improve conditions in each district. There was always some rivalry between districts. It kept the CDOs on their toes. The regular departmental meetings we had were always exciting for we never knew what would come up next. The bosses were not spared the sharp edge of the tongues of our bright young men and women. Perhaps the climate of opinion was changing in Hong Kong. I do, however, believe that the establishment of this scheme acted as a stimulus to a new appreciation of the importance of a government, even a colonial government, seeking and maintaining the support of its citizens.

Sir Ronald Holmes

This was the last time I worked under Ronald Holmes. He was a classics scholar and very quick on the uptake. He had joined the Colonial Service before the war and was learning Cantonese in Hong Kong when the war broke out. When the war came to Hong Kong, he — Eddie Teesdale — and a few others were required to stay behind the Japanese lines at the time of the surrender. They did some demolition and then made haste to get into China. I only once heard him talk about this escape when he described his utter exhaustion on reaching a stream near the border and plunged in. During the war he was in China, a key member of the British Army Aid Group which kept track of what was going on in Hong Kong. He went down himself as far as the hills behind Kai Tak to study the look of the town. He was awarded an MBE and MC in 1943 for his work in China.

All of us who had the experience of working under Ronnie found him an inspirational leader. One trick he had was to approve your drafts with scarcely an amendment. This put you on the spot for you knew that you had to draft in the knowledge as the paper was unlikely to be improved, so it had better be good. I once wanted to make a rather revolutionary proposal for organizational change and drafted a minute of a few lines to him. Just before I signed it, I realized that he was no longer my boss as he had been posted away. His successor was much more pedantic, so I scrapped my few lines and instead wrote a two-page justification for what I was proposing. It got through. Ronnie could understand problems with clarity and would lead us to think his ideas were ours. We all spent hours chatting to him in the evenings or at weekends and he never seemed to get tired of our importunities.

He stayed on after he retired to be Chairman of the Public Services Commission and then finally left Hong Kong to live in Corfu where his widow still maintains a beautiful home and garden.

Chinese marriages

I had been due for leave at the end of 1969 and on return was again posted to be Deputy Secretary for Home Affairs. This was familiar work with the City District Officers who were now well established. For a period in 1970, the Secretary for Home Affairs, Ronald Holmes, acted as Colonial Secretary and I acted as the Secretary for Home Affairs in his place. This took me into the highest echelons of government for a few months. The Secretary was, by his office, a member of the Executive and Legislative Councils and also of the Urban Council. I had enough sense not to throw my weight about in any of these bodies though I did round on some of the attacks on the government in the Urban Council annual debate.

Concubines

One curious little statutory duty threw a light on social development in Hong Kong over the years. This was the determination of the date on which a new law relating to marriages was to come into force. Until then lawful marriages, with implications on the rights to property when the husband died intestate, could be either those registered with the Registrar of Marriages after a due civil or religious ceremony, or they could be in accordance with Chinese custom, or any other custom for that matter. The traditional Chinese customary marriage involved lavish dinners and a number of ceremonies that were not codified but well understood. In accordance with Chinese custom, it was quite proper for a man to take two, three or more wives, commonly called concubines. Again custom required procedures, the chief of which was for the concubine to take tea with the principal wife. The concubines had legal rights to succession when a man died without making a will. As wealthy men seldom made wills because of a superstition that this would hasten their passing, this law was a real protection for the concubines in the face of rivalries after the man of the house passed away. The custom was so well entrenched in Chinese society that second or third wives were not social outcasts and were even invited to Government House. To this day, an old friend of mine always takes his three wives, two of whom are cousins, to every social occasion he attends.

Several attempts were made to abolish customary marriages, but too many important people had concubines and the custom was securely established. I had been vaguely aware that committees had recommended change, and had their recommendations set aside, that eventually some progress had been made in drawing up laws on marriage and intestate succession, but I had not followed progress in detail until this short period as Acting Secretary for Home Affairs in charge of the legislation.

By now, public opposition had almost vanished and for a reason that was not at first obvious. In the early postwar years, there was only one marriage registry and that was in central Hong Kong. It was such a bother to register marriages that most marriages took place in accordance with Chinese custom. The Registrar of Marriages (who also did births and deaths) took compassion on his bridal customers and gradually opened more and more marriage registries. By the late 1960s, nobody had to go further than to his local market to find one. As these offices became more accessible, the brides found that if they married in accordance with this new legal procedure, they could only be divorced after prolonged and costly legal fights in the courts. Furthermore, the courts would see that wronged wives were provided for. A marriage in accordance with Chinese custom was not registered anywhere. Divorce could be easily secured by the husband. Moreover, there was no legal protection for the wife in the case of such a divorce. Brides everywhere began to insist on the new form of marriage. Before long, the standard marriage came to combine both traditions. The family and close friends went to church or the marriage registry for the formal statutory procedures. In the evening, huge wedding feasts were held for friends, relatives and as many distinguished acquaintances as could be mustered. The feasts cost as much as the bridegroom's family could afford and took place in hotels, ballrooms or anywhere a crowd of up to a thousand could be sat down to a feast of a dozen or more courses.

The laws, which abolished the rights of concubines in marriage and in succession to property and which recognized only marriage in the registry and permitted only one lawful wife, had been passed but not yet brought into force. The subsidiary regulations had hit a problem in preserving the rights of concubines who had been taken before the law came into force, for there was no intention to interfere with their rights. Neither customary marriages nor concubines were registered anywhere. Suggestions were made to provide registers under the new law with the worthy motive of allowing voluntary registration to preserve the rights of the concubines. This was going to prove embarrassing. There were too many unofficial concubines that the wives might be aware of, but who they had not taken tea with and so could not be recognized in law. Nobody wanted to create a mass of quarrels about who was and who was not a lawful concubine. The problem was ducked on the assurance by the lawyers that whether the concubine was formally registered as such or not, her rights depended on the facts relating to the way she had been taken into the family and whether this had taken place before the new laws came into force. There was no need for special registration of concubines.

Fortune-teller to the rescue

With this last problem out of the way, the law could be brought into force on a 'day fixed by proclamation of the Governor'. I had to suggest the date. My advisers were confused. No festival would be appropriate, though the romantic Mid-Autumn Festival was nigh. Nobody could think of a logical way to determine the day. It really was of no significance as there were no customary marriages taking place without being registered as lawful marriages. In the end, I decided to seek the advice of a traditional fortune-teller. Many well-to-do, and many less well-to-do, constantly consulted fortune-tellers. By studying the *tung sing,* a fabulous book prescribing things one should or should not do day by day, a fortune-teller was able to suggest propitious days for doing things — moving house, getting married, starting a business, burying a relative, or almost any activity needing to be done on a lucky day. This was a challenge for him but, undaunted, he announced that the proper date for the Governor's proclamation was 7 October 1971. And so it came to pass that this date of no apparent significance in Western or Chinese calendars is enshrined in the law as the day when Chinese customary marriage ceased to carry any weight in Hong Kong law.

12

Typhoons, Sailing and Long Leaves

Before returning to the New Territories for the last time, this seems to be a good place to write about typhoons, and a bit about what we did when we were not at work.

Typhoons seem to be caused essentially by high sea temperatures out in the Pacific to the east of the Philippines. The hot air rises and cooler air rushes in rather like the water swirling down the bath plug-hole, but with the whole system upside down. The circulation can be hundreds of miles across and, north of the equator, is in an anti-clockwise direction. The typhoon can sit still or move on an erratic track, usually between west and north, at a speed of up to twenty miles an hour. The eventual tracks of typhoons cannot be predicted, but short-term forecasts can now be made. The destruction can be so great that a crude but effective warning system has been in force for years. This involves a series of typhoon signals, the term dating from the days when the only way of disseminating the news was by hoisting shapes from a mast on the southern tip of the Kowloon peninsula and at outstations, including Island House in Tai Po. The signals are numbered so that Number 1 just warns that a typhoon is in the area and could strike. There are now only four other signals numbered 3, 8, 9 and 10. The intervening numbers were used to describe the direction from which the wind was expected but were abandoned as they gave an illusion of increasing strength. Shops and offices close on the hoisting of Number 8. Although many typhoons have winds no stronger than a European gale, you just do not know when winds will reach twice this strength — a higher speed than that reached by a human body in free fall. The signals are taken seriously.

The 1906 and 1937 typhoons

We all knew the dates of the worst typhoons. The pre-war ones were in 1906 and 1937 when tens of thousands of boat people perished. Island House was being built in 1906. The District Office consisted of a strong room and a matshed, or bamboo structure with a palm leaf roof. After the typhoon, it was just the strong room. In 1937, big ships were washed up on the city waterfront and again there was tremendous loss of life among the fishermen who lived the whole of their lives on their boats. In the 1937 typhoon, Tolo Harbour was assaulted by a tidal surge. This happens when the wind is from the north-east blowing the sea down the channel into Tolo Harbour, during the approach of a typhoon, coincides with a particularly high tide. On that occasion in 1937, the sea level rose some fifteen feet above its normal high tide level, causing great loss of life among the fishing boats which were carried inland and smashed to bits.

It was after the 1906 typhoon that the government built a number of typhoon shelters for the fishing fleet. These were sea walls round an area of sheltered water to which boats of all descriptions swarmed as soon as there was warning of the approach of a typhoon. Typhoon shelters do offer protection from the seas, but nothing can provide shelter from the winds.

Postwar typhoons

After the war typhoons were given names, at first only girls names but now men's names are used too. Typhoon Wanda in 1962 brought another tidal surge into Tolo Harbour and we were living in Island House. It struck at night and took the sea nearly as high as the 1937 disaster. We found fisher families who had lost their boats taking shelter on the island and brought them into the house. Our servants were astonished to discover that, though they were Chinese, they could not understand a word they said. This was a time of depression in the shipping industry and a number of cargo ships were laid up in Tolo Harbour. Every one of them was swept onto the shore and found the next day stranded high and dry.

The Assistant District Officer (ADO), Trevor Bedford, was out and about among the boat people below his house just across from Island House. At the height of the storm, he took shelter with a few others under an embankment adjoining the typhoon shelter. The sea had risen above the protecting wall and had already cleared the stalls on it that served the boat people. The ADO found a fridge washed up near him and, on opening it up, was delighted to find some cold beer that he and his helpers enjoyed. What he did not know was that his wife had a house full of fishermen's families. A baby was born. When they left, the poor man found that all his towels and clothes had been carried off by the grateful fisher wives.

Typhoon Rose in 1971 was the last one we experienced in Tai Po. This one sat still due south of Hong Kong for hours, getting fiercer and fiercer. When it moved, it came straight for us. I was District Commissioner at the time and took up my post in the Tai Po District Office that night. We were afraid of another tidal surge as there was a very high tide due and the wind was coming from the east. During the night, the various forms of communication went dead one by one. The first to go was the civilian phone. This was followed by our departmental wireless system when the aerial was blown away. An army telephone through which we could eventually reach the civilian network kept going longest, but it too went dead.

In the early hours we had no communication, so I thought I would go home for a while. The wind was still at its height and the noise in the trees round the office was terrifying. We got into the Land Rover and got down to the causeway leading to our house. There we were completely blinded by the wind and the rain. We could barely make out the road underneath us. It would have been folly to try to drive along the causeway, so I went back to the office and lay down among the others on a camp bed. When I got home at six in the morning, the house was silent. I found the drawing-room flooded and curtains hanging over the stairs. My wife was slumped on the bed in the main bedroom in exhaustion. The upstairs verandahs were six inches deep in water and flooding into the adjoining bedrooms. My wife told me that in the middle of the night she had noticed dust and water falling from the ceiling. She picked up the two children who had come to her and evacuated the main bedroom. Then there was a terrific explosion. She had had no sleep until she heard me coming in. She was so relieved that someone else was about that she dropped into a deep sleep, slumped over the piled up bedding.

The explosion she heard was the roof being blown off. We found tiles blown across the house, the lawn and the tennis court and embedded in tree trunks.

Island House became a proper island again for a few hours. When the winds went down, we found that the little causeway had been breached and there was no way in or out that was not blocked by fallen trees. One of our neighbours' boys found a couple of newborn mynah birds in one of the fallen trees. One died shortly after being rescued, but we reared the other to maturity and enjoyed the way he would imitate all manner of sounds, including our remarks.

The last typhoon during my service struck when we were living in a penthouse thirty-four floors above the street. We expected the noise and were rather pleased to see how little water blew under the windows. What we were not prepared for was the swaying of the building. In theory, we knew that tall buildings were meant to sway in high winds, but it was disconcerting actually to experience it. A lamp hanging over the stairs started swaying as if in a ship at sea. A gust would give the building a vibrating shake from which it recovered with a gentle sway like that of a small boat at anchor. Once we realized the building was not going to collapse, we settled down again. That storm was in 1983. Number 10 signal was not hoisted again until 1999.

Sailing

It was not all work. We all had some form of recreation for relaxation, though not always the time to enjoy it. Mine was sailing. At first, it was on other people's boats where I spent many a happy day out or, later, a weekend afloat. One summer, we looked after a sampan belonging to a friend who was on leave. We met up with a hiking friend, Donald Luddington, who liked to boast that he could carry everything he needed with him and he certainly had all the makings of excellent cooked rice. 'What have you got that I cannot carry?' he asked. I opened the bow locker where several cans of beer were cooling on a large block of ice.

The pilot cutter *Swallow*

In 1967 another administrator, Hal Miller, and I decided to buy a pilot cutter. This was really a peculiar form of sampan, thirty-two feet six inches long and seven feet six inches slim, to enable it to be towed alongside ships. Pictures of these vessels are to be seen along the waterfront in photos from the nineteenth century. We found one in Causeway Bay typhoon shelter and paid, I think, $2,000 (£125) for it. It had no engine so we began a search for a second-hand one. I trailed round engine shops in Shanghai Street near the Yau Ma Tei typhoon shelter and Hal tried Ap Lei Chau where a large fishing fleet was based. He thought he was having success when an old man said, 'Yes, second-hand engines of six or eight horsepower were available.' 'Fine,' said my friend. 'Let's see one.' 'But we haven't been introduced!' said the old man and who can do business without proper introductions? We gave up and got a fine new little four horsepower diesel engine. This was installed and we sailed forth on our maiden journey to Hebe Haven, a popular anchorage in the eastern waters.

The two of us shared the boat for a year or two until Hal decided to resign and leave Hong Kong. He settled in England, went into parliament and retired with a knighthood. I bought his share in the boat for a song. I sometimes shudder to think of the journeys we made in this frail craft. Being so long and slim, she would do a good seven knots under sail and engine, which was more than some of the fine more conventional yachts. On one occasion, we headed into a strong north wind, coming out of Long Harbour into Mirs Bay, and shipped two substantial waves. They seemed to slide off, but when we anchored, we found the two bow compartments flooded almost to the decks and everybody's bedding and clothes were soaked. On another occasion, I was returning to Hebe Haven from Mirs Bay in a strong south-westerly breeze. My crew was my wife and one of our daughters, both immobile with seasickness. I could not get a good view of the land and was horrified to find myself making a passage south of Town Island where I had never been before because of the large number of tiny crosses on the chart marking submerged rocks. We survived.

On another occasion, we had been on holiday on Cheung Chau Island to the west of Hong Kong. I had an accident when chopping down some undergrowth and the damage had been repaired in hospital in town before we were due to return. When the time came, a typhoon was approaching. The anchorage at Cheung Chau emptied for it was not safe in a typhoon. I rang a sailing friend in town, Kevin Palfreeman, and he agreed to come out to help us sail back. We set off when Number 3 typhoon signal was up with an increasing wind from the south-west. I do not think the little boat ever went so fast back to Hong Kong and right through the harbour.

Outside on the east, we passed fishermen who waved to us to go back, but our anchorage was still a few miles to the east. With the strong west wind, I was not worried about going through the Buddha's Head strait where one usually met rough water on entering the open sea for the wind was behind us. Sure enough, there were no waves, but the typhoon had set up such a swell that we were almost going through breaking seas in the strait. We met two big swells head on and were through.

We had many a pleasant, but much less adventurous, weekend camping on the boat under makeshift awnings. The boat was nearly lost in a typhoon when I was out of town and so was the man who was looking after it. I managed to get it repaired but was due to move into town, so I sold it for the price of the repair bill.

Yacht *Wind Song*

A major acquisition was made in 1974 when two civil service colleagues, Bim Davies, Alan Britsow and I, bought a fine thirty-six-foot Bermuda rigged yacht, *Wind Song,* designed shortly before the skeg keels came in. She had just completed a China Sea Race to Manila in the Philippines and was up for sale. We had all had some sailing experience but had never raced a boat of this class. The racing season in Hong Kong is during the winter when the north-east monsoon usually provides good wind. We raced practically every week but made time also for cruising with families. Bim Davies was even able to persuade a regular crew member to marry him. On races we usually had one or more experienced sailing men who taught us a great deal. The highlights of the racing were the monthly overnight races which started on Saturday afternoons and finished any time from breakfast time to the early evening on Sunday. We did win one small cup. We were too inexperienced and our boat of too early a design to do really well.

By the spring of 1976, we felt we were able to enter for the China Sea Race to Manila. We had put in a great deal of training. The start was uneventful but during the night a cold front came through and we had a gale on our quarter. The sea was very confused and we did an accidental jibe which tore the mainsail along the whole of its foot. What an end to all our hopes! Not deterred we hoisted the try-sail, a very small piece of canvas few have ever seen in action. With this and a small headsail we tore through the sea, passing a couple of other yachts which were probably over canvassed. We had no sewing machine but did have a palm and needle; a determined crew sewed up the sail in a secure but not very beautiful manner. This took nearly all night and in the morning we felt the wind had moderated enough to try our mended sail, albeit with a roll in it.

It is typical of this voyage to the Philippines at this time of the year that you get a fierce cold front at some early stage of the race and then run completely out of wind as you near the Luzon coast. We found ourselves in such a calm, just sailing with a gossamer-thin headsail, but we were moving. The direct course kept us well out to sea, but I thought we should make up for the coast. The extra distance would be made up by taking advantage of the land and sea breezes we should find there. We hit the coast at 10 p.m. in a dead calm. By mid-day the next day, we had moved a quarter of a mile. To measure the distance travelled, we trailed a small Walker Log, a propeller attached to a string which clocked up the miles in a remarkably accurate manner. I looked over the stern and found the string hanging vertically down. We were absolutely stationary. Several of us had a swim for it was very hot. Yachts who kept out at sea had light airs but at least they kept sailing. As we made our way slowly down the Luzon coast, we saw ahead what looked like the wreck of a yacht. One of our competitors had indeed run aground on the notorious Palauig Reef which extends several miles out from the shore. They declined assistance and came in even after us. Off Subic Bay, we had occasional brisk breezes and calms. During one of these calms, we had more swimming until one of us seemed to fly out of the water scarcely touching the ladder. He had seen a shark in the murk and did not wait.

As we finished at Corregidor Island, some twenty miles from the Manila Yacht Club, we were passed a case of ice-cold beer. We had rationed ourselves to one can a day each which we had frozen before leaving Hong Kong and were now beer dry. Our boat had no fridge but a capacious icebox which was by now only slightly cooler than the cabin. Needless to say, we were all merry as crickets after a few minutes. I had been navigating, but another crew member offered to take us in. I was only too glad to be left with my cold beer and some tins of sardines, all we had left in the way of food. After an hour, there was a cry of land where it should not be. Our course had been laid off exactly 90 degrees from where it should have been. We arrived at the yacht club some time in the early hours, more than seven days after leaving Hong Kong, and simply slumped down where we lay. In the morning, our wives came down and were horrified to see this stinking mess of sweaty, unconscious bodies.

We were delighted to be woken up, to shower and to eat a colossal breakfast.

Vanguard in the Admiral's Cup

After the summer, I was asked to join a yacht starting to train to race in England as one of a team of three representing Hong Kong in the competition for the Admiral's Cup. The crew were all experienced sailors but none of them could navigate. I had taken to this esoteric art in 1974 when crewing on a boat returning from the China Sea Race of that year. On that occasion, none of the four of us had any real experience of ocean navigating. I claimed priority because I had had Mary Pera's excellent book for two weeks while the rest were reading it for the first time. In those low latitudes, it is very difficult to get a good position from the sun because it is either due east in the morning or due west in the afternoon. For a short time round noon, it does make the transit between east and west, almost overhead, but you have to be quick to get lines on the chart that cross at a reasonable angle. We did not even try to get a position from the stars. Not only were we very inexperienced, but near the equator you only have a few minutes at dawn and dusk to get your sights. We never did get a good fix. We homed in on Radio Hong Kong and a portable radio that had something of a directional aerial.

By 1976, I had acquired a sextant and, from our garden on the Peak, had taken endless sights of sun and stars reflected in a saucer of oil. My position lines did at least hit Hong Kong Island, but it was a long time before I could put lines within half a mile of the house. I did, however, feel confident enough to accept Bill Turnbull's invitation to join in this Admiral's Cup venture — and there was nobody else. Navigating in Hong Kong waters was just a matter of knowing the islands. All the shores were steep too and nobody took any notice of the small tidal streams. You were either afloat or on the rocks.

Vanguard was a new yacht of novel design by Ed Dubois, a naval architect who has since made a reputation for the magnificent huge motor yachts he designs. The venture was the enterprise of David Lieu, a shipping magnate who really preferred power boats but who wanted to see what could be achieved with the right team. Bill Turnbull, a prominent Hong Kong solicitor and one of the leading big boat sailors, was the man putting the venture together. He had sailed his boat in the 1975 Admirals Cup and had a very experienced crew.

The summer of 1977 was a glorious one for me. I set off in June for a long leave and joined the yacht in the Hamble. The Admiralty Chart Agent in Hong Kong had supplied me with a complete set of charts of the Solent and the Channel and the waters up to the Fastnet rock. Brooding over charts and tide tables was one thing, but it was another matter to tackle the problems in real life in these unfamiliar waters. A very experienced English Olympic sailor, John Oakley, who knew the Solent like the back of his hand, joined the crew and was able to provide all the tactical navigating for the races off Cowes. We also sailed in a number of cross-channel races. At sea, the theory was that you could get good positions with little hand-held directional radios from radio beacons along the coast. I had tried this in Hong Kong and found the wretched instrument a great trial. That had not mattered in Hong Kong but here, these radio beacon fixes were the only thing we had to check on our dead reckoning. The landmarks were unfamiliar. The light on one buoy, off Brighton, was so tiny that it looked, as one of us said, like a fisherman having difficulty with his lighter. I got Ordinance Survey maps of the area and drove round the downs behind Brighton looking for some landmark you could recognize from way out at sea. I came to the conclusion that the best would be for someone to set fire to Rodean School which would have given us an excellent mark to aim for.

Navigating for races that crossed the channel involved painstaking study of the excellent tidal stream atlases you could get. I had acquired a fine new navigational calculator and spent hours calculating courses for all sorts of speeds and times of departure from the English coast, making a calculation for each hour after the start. There were a great many variables, but I hoped that one of the calculations might come near enough the mark to be useful. Needless to say, my high-powered sailing friends thought this was all a lot of nonsense. It did, however, pay off in the Cowes-Dinard Race of 1977. We left the English coast near Portland Bill within five minutes of one of the possibilities I had envisaged. We were reaching along at a steady six knots in a light breeze on the starboard tack. I gave the skipper a course and we maintained this speed with most unusual constancy. All night long, we seemed to be far to the west of the fleet. I was constantly asked if I was sure I knew what I was up to. In the morning as we approached the coast of Guernsey, we saw the whole fleet still lying way down on our lee to the east. The difference was that while we were still reaching along on the course we had sailed all night, they were now having to beat up against one of those strong channel flood tides. Although by no means the largest yacht in the race, we were first round Les Hanois light at the western point of Guernsey after only one tack of about fifty yards. Luck, you might say. Skill I said!

I had better cap that story with one that is rather less creditable. A friend from Jesus College rowing connections, Peter Bell, had lent us his yacht and strong son, Simon, for a family cruise in the Channel Islands. After a splendid week's sailing, we set off back from Cherbourg overnight. In the morning we were approaching the Isle of Wight, as planned. It looked as if we were going to get in rather early for the owner's family. I identified St Catherine's Point, at the southern extremity of the Wight, on our port bow. We bore away, against the flood tide but with a good quartering breeze. I wondered about taking a radio bearing to make sure that the point was St Catherine's. The thought of wrestling with the little black box listening for the signal 'SC' from the point was too much bother. I felt sure I knew the mark. After some considerable time, the Needles still failed to appear but the coast still stretched away to the west. Eventually, the strong son said, 'There's Portland Bill.' Its outline was unmistakable. My 'St Catherine's Point' was in fact St Alban's Head, way to the west of the entrance to the Solent. We went about to retrace our course. The trouble with headlands is that they do not look like headlands when you come straight at them. I had only seen St Alban's Head during Fastnet races when you approach from the Solent passing well out to sea. The point looks like a rather featureless hill flat on the coast. On the other hand, I had been round St Catherine's Point several times on Channel races, or the Round the Island race, when it really does look like a point as you approach from either east or west. Well, I now know that St Alban's Head really does look like a respectable headland from the south. A feeble excuse you might say with justification.

By now, the tide had changed and was against us, as was the wind. Far from waking up our owner at the crack of dawn, we only arrived in time for a late tea.

The Admirals Cup is run in alternate years when teams of three yachts that represent their countries compete in a number of races to gather points to fix the final finishing order. Hong Kong had a team in for the 1975 cup when they asked me to be the team manager. I did this though I had no idea what a team manager was supposed to do. The sailors were all more than capable of managing themselves. In 1977, I was navigating on *Vanguard* which was one of the Hong Kong yachts. We found we could hold our own against all but the top American boat. We did reasonably well in the Solent races and the cross-channel race, so that we went into the Fastnet race as third in the fleet. This is a race of fearsome reputation which I had done for the first time in 1975 with a friend of my sister's, Dr John Graves, in a small thirty-two-feet yacht. On that occasion, we had a rough start to the race. We stood well out to sea past Portland Bill to avoid the very rough overfalls that spring up off that point when the tide goes against the wind. By the time we got to Land's End, we were in a dead calm but eventually had quite a reasonable trip round the rock and back.

In the 1977 Admiral's Cup, we got off to a good start and squeezed past Portland Bill against the tide, only a few feet off the rocks. After Land's End, we found ourselves hard on the starboard tack well ahead of our American rival as we headed for the rock. I took some sextant sights of the American's mast and had to confess that he was slowly overtaking us. There was scarcely any wind where we were. Should we tack and hope that the wind would fill in from the south, or hang on in the expectation that the new wind would come from the north? The forecasts were no help for we were looking for only a tiny improvement in the wind. We were not gaining on the American and so our skipper decided to risk looking south for wind. It turned out to be the wrong decision as the wind, such as it was, did come from the north. That was one of the slowest Fastnet races there has been. To save weight, boats carried only the minimum stores and all were running low on food towards the end. I announced that we had plenty of tea bags and plenty of butter but not much else. 'Buttered tea bags!' muttered John Oakley. Someone must have heard, for when I went below, there was a dish of buttered tea bags. John did munch one, but the rest went over the side.

Ceil III in the 1979 Fastnet Race

In 1979, I was working in London and Bill Turnbull was racing a smaller boat not in the Hong Kong team. He asked me to join him. We had some good racing during Cowes Week in the Solent when at least two small depressions swept through the fleet causing havoc. The Fastnet Race started in moderate winds, but I had seen another depression forming far out in the Atlantic to the west. I said we might be in for some rough weather if this were to cross our course. There was not much wind in the early part of the race. Following the successful precedent of the 1977 race, we decided to pass Portland Bill close in. As we approached, the wind faded away and we were sailing very slowly. When the tide is flooding, that is flowing to the east, past the Bill, it forms a back eddy close in shore so that you can creep up to the point with a favourable stream. On the point itself, there was no escaping the adverse tide. If you can get past, you can save several miles on the run to Start Point. All went well until we got to the point when there just was not enough wind to get us past. We drifted back and tried again, and again failed to get past. I think we made three tries, after one of which we allowed ourselves to drift rather too far out to sea. We found ourselves at the edge of the overfalls. This was an amazing sight. There we were, with practically no wind, being thrown about by large smooth waves — they must be frightening in a wind-against-tide situation. We went back in shore and eventually got round the point as the tide slackened. We wondered if those who had kept out to sea were faring any better, but I think not. We could see them sailing along in fine style but being carried backwards by the tide just as fast. The wind picked up and we had a good sail past Start Point and the Eddystone light. At this time, we could just carry a spinnaker on the port tack but were clearly heading for Lizard Point. On the other hand, there was a raging ebb tide sweeping out of the bay. Would it carry us far enough to windward to avoid the point? It seemed to but as we sailed past, I asked one of our crew how far he thought we were off the Lizard. 'About a mile,' he said. 'That is just where a patch of rock is marked on the chart,' I replied. We had a few very anxious moments.

It was not until we were well on our way to the Fastnet Rock, and the sun had gone down, that the weather deteriorated. One by one, we changed to smaller and smaller headsails until we had none at all. We were still overpressed and were debating going down to the tiny trysail. The skipper decided to tack away towards the east. The sea was so rough that the tack ended with the sail carrying the runner away, so that we now had a flapping main sail with the sheets in the wind. When the main was lowered and tied down, it was so calm with no sail at all that Bill decided to lie to without any sail until things quieted down. We lashed the tiller down to starboard and left the boat to its own devices. She behaved beautifully. We were lying more or less across the wind and waves. After a while, the bows fell away to leeward and we started to gather speed. This brought the rudder into play so that we rounded up until we stopped more or less in our starting position. My job was to be cook, as well as navigator, so I busily prepared a huge pot of mixed stew for the exhausted crew. Imagine my disappointment when they all turned it down. Two were so seasick that they got seriously dehydrated and could not get out of their bunks for twenty-four hours. Two others were just very sick. Bill, who always got sick the moment the boat sailed, for some reason felt no qualms at all. I was doped up with a mixture of pills that a sailing doctor in Hong Kong had read about being used to prevent sickness in space. One ensured you did not get sick but would put you to sleep. The other was a pep pill which kept you awake. The trick was to get the balance right.

We lay for eight hours in this way. Once or twice a breaking wave crashed down on us, knocking us over until the mast was horizontal and sweeping the whole boat down its front. We were lucky not to be knocked right over. Although practically everything was shut up, we did have a small portion of the hatch open. If we had capsized, we should have been in trouble. I have a clear memory of the bright sunlight that came through the clouds for a short time in the early morning. The whole sea was heaving about with vast stretches of water, the size of football fields, tipped up at an angle as the swell went through. A helicopter passed and we radioed that we were not in need of help. A fishing trawler approached but fortunately did not try to come alongside for he would have smashed us up. The first sail up was the small trysail which did give us some control. I had the unenviable task of trying to beat into the wind with this sail. I did make some progress but I could not get very close to the wind or make much speed.

As the day wore on, the wind abated and we had a pleasant sail as we tidied up and fixed up a means of managing the boom. We rounded Fastnet Rock in light airs and had a fine sail down to Bishops Rock light off the Scillies. Another helicopter spoke with us then. We were able to pass him a phone number to call so that a message could be passed to the skipper's wife back in Hong Kong.

Our troubles were not over yet. A Royal Naval frigate warned us that another gale was approaching, and sure enough it came upon us as we were approaching the finish at Plymouth. I had taken a fix in clear sunshine and was below reading a book when the skipper called for me and asked me where we were. The weather had completely closed in and you could not see more than a few yards. We had no radar. We raced towards Rame Head, at the entrance to Plymouth Sound, on the starboard tack, just carrying our spinnaker as close to the wind as we could sail. We had no sight of the land. I hoped that if we were going to hit the peninsula, we should have time to go about. Fortunately, we cleared the head without seeing it and were able to spot the shore on the other side of the Sound in time to bear away and sail over the finishing line.

Sixty-three boats started the race in our division. Six finished. We won our division. We were lucky.

Fifteen people lost their lives in that race. As a result of the heart-searching afterwards, rules were tightened up. I had been alarmed at some of the sailing we had seen in the Solent during the smaller gales that went through in Cowes Week. Clearly, some were not experienced enough to cope with extreme conditions.

Communications were chaotic during the race. None in the Hong Kong Admiral's Cup team came to harm though one man was washed overboard and got back with his harness. In Plymouth, some had got wind of a story that we had been lost. When my wife and children turned up, they were treated with immense kindness by the Hong Kong sailors, though without being told of the rumour. The radio message we had passed, as we rounded Bishops Rock, had led to a phone call to Hong Kong where the skipper's wife got it at three in the morning. The *South China Morning Post* arrived a few hours later with banner headlines that we were missing.

Four-year tours

No account of life in the Colonial Service would be complete without a few words about our long leaves. When I went out to Hong Kong, we were on four-year tour followed by seven months' leave. The month-long sea journey each way did not count as leave so one might be away for nine months, though I never was in practice.

This was a regime designed for rough life in the tropics when sea travel was the only way to make such long journeys as that to Hong Kong. When I went out, air travel was rare. It was sea and it was P&O and P&O expected first-class to travel in style. In 1950, we dressed for dinner every night at sea though in port we could wear a lounge suit. By my first leave at the end of 1954, we could wear a suit at sea too. We were now a family of three and still on P&O with an infant. These ships carried a good many families and so had good provision for infants in a nursery. We called at Penang where we met my sister and her husband who was doing his National Service as a doctor in Kota Bahru in Malaya. In Ceylon, we met a college friend of my sister who took us round the sights. Car dealers in Hong Kong used to arrange for the delivery of a new export car to meet the ship at Tilbury. We had an enormous amount of luggage which an enterprising taxi-driver said we should never get in the car — he would take it and follow us. As the luggage disappeared into the car bit by bit, he muttered, 'Pity to spoil a new car with so much luggage.'

That winter seemed cold after nearly six years in the case of my wife. We toured relatives, many of whom had not seen each other for years. We went on our first skiing holiday and found it a wonderful experience. I also renewed contact with the rowing world. In the spring, we followed the Jesus College boats as they rowed down the Thames from Reading to Putney over three days, a row I had done in 1947. Our job was to carry the luggage of the two crews. We also went back to Cambridge where I coached the Jesus College Second May boat — I did not feel sufficiently in touch to try the First Boat. It was a good year. The First Boat went Head of the River and the Second Boat made four bumps, all of College First Boats, in the middle of the First Division. It had never happened before and never since. The Bump Supper in Hall was as riotous as it had ever been and the bonfire, when an old boat was burnt and beer was provided for oarsmen from other colleges, unchanged in style from my undergraduate days.

For the return journey to Hong Kong, we had booked to travel by the Italian Line, Lloyd Triestino. The great attraction was that these ships were air-conditioned. The ship sailed from Genoa so we drove our new car on a continental round trip through Paris, Lakes Maggiore and Garda, to Venice, Pisa, and Florence. My younger sister travelled with us and was a great help with the two-year-old infant. My wife sailed from Genoa with the baby and the car, but I was required to fly. I said goodbye to them in Genoa, took a train to Rome and flew from there. In Rome, I saw some of the sights and paid my bill at the hotel. The airline, BOAC, would pick me up late in the evening. I thought a good dinner would round off the trip excellently but was dismayed to find I had had my pocket picked. I had only 250 lire for supper. This was not quite such a trivial sum it is now but certainly not enough for the meal I had planned. At a fast food counter, I watched others buying all sorts of mouth-watering food but found I only had just enough for a cheeseburger. Once on the plane, I was in luxury again.

Our second leave was four and a quarter years later, this time with three youngsters aged six years, two years and two months. The six-year-old should have gone to school, but we were travelling so much that this was not possible. Instead, I bought a good range of books and teaching materials and we sweated away at the three Rs. On this leave, we hired a caravan and so were able to travel more freely. We did another skiing trip with the six-year-old and the baby but could not quite repeat the thrills of our first experience. My wife's parents were only too pleased to have charge of the two-year-old.

The end of sea travel

As air travel became more common, our terms of service were changed. We could still go by sea but the leaves were greatly shortened so we nearly all went by air. Sea travel too had changed. One colleague on retirement decided to fly to Australia and go by P&O to England. His wife bought beautiful dresses for the evening social life. On board they found that not only was a dinner jacket no longer required, but that it was as much as the stewards could do to prevent passengers turning up in their swimming trunks. First-class air travel was no longer automatic for all in the Administrative Service. I was lucky enough to get promotion just fast enough to keep ahead of the increasing level of seniority required to be entitled to first-class air fares. We had considerable freedom in arranging our journeys so long as the cost did not exceed the fares we were entitled to. In 1963, my wife took the two girls on a round-the-world trip though I had to stay at work a little longer. I did my last homeward trip by sea that year. The air journey to England then involved as many as five stops in propeller-driven aircraft vibrating all the way. We did one journey in the first jet liner, the Comet. This superb plane flew without vibration but still had a few stops. We were lucky not to be in one of the two that crashed, due to metal fatigue round the windows, before the service was withdrawn. On two occasions, we included a Mediterranean cruise from Venice to Athens and once we went up the Rhine on a river steamer.

Health

Life in Hong Kong before the war was hard on health. Conditions were revolutionized over the years we have lived here. I believe the greatest transformation was air-conditioning. In my early years, people would retire about as soon as they could. Many police officers retired at the age of forty-five. Researching our service in 1971, I found that only two of my seniors had worked to the full retiring age of fifty-five. By the time I was due to retire, our aim was to stay for one or more extensions. We did not sleep in air-conditioning at home until 1967, seventeen years after I started. The buildings were more airy but nothing could alleviate the heat and sweat of a still summer night. Work the next day was often a struggle. In the New Territories, we would sleep outside on a screened verandah from about May to November, except when it rained. The period also saw the elimination of diseases that had killed so many in the old days. In our early years, we had to carry valid certificates of inoculation against typhoid and cholera and vaccination against smallpox and have annual X-rays to check for tuberculosis. None of these is necessary now. Tuberculosis was suppressed by BCG vaccine administered to all babies at birth. Today, several of us continue to live in Hong Kong after retirement where health problems are no different from those in a temperate climate for the very good reason that we spend much of our time in an air-conditioned temperate climate.

13

New Territories Commissioner

After my short spell as Acting Secretary for Home Affairs, I was posted to the New Territories as District Commissioner. For years, I had looked forward to the distant day when I might become senior enough to be considered for this post where I confidently expected to serve out my time. It was quite senior enough to retire from with dignity for it carried with it a seat on the Legislative Council. It was not a post that many of my colleagues coveted because the New Territories was still a world unto itself. New Territories affairs were still outside the knowledge of people, and officials, in the urban areas. I had been away from these affairs for some years and had a good deal of catching up to do.

The tanneries

I landed in trouble straight away. The tanneries had to be cleared. Leather tanning is classified everywhere as an 'offensive trade' and so it is. The stink of hides and the chemicals they were treated with before they were hung out to dry was enough to keep everyone away. The damage to the environment, a word scarcely heard then, was appalling. The waste liquid was simply discharged into the streams with all sorts of heavy metals. These tanneries were illegal in the sense that they operated on land restricted for agricultural use. What was even worse, they lined a stretch of the main road to the golf course! The operations had grown into a substantial industry. Nothing my predecessor did could contain their growth. The tanned leather was in great demand by a thriving leather manufacturing industry. There was a brisk export trade in leather goods. Leather garments were never subject to the quotas imposed on the export of other garments. Hides were being imported from as far away as Indonesia.

It was decided that the situation could no longer be tolerated. As the industry involved an improper use of agricultural land, the government would be within its rights to re-enter all the leases and, once the land reverted to the Crown, the operations could be cleared. There was, of course, no question of acting precipitately. It was recognized that the industry, if properly operated, would make a legitimate and valuable contribution to the economy. An area in Kwai Chung, near to the main urban areas, had been designated for offensive trades. Land would be offered for auction specifically for tanning. Factories built there would be required to comply with reasonable environmental restrictions and the effluents from the factories would have to be properly treated. These proposals were not received enthusiastically by the operators, but they knew the game was up. One or two lots were sold for the new factories, but the mass made no move to prepare to relocate. It was time to get tough. Government agreement was given to the re-entry of all the agricultural land occupied by the tanneries and they would be cleared, whether they had made provision at Kwai Chung or not.

This was the point at which I took up my new responsibilities. At the end of my first day's work, sitting in the car on the way back to Island House, I signed the hundreds of memorials of re-entry of all the old paddy-fields.

The tanners recognized defeat and moved out quietly. The land was cleared and the mess covered up with earth. As to the great tanning industry that had blossomed so vigorously in Hong Kong, it vanished. I believe some tanning continued for a while at Kwai Chung but the restrictions were costly. Tanning moved to China and Indonesia where noses were less delicate and governments less concerned about the environment. The story had close parallels to the ship-breaking industry which enjoyed a brief period of prosperity. Nobody can say that entrepreneurs were lacking in Hong Kong.

Village Representatives mass meeting

I had not known that shortly before I took up the post, there had been a mass meeting of the entire body of Village Representatives from all over the New Territories, about a thousand of them. This meeting had produced a short list of demands that the Heung Yee Kuk presented to me. This was almost a village uprising, yet nothing was known of it in town. To mount such a meeting was an undertaking of some magnitude. It must have involved a good deal of organization and generated a good deal of heat. I sensed real trouble and a rocky start to my romance with the Heung Yee Kuk.

I studied the demands carefully. They contained such wording as 'the government must cease to expropriate villagers' land', and so forth. They all looked quite reasonable when stripped of the violent verbiage but could also be read to make quite impossible demands of the government if read in a more critical sense. The imprecise wording seemed to me to be the key. I invited the leaders of the Heung Yee Kuk to a meeting. The Chairman was Chan Yat Sun and the others were the same crowd that led New Territories opinion to support us when dealing with the 1959 coup of the Kuk. They were friendly and not aggressive — a little sheepish if anything — for they knew the demands were not worded in the politest of terms. I thanked them for calling and said I had read the demands carefully. I said they seemed reasonable and that I would accept them all. 'Now,' I said, 'just what do they mean?' And we got down to serious discussions on the grievances that were at the root of the problem.

Village housing

The most serious problem related to traditional village housing. New Territories villages were still largely one-clan or two-clan villages. As sons grew up, they had always been able to build themselves a village house on their land in accordance with the orderly layout of the village. Daughters always married outside the village and relied on their husbands to build for them. This had been the custom for generations, but now it had become impossible for villagers to build houses in their villages. Our procedures prohibited the granting of land for village houses to those who needed it. The land had to be sold by public auction. Anybody could bid, yet it was unthinkable that anyone not of the village clan could build a house in a village. Some District Officers had got round the problem by conducting public auctions in the villages, which were miles off the road system, at the crack of dawn so that nobody but those who lived in the village could take part. Another trick was to issue 'temporary structure' permits which District Officers could do without auction, but these gave no title to the land and did not result in permanent structures. Clearly, some policy change had to be made.

The major change that we agreed was that auctions should not be required but that the only people who could be granted land by private treaty would be genuine villagers — a term that we defined as being male descendants of villagers who were inhabitants of the village when the New Territories lease was signed in 1898. In a less settled and less organized society, such an agreement could be subject to widespread abuse but such was the cohesion of village life that nobody dared to masquerade as a villager who was not one. He would be spotted immediately.

Next, we tackled the question of the reach of the Buildings Ordinance which controlled the construction of all buildings in Hong Kong from skyscrapers to the humblest village house. It was clearly impossible to require the participation of authorized architects, who had to be responsible for the construction of all building works. There were no authorized architects in the New Territories. They were all on Hong Kong Island. The same applied to authorized contractors, none of whom was found outside the major towns. What we were talking about was the construction of simple two-storey houses by local contractors who were perfectly capable of putting up structures that would not fall down.

The Buildings Ordinance Office was only too pleased to be shot of these buildings, but they needed a clear definition of the building we were going to exempt from the Ordinance. The term 'village type house' had been loosely used to describe them. For years there had been arguments about the definition of the 'village type house', for in fact a great variety of houses was to be found in various parts of the New Territories. One of my learned predecessors, Ken Barnett, had written a two-page definition of what a village type house was. I cut through the sometimes esoteric arguments by dispensing with the term 'village type house'. Instead, I suggested a simple definition by fixing the maximum dimensions of the 'small house' as covering not more than seven hundred square feet and being not more than twenty-five feet high, allowing a two-storey structure with a cockloft on the ground floor. We also laid down some simple requirements relating to septic tanks and so forth which could be readily understood by rural contractors and be easily checked prior to the issue of an occupation certificate.

No general rules were laid down in respect of the location of the houses, but they were to be in the environs of the villages and decided on the basis of discussion in each case.

To bring the small house policy into action did not, for the most part, require legislation. It was a matter of approval of the new rules for a private treaty grant of land. One set of regulations by the Governor in Council was required. This was to exempt the small houses from the provisions of the Buildings Ordinance. The regulations were quickly drawn up, made and published in the Government Gazette. None of this attracted any attention, but I very much wanted publicity for this radical improvement of village administration. After the Governor in Council has made regulations, they do not come into force until they are laid on the table in the Legislative Council. On the laying of papers, a debate can take place. I suggested therefore that when the regulations were laid, I should make a speech. Nobody else would. This was agreed. I rang my friends in the Heung Yee Kuk to tell them of the occasion and urged them to attend to witness the triumph of their agitation. This they willingly did, though none of them had ever attended a meeting of the Legislative Council before and most had only very limited English. Our little drama did attract the press in a way that an ordinary press release would never have done. The scheme was well and truly launched.

A further element in the policy was to regularize the tenure of the many so-called 'temporary structures'. Some of the buildings allowed under these permits had been lived in for decades. There was nothing temporary about them. They were authorized as one way of allowing villagers to build houses without the formalities of auction and statutory plans. We agreed that anyone living in a temporary structure which had been up for ten years or more could turn his tenure into ownership of a small house plot. I particularly remember a row of shops near the pier on Ma Wan Island which had been on temporary structure permit since before the war. They were a decrepit collection of wooden huts but obviously serving a useful purpose. Once the shopkeepers had been granted ownership of the land, they built a fine row of excellent village shops with the family living upstairs.

This began to happen all over the rural areas of the New Territories. We cut procedures to the minimum for there was a terrific pent-up demand for legitimate development. The appearance of the rural areas changed dramatically. Wooden sheds with tin roofs disappeared and in their place sprang up neat little houses of modern construction. In about nine months, we were able to issue the thousandth building licence for a small house. We had a little ceremony and gave the proud owner a suite of furniture to mark the occasion. In terms of the space allocated in public housing, the villagers had built housing for some fifty thousand people without a cent of public expenditure — in fact there was a small amount of revenue for the land was not granted free.

The small house policy was worked out and implemented in a matter of about six weeks. My Acting Deputy, Patrick Williamson, did the detailed work and he did it speedily and effectively. I felt that I should emphasize to the Kuk that we should be bound to find snags in its implementation. I added, in a threatening way, that if the scheme was abused, we should scrap the whole thing. They understood. In a review after one year, a number of small points were settled. One, which was not, was the almost universal practice of extending the ground floor cockloft from 50 percent of the floor area to 100 percent as soon as the occupation certificate was issued. This really involved the two-storey houses becoming three-storey buildings, so I suggested this be considered further and left for the next review so that we should have something further to discuss then.

I cannot pretend that the small house policy was without its critics. These were not found among the villagers but among my fellow officials involved in land administration — mainly because the villagers had such freedom from regulation. The definition of a small house was deliberately made simple and precise. I knew perfectly well that it would not be long before some enterprising architect would design pleasant little buildings that fitted the rules but looked nothing like a traditional village house. Sure enough a Spanish-style house began to appear with lovely tiled half-roofs. They were a great improvement. What was less satisfactory was that once some villagers got an Occupation Certificate, they sold the buildings to rich city slickers. This was an abuse that has taken some time to deal with, but I cannot say the result has been seriously damaging to the development of the New Territories. I still maintain that the principal result was a very considerable improvement in the standard of housing that the ordinary villagers have been able to enjoy. The old system stifled building in the interest of rules that were totally unsuitable for the rural environment in which they were meant to operate. They caused much of the squalor in which these people had to live. If some of them have made money out of the policy, I do not grudge it to them.

Another land problem that we dealt with resulted from the realization that the development of small towns was now becoming inevitable. Layout plans were drawn up covering considerable areas round the principal urban centres and within these areas no development was allowed except in conformity with the plans. The fact that the government moved very slowly to stimulate the development by building the infrastructure of roads and so forth meant that land within these layout areas was frozen. Outside the layout areas such demand, as there was, could be largely met by the small house policy and some larger sales of land for substantial development. The Kuk pointed out that we had frozen land inside layout area but would be certain to need to resume it for urban development in due course. How would it be if they were to surrender land within a layout area for the grant of building land outside where we would allow development? Again, this seemed reasonable. We did allow some development outside the layout areas. There was no reason why we should not accept the surrender of land we should need one day, when its value would be many times what it was worth today, in exchange for grants of land outside layout areas which was lying idle anyway. So it was agreed. I do not think that much development took place under this scheme, principally because it was so difficult to find anywhere where we would agree to grant land for development. One well-known case was the early development of Discovery Bay on Lantau Island. This was based initially on the use of land bought for a cattle quarantine holding area when some entrepreneurs wanted to import Australian cattle on the hoof. The scheme was not a success, but the owners sold to a developer who had a vision of a city suburb accessible only by sea. Much of the additional land required in the early stages was granted in exchange for the surrender of agricultural land within the layout area of Tuen Mun where no development was taking place.

The Sha Tin racecourse

Postings to various appointments were often too short to get anything done. It would take a few months to work out what the new job was all about and then a year or more to get the money and law for any new initiative. Just as implementation started, you were moved to another post. Occasionally, it was possible to influence events at the very beginning of a project and one such was the Sha Tin racecourse. It was while I was

District Commissioner that agreement was given to the Jockey Club's plan to build a new racecourse in Sha Tin. This would involve considerable reclamation of the bay called Tide Cove. Now fill has to be found to reclaim land and this fill comes from what engineers called 'borrow areas'. I took exception to this term and would not let any of our people use it. There was no element of borrowing at all — certainly nothing was ever returned. I said the areas from which earth was to be fetched could be called either 'devastation areas' or 'development areas'. I had seen the devastation wrought in the areas from which earth and rock was excavated for the Plover Cove dam. The Chinese University was given one of these areas and had to spend millions on site formation which could have been greatly reduced, had more thought been given to the way in which earth had been dug out for the dam. The other Plover Cove 'borrow area' was at Wu Kwai Sha at the foot of Ma On Shan where the mess left was so unsightly that millions were spent to reform the site and plant trees until the whole area was absorbed into the new town. I did not want any new mess left from the reclamation for the racecourse.

Bernard Penfold, who was running the Jockey Club, was sympathetic and readily agreed that the conditions for the extraction of the fill should include provisions requiring the Club to form the land in a way suitable for subsequent development. Today, some very pleasant low-density settlements are found on this land with a fine view over the racecourse.

The other agreement I reached with Bernard, before anyone else thought about it, was that the Jockey Club, not the government, would develop the infield. I suggested this because, at that time, the infield at Happy Valley, which was managed by the Urban Services Department, turned into a dust bowl at the beginning of winter each year as the grass was worn away by the football players. I knew the Jockey Club would not let this happen. Bernard grasped this opportunity and built a fine park on the infield, with trees, ponds, shrubs and lawns, before anyone in the Urban Services Department realized what was happening. Their protests were too late. The park is quite rightly called Penfold Park.

Liaison with the military

The land border with China formed the northern boundary of the New Territories. During the 1967 troubles, the border provided its own excitement as I have already described. One of the results of the border problems at that time was the setting up of a tripartite organization comprising the police, the army and the civil government which came to be called PAGENT. The police Assistant Commissioner, the Brigadier in command of 48 brigade of Gurkhas and the District Commissioner were the representatives who met together regularly. I found this group both interesting and valuable and I think the others did too. We all happened to like each other. Many a little problem which could have led to rivalry was easily dealt with.

Control of the border itself probably took up most of our time. We decided for a start to count the number of holes in the border fence. This was a stout but uncomplicated chain-link fence with some barbed wire along the top. At several points along the border, fields on the Hong Kong side were owned by villagers on the Chinese side. As far as we were concerned, the land was still owned by the registered owners in the villages and not by the communes who owned all the land in China. Farmers crossed the border daily to till their fields. There were a few gates left open for this purpose by day and shut by night, but some were a little inconvenient. What could be more natural than to lift up the bottom of the chain-link fence to make a short cut? During the 1967 disturbances, after one of the border incidents, the border was closed by order of the Hong Kong government. The aim was to block the normal crossing points for commercial traffic, but the order was found to apply to the gates used by the farmers. The Chinese protested. The farmers could not get to their fields. The crops would be ruined. The villagers would starve. A mob assembled at one of the closed gates. The fact that only a few yards from the closed and locked gate there was a well-worn track to a hole in the fence made no difference to the heart-rending cries of the villagers, who were cut off from their land. That little problem was settled by some face-saving formula that led to the opening of the gates and the resumption of the use of both gates and holes in the fence.

In 1971 the border was quiet. There was a little smuggling and some illegal immigration, but controls on movement in China were so strict that few could get as far as the Hong Kong border. We did look at the border fence. The Gurkhas counted two hundred holes in it. None of us was unduly worried but we did put in hand a programme of repair to the fence and opened a few more gates.

PAGENT was a model of effective co-ordination on security matters. For most of the time, things were quiet and our meetings did not deal with weighty matters. We met as a routine. We got to know each other and something about each other's organizations and operations. The result was that when there was trouble, as for instance during a typhoon, all three organizations could bring their forces to bear speedily and in an effective and appropriate manner without wasting time in parochial arguments or trying to do each other's job.

The armed forces from Britain were an essential component of Britain's rule in Hong Kong, yet most administrators seldom came across them. The exception was among those working in the New Territories. Both in our work and in our social lives we saw a good deal of these soldiers and, in the early days, the Royal Navy too. We had come to Hong Kong for a lifelong career. The army were on a posting for two or three years. Some returned from time to time. It was immensely satisfying to see a bright, energetic young Brigade Major come back as a Brigadier and eventually as Commander British Forces — I am thinking of Derek Boorman who went so cheerfully through this process of promotion. We could not rival the colour of their Beating of the Retreat or the guest nights at their messes, but they did join in our Dragon Boat festivities and agricultural shows.

A much longer-lasting mark of the British forces is the basic network of roads in the New Territories. The Hong Kong government was not interested in developing the New Territories. It did not build any new roads of consequence before the roads were required for waterworks construction. These gave access to Lantau Island and the Sai Kung peninsula.

The first roads in the New Territories were built for defence purposes, the first being the main circular road. This left Kowloon from Sham Shui Po through Tsuen Wan, passing Castle Peak, Yuen Long and San Tin to Sheung Shui with branches to Man Kam To and Sha Tau Kok on the border, before returning through Tai Po, Sha Tin and back to Sham Shui Po. Another defence road was built from Kai Tak through the length of the Clear Water Bay peninsula to a gun emplacement overlooking the eastern sea approaches to Hong Kong.

As the main circular road was intended to facilitate the movement of troops, it avoided the centres of population. Of course, this new facility was just the thing to stimulate development. The road did not go through any settlement near Yuen Long, but soon after it was built, the citizens of the area established the Hop Yick Company to take advantage of it. This developed into Yuen Long town. At Castle Peak, the road was on the opposite side of the river estuary from the town of Tuen Mun, so a San Hui, or New Market, was built alongside the road. Similarly at Tai Po, the Old Market was found to be on the wrong side of the river from the road and railway, so the tycoons of Tai Po and surrounding villages set up the Tsat Yeuk, or Seven Districts, to build Tai Po New Market. In Sha Tin, the District Officer, Brian Wilson, issued a block of temporary structure permits to the man who owned the paddy-fields by the railway station.

Even after the war, it was the military who did the road building. New short cuts from Kam Tin through the Lam Tsuen Valley to Tai Po, and to Fan Ling past the golf club were called Route 1 and Route 2, later known as the Lam Kam and Fan Kam roads. A jeep track was built from the Clear Water Bay Road to Sai Kung as a reward for the spirited resistance during the Japanese occupation. Plans were drawn up for a road over Tai Mo Shan to provide a link to a proposed new airport at Ping Shan, near Yuen Long, but were dropped when the airport idea was abandoned. The army dug out these plans and built a much more ambitious road over Tai Mo Shan from Tsuen Wan to Sek Kong called TWSK from which a jeep track led to the summit of Tai Mo Shan where radar was installed. The last road built by the Gurkha Engineers was the one from Luk Keng to Tai Mei Tuk across the Sha Tau Kok peninsula, running through what is now a beautiful country park. No new town has sprung up on this road.

Sir David Trench

It was not until I became District Commissioner that I came at all frequently in contact with the Governor. David Trench had been in the Hong Kong Civil Service before he became High Commissioner of the Western Pacific, so I did know him before he returned as Governor. He had also been at Jesus College in Cambridge so that he would entertain former members when we had a visitor who was a contemporary of his. All this meant that he was not quite so awe-inspiring as previous governors had been. He was our last 'colonial' governor, that is, the last governor who had made his career in the Colonial Service. As such, he was used to championing the interests of the people of the place where he was working against the tendency of London to give more importance to the interests of Britain. Later, when we started getting diplomats as Governor, some of us were afraid that they would tend to give British views more importance than those of Hong Kong. We need not have worried. It was no secret that David Trench had formidable battles with the Foreign and

Commonwealth Office who had taken over the British government's responsibilities for colonial government from the specialized Colonial Office. I remember on one occasion when the Minister responsible was to visit Hong Kong, I asked at one of the weekly meetings which the Governor had with a few heads of departments, whether we should make any preparations for the occasion. 'Rubbish,' he said, 'this is of no real importance.' During the 1967 disturbances, he stood no nonsense from those breaking the law, whoever they were. They would be dealt with in accordance with the law. If they had been tried, convicted and imprisoned, they would stay in gaol even when he was put under pressure in the case of the man was from the New China News Agency. I was surprised to hear someone say he had been so frightened that he had gone on leave at the height of the disturbances. Nothing could be further from the truth. He was due for leave and was damned if a bunch of communists was going to disturb the arrangements. The same applied to all other senior staff for he was determined to maintain things as usual. I remember him as a direct, no-nonsense administrator who was able to continue to maintain personal relations with people he had known as a much more junior man long after becoming Governor — such as those in the curious little Cosmo Club. He took a great interest in the Royal Hong Kong Defence Force. He enrolled as a pilot in the Auxiliary Air Force though I think the only time he was able to wear his wings, as a qualified pilot, on his uniform was during the ceremonies for his departure.

Ten-year housing programme

Murray MacLehose succeeded David Trench in 1971. His ten-year housing plan was one of the most significant initiatives of his term as Governor. Housing policy was in a muddle. There were several programmes split roughly between Resettlement and Housing Authority. Resettlement was solely for squatters who had to be cleared to make way for development. The Housing Authority aimed to provide adequate housing for poor people in need of housing. You could apply for Housing Authority housing but not resettlement.

The fundamental problem was that so many people had been made eligible for public housing that there was no possibility of demand being satisfied in any reasonable time-scale. MacLehose believed that we could go on clearing huts for a maximum of ten years but not much longer. He called for a plan to provide adequate housing for everybody within this ten-year period. His call was made in the early summer of 1972 and he wanted to announce the new plan in his October speech.

Adequate housing was defined pretty simply as permanent housing at not less than thirty-five square feet a head — a figure that had been on the statute books pre-war but had been abandoned after the war as being unrealistically extravagant. Although none of the housing experts could be bothered with housing for the people of the rural areas, for once the New Territories were not left out. I got in on the discussions as District Commissioner, New Territories, since it was obvious that much of the new housing had to be built in the New Territories. I was particularly cross because the 1971 Census had shown how neglected the rural areas had been in the housing bonanza that the urban areas enjoyed. There had been some squatter clearances in the rural New Territories, that is, the New Territories outside Tsuen Wan, so there was one resettlement estate in Yuen Long. Admission was only for squatters whose homes had been demolished for some development — mostly road building. The Housing Authority had not built a single unit of accommodation in the rural New Territories. In the urban areas, the Housing Authority had built housing for a population exceeding the total population of the rural New Territories. Furthermore, it scarcely needed the census statistics to show that the rural population was very much poorer than that of the urban areas.

I was determined that this imbalance should be redressed. I made a point of understanding all the complicated figures that the housing experts produced and kept on inserting my rural area requirements. These were peripheral but the main exercise was fascinating. Donnithorn, builder of Resettlement Estates, Ted Pryor, the Town Planner, and Donald Liao, the Housing Authority chief, would sit round maps sketching in vast estates, adding up the figures until they matched the estimates of the inadequately housed.

In order to show the experts the needs of the rural areas, I took the housing chiefs off for a weekend on the District Office launch, touring some of the island communities. Our problems were trifling compared to those of the urban areas and all agreed that they could readily be solved in no time. They weren't, but that is another story.

Eventually, the back of the envelope figures were assembled into an Executive Council paper and in October 1972 the Governor announced his ten-year housing plan which was to be accomplished from 1 April 1973. It was a moment of great excitement.

Of course, things did not work out as envisaged in those few weeks of planning. To this day, you will find those involved with housing in the early 1970s saying that MacLehose's requirements were quite impossible to meet. They probably were, but the initiative and drive of the Governor got the new town programme into top gear. The whole scale of development changed. New administrative organizations were set up to keep the output up to scratch. New towns were developed with their full complement of infrastructure and social support in one coherent programme, unlike development hitherto where parks, schools, roads, clinics and so forth had to be argued for separately in their own programmes. That continued to be the case in the urban areas which now came to be left behind, until the same overall development systems were set up for them.

I had no idea that my time in the New Territories would be ended before the development got into its stride. I was sorry to be moved out of the New Territories just as things were at last getting moving. Now that real money was being invested in the area by the government, there was no doubt that private investment would follow and the whole scene would be transformed.

The end of rustication

After two and a half years as District Commissioner, I felt settled in a worthwhile and interesting job. Things were moving fast and the Governor had just announced a ten-year programme for the building of new towns. The nature of the New Territories was about to change dramatically. I had been involved in the planning of these new towns in the New Territories. I felt at home with the villagers and the developers which they all wanted to become.

I had made many friends among the villagers and was supported by a congenial, friendly and able staff headed by Ian Macpherson as my deputy. District Officers I think of are Patrick Williamson in Yuen Long, John Warren at Tsuen Wan, Harnam Grewal, one of our few Hong Kong–born Indians, at Tai Po, Tony Eason at Sai Kung and Harold Kwok in Islands. In the Head Office, we had the lively Ophelia Cheung and the wild S. J. Chan. Shortly before I left, Anson Chan came to us after a thin time in the Finance Branch, adding quality to the countrymen. All later had successful careers. I was lucky to have their support when they were rising fast. All have been good friends since.

I did not want to leave all this.

Alas, I was to be whisked off to be Secretary for Home Affairs just as the new programme was getting into top gear. I had resisted a proposal to move me to run the Establishment Branch in the Secretariat a year before. Perhaps that was not a wise move as the job of Establishment Officer in charge of all government personnel matters was difficult and prestigious. A successful stint here could lead to greater things. It was a challenge, but I felt that the New Territories job required continuity. There had been frequent changes in the post before I arrived and I argued that this should cease. The move to Secretary for Home Affairs was a promotion. My old mentor, Ronnie Holmes, said, 'You cannot turn down a promotion.' And Sir Murray MacLehose was not a man you took on lightly. I succumbed. As it turned out, the promotion resulted in a move to a smaller house, albeit on the Peak, and a slight diminution in pay for the District Commissioner had two domestic servants to help with the entertaining while the Secretary for Home Affairs had none. I had no idea that this was not to be my last move.

14

Life Near the Top

The Independent Commission Against Corruption

My move back to town was a minor consequence of a major new initiative that the Governor, Sir Murray MacLehose, had decided on. This was to mount a serious attack on corruption in the government, particularly in the police force. The Secretary for Home Affairs, who was now Jack Cater, was to head a new Independent Commission Against Corruption, and I was to be Secretary for Home Affairs. When the move took place, even the name of the new organization had not been decided. All Jack Cater had was an office. Starting from scratch, he built up an organization that took on the entrenched, syndicated corruption that saw police not only condoning vice but actually running it. Of course, not all policemen were involved. Some of the very fine crime fighters joined the new commission which, in addition, took on corruption found in several other departments where permissions had to be granted for profitable activities. The utilities and other 'public bodies' were also drawn in.

I was staggered by the state of affairs that was gradually revealed. The police had done sterling work in keeping the peace during the 1967 disturbances. Indeed, had it not been for their steadfastness, the history of Hong Kong would have been completely different. They had been granted the honour of being named the Royal Hong Kong Police Force in recognition. One of the most stalwart officers in those troubled times was Peter Godber, a senior policeman, whose daring and resolution we all admired. As the new commission got into its stride, the scale of corruption in the police almost passed belief. It was not long before over a hundred policemen were removed from their duties because they were being investigated. One of the most senior and most corrupt officers was the gallant Peter Godber who proved to have pulled in millions in corrupt takings. Even today, I find it difficult to contain the horror and disgust I felt as the state of affairs came to be exposed.

Although I saw and admired the success of this initiative, I was not part of it and cannot give a sensible account of its development. The Governor, Murray MacLehose, and the Commissioner Against Corruption, Jack Cater, must be owed an enormous debt of gratitude for transforming those parts of the police and civil service where structurally embedded acceptance of widespread corruption had seemed to be beyond redemption.

The new Secretariat for Home Affairs

My introduction to the new job was to plunge straight into the social and ceremonial obligations. On the first night, I was to join the Tung Wah Hospitals in their annual charity ball to welcome the Governor. I saw the Directors again the following Sunday during Remembrance Sunday ceremonies. Tung Wah, the oldest charity in Hong Kong, was founded in 1870. Its directors have always been respected and well-to-do businessmen. In addition to raising money for their charity, whose institutions are now largely financed by the government, they do a great deal of personal welfare work in their hospitals, schools, kindergartens, old people's homes, and so forth. There seems to be no limit to their reach. Originally founded to build a hospital, the charity has always maintained the closest of relations with the Home Affairs Secretariat. A Tung Wah chairman (for in those days they were all men) will have served anything from five to ten years before rising to this position. During his term as chairman, he will find himself in an almost full-time job, not only personally involved in the administration, but also engaged in a non-stop social round drumming up donations. Not everybody can spare the time. Not everybody can maintain the personal detailed interest in the activities of this large organization. At the end of his or her one-year period of office, he or she will still maintain a lively interest in the group's activities. As Secretary for Home Affairs, I was chairman of the advisory board to the Tung Wah and so soon built up a close association with the directors. When I eventually retired,

I was given the great honour of being appointed an honorary member of what must be the most exclusive association in Hong Kong. Only one new member can join each year, as membership is confined to past chairmen of Tung Wah. To this day, I attend their regular lunches and functions and my wife is very much at home with the Tung Wah wives. The chairman of this body is Leo Lee who has not only been involved in welfare work all his life, but was chairman during the Tung Wah's centenary year and has in addition done so much to improve trade of Italy and France with Hong Kong that both those countries have honoured him with their highest awards. Other past chairmen are household names in many circles and all retain a lively interest in the work of the charity.

The Secretariat for Home Affairs in 1973 was not the department I knew in 1971. Then it included the City District Officers, now these were to be found in a new Home Affairs Department. If that sounds like a muddle, it was. The idea was that the great man should be freed from day-to-day worries so that he could concentrate on important policy matters. Eric Ho, the Director of Home Affairs, the head of this new department, naturally wanted to behave like a head of department and saw no need for the Secretary to peer over his shoulder all the time. Fortunately he was a man I liked, and thought highly of, so we managed affairs without rancour or poaching on each other's territory. Years later, the two organizations were joined together again and have split again.

The chief concern of the Secretary was the government's public relations and communications with the public in general. He also had to oversee policy on culture, recreation and sport and, for a while, he even had responsibility for the government's policy on environmental protection. As an *ex officio* member of the Executive and Legislative Councils, he tended to become involved in all manner of policies and activities in times of difficulty.

Press, radio, television and publicity

For professional public relations work, there was an Information Services Department headed by Nigel Watt and staffed by professionals who, being better paid than press professionals outside the government, were able to keep our end up in the endless tug of war between the media and the government. They also did very good work on straight publicity for campaigns that we ran. Whenever there was anything of a crisis, we would get our heads together, but generally they ran their own operation with verve and expertise.

Radio Hong Kong, whose name we changed to Radio Television Hong Kong because of their considerable output of television, was another matter. Here was a powerful medium which would only be listened to and be credible if it operated with editorial independence. Yet, the director and his staff were civil servants answerable to the Secretary for Home Affairs. Some of my colleagues would jump up and down at the slightest hint of criticism of the government emanating from RTHK. Fortunately, the conduit between them and RTHK was me. I would take the slings and arrows fired at RTHK, smile sweetly, and keep mum. The director of this government radio and television station when I took up the post was James Hawthorn, a pretty independent-minded chap with a good many bright ideas. Of course, he gave time to our critics but he also ran, for instance, an excellent soap opera long before East Enders or Neighbours was heard of. It was popular and had good audiences. It also had excellent, low-key, messages urging good social behaviour — not three cheers for the government but subtle attacks on social ills from drug-taking to petty theft and even littering. RTHK also operated in a competitive field. We had no television station of our own but did have powers to require the commercial stations to broadcast a certain amount of RTHK output. The stations grumbled like mad about government shoving programmes into their schedules, but they were rather pleased with the ratings they got from RTHK's work. I will not pretend we had an ideal setup but, given the constraints of a colonial government, I think we managed the delicate balance between control and independence very well. That James went on to be the BBC's head of the Northern Ireland service when the mayhem there was at its height speaks volumes for his ability, tact and strength of mind.

We also spent a good deal of money on educational television because it is an extremely effective way of improving teaching methods. At first, this was run by the Education Department and they made a good start. As the output expanded from primary to secondary education, both television and educational techniques became more sophisticated. The Director of Broadcasting argued that the operation should be transferred to his department while the Director of Education said it was education and that was his field. The arguments were finely balanced, but I came down in favour of centralizing the government's television output and the Chief Secretary, Denys Roberts, agreed. This was one of the few interdepartmental struggles that I was ever involved in. Both protagonists were good men and had the support of their people. The transition was accomplished in the end without bad feeling.

Insoluble problems

Murray MacLehose was a great man for tackling obviously insoluble problems. I have already written about his housing initiative and the new drive against corruption. Two lesser initiatives had a less dramatic but still far-reaching effect on the community. These were the Clean Hong Kong campaign and the Fight Crime campaign.

Cleaning up a big city which has got used to living with filth in the streets requires a major change in the mentality of its citizens. It also needs real money to be put into the cleaning operation. Both these were done. A publicity campaign dominated government public relations. Litter-bins were put out every fifty yards. New laws against littering were enforced. Black spots, which it was nobody's job to clean, were cleaned and, in some cases, turned into little urban sitting-out areas with trees and grass. The campaign had started in 1972 and was still being carried on when I was moved.

One of the most effective initiatives in this campaign was the launching of Mutual Aid Committees. Left to themselves, people who live in multi-storey buildings do not develop the most socially happy responsibilities for communal facilities. The buildings tend to go to rack and ruin. The postwar replacement of all private residential buildings, which was accomplished with astonishing speed, left Hong Kong with thousands of buildings each with hundreds of flats that were individually owned. Management remained in the hands of the original developer who had sold all his interest. The result was widespread neglect of the common parts of buildings and, as these were tall buildings, the lifts were an important part. We did legislate but found no way round the problem that tenants could not commit their landlords to expenditure on improvements. Laws were passed to make it fairly straightforward for owners to band together to form owners' corporations which did have powers to impose charges on owners for improvements. Still, the problem of blocks largely occupied by tenants remained. A bright idea was developed in the Home Affairs Department by, I think, Martin Rowlands. It was to promote the formation of Mutual Aid Committees. These bodies were composed of residents of blocks of flats, whether they were owners or tenants. They had a legal existence but had no legal powers to levy charges. With our encouragement, a few were set up to see how moral suasion would raise the money for improvements. They were a great success. A major publicity campaign was then launched to encourage residents to form these committees. Part-time staff, many of them school teachers, was engaged to go round the blocks talking to residents about the idea. They were well received. Although a few buildings generated their committees without assistance, this assistance usually led quickly to the formation of a Mutual Aid Committee. In no time, over a thousand were formed. The astonishing thing was the readiness of residents to contribute to common expenses even without any force of law behind the committees. The improvements to building entrances and lifts were not only pleasing but helped to reduce petty crime.

The Fight Crime campaign was another drive to change mentality. The aim was to get people to report crime and to take sensible steps to prevent it. The magisterial thrones of the inspector on duty at police stations were demolished. Friendly Neighbourhood Police Posts were set up in little plastic cabins. People were urged to report crime. Police Community Officers were appointed. A television programme called *Junior Police Call* grew into a major youth movement which Drew Rennie, in the police, and James Hawthorn, at RTHK, masterminded. Police pay was boosted and training was oriented towards getting the public on side. This might all seem at odds with a police force which needed a new independent commission to root out corruption. The fact was that the force was a large one. Both elements existed at the same time. Some were real villains, but there were others who were fine humanitarians and only needed the new initiative to bring out the best in them.

As Secretary for Home Affairs, I found myself Chairman of the Fight Crime Committee. This had been going for some time, so it had settled into something of a routine. The major reforms had been achieved, but we still managed to continue to listen to new ideas and at least try them out if there was any possibility of their being useful.

The Consumer Council

It was in the mid-1970s that inflation began to bite. This was a side effect of the oil embargo which had such devastating effects not only on us but on Japan. What hit the Hong Kong people was the steep rise in the price of rice. It had been stable for twenty years but was now increasing by the day. In order to ensure that there was always a sufficient store of rice in Hong Kong, the government had restricted its import to a limited number of importers who, in consideration for this monopoly, agreed to hold stores well in excess of commercially prudent requirements. The public began to fear that these importers were using the excuse of inflation to increase their own profits. Rice on sale today had been purchased three months ago at prices much lower than those of today. It was being sold to retailers at today's price with the importers gaining a clear profit arising from the three months of inflation. MacLehose took action. He decided to set up a Consumer Council and told me to get on with it — in fact I was not to go to Manila to crew a yacht back from the China Sea Race unless the Council was in business before I went. The Council was set up on 1 April 1974. This was an innovation which we had not seen before. This body was chaired by Y. K. Kan, the Legislator who had done so brilliantly in transport matters. His administrative secretary was one of the livelier first District Officers who had worked in town and country, Patrick Williamson. The decision to set up the Council was taken in the Executive Council one Tuesday. The first meeting was held in the following week. The Council had no powers and was, indeed, in some danger of being sued for some of its pronouncements. When one member asked the chairman if the secretary was legally protected when he made some of his statements, he replied that he had assured the secretary that if he went to jail, he, the chairman, would visit him daily. The boldness with which this group tackled profiteering with nothing, but public fury to back them was amazing. The pricing racket stopped and the profits of the importers were reined in. I was able to go to Manila. The Consumer Council has gone on from strength to strength, but it owes a great deal to those pioneers of consumer protection who had no experience, no law, no staff — just supreme confidence.

The onset of leisure

A new challenge was emerging from an unexpected quarter. People actually had leisure. Hitherto people worked until they dropped. When they looked for a job, they asked not only about wages but about overtime. If one job did not keep them busy enough, they took two. For a few days at Chinese

New Year and perhaps at the Dragon Boat and Mid-Autumn Festivals, they might get time off. Otherwise, they worked seven days a week throughout the year. I am not talking about the government offices or the big business houses where the norm was a five-and-a-half-day week with a day off on Sundays and some seventeen general holidays. Employers were not required to give these holidays to industrial or construction workers or the general mass of the poorly paid. For some years these people had to be given ten days off in the year on specific festivals, but the working week was still seven days.

By the mid-1970s, people were coming to prefer a little leisure rather than the extra wages. Some people other than office workers and civil servants were actually taking one day off every week. This was becoming sufficiently common to enable legislation to be introduced in 1976 to require employers to offer their employees four days off a month. They did not have to stop work if they did not want to, but the offer had to be made. It was quite lawful to offer a little extra to a man not to take the time off. It was a later battle to introduce the law requiring that the offer be increased to one day a week. A legal requirement for a few annual holidays came much later.

It was also during the 1970s that primary and secondary education became available for everybody who wanted it. Primary education became universal in 1971 and secondary in 1978. Before 1971, there was great competition to get into school. Private schools of indifferent quality made good profits. Charitable bodies set up recreation centres for children without school but had to be careful not to teach them so much that they became, in law, 'schools' and had to comply with all the regulations that applied to schools. Entrance to publicly financed secondary schools was a matter of passing a competitive examination. Children who failed to get in left school at the age of twelve, but they could not work legally until they were fourteen. Many of these children took to petty crime. It came to be believed that once there was adequate secondary school accommodation, juvenile crime would disappear. Of course, it did not. A survey showed that most of the children picked up for petty crime had started on their careers of crime when they absconded from their primary schools. But what could a youngster do after school or after he left school when jobs were beginning to leave him with leisure?

Recreation and sport

The unaccustomed luxury of leisure created an opportunity — for mischief if we were not careful. Energetic young people had no outlets for their energies as there were few sporting activities. The Governor set up a new body called the Council for Recreation and Sport and made the Secretary for Home Affairs Chairman. The emphasis was on recreation rather than organized sport as the sporting hierarchy was somewhat stultified. Executives in some sports associations did very little to promote their sport. The new Council was after the masses of youngsters who simply wanted to have fun. The Education Department had a number of very able and enthusiastic sports administrators. They proposed that we should establish a Recreation and Sports Service which was not school-based but district-based. The aim would be to organize mass recreation and sporting activities. Thanks to the Urban Council, there were plenty of recreation grounds, but there was no organization to help people use them once they had left school.

The scheme was headed by Mike Caswell and Betty Mair and proved instantly popular. Betty indeed went on, long after retirement, to organize all manner of sports and recreation for companies and public bodies that had no such expertise. Some of the sporting associations joined in. On public holidays and during the summer break, sporting and recreational activities were organized everywhere and the Jockey Club produced money for the expenses. The City District Officers joined in and drew in the local leaders as well. At first, the games were just one-off functions but gradually teams were built up and inter-district competitions were arranged.

The Jockey Club proposed that outstanding sportsmen should be catered for at a central facility. This was the Jubilee Sports Centre at Sha Tin. Public donations were raised on the occasion of the Queen's Silver Jubilee, but the bulk of the capital and all the running expenses were born by the Jockey Club for some years. I found myself on the board of this body. We did not have an easy time. Hong Kong people put far more energy into making money than into sport at an international level. Gradually, we began to find an occasional outstanding athlete. Our coaches were first-class and slowly the athletes got used to the idea of training for long periods. Some of the best could not do this because they had to work, so Howard Wells, who was head of the centre by the time I joined it, instituted scholarships for some of the top athletes. It was interesting to see which sporting associations took advantage of the new centre. They were not always the obvious ones. Football, gymnastics and fencing, I remember, but athletics had a bad time as did table tennis. Rowing, which was exclusively an expatriate sport for a few old rowing men, not me included I am sad to say, took off because of the effective and energetic leadership of a handful of enthusiasts, led by Bob Wilson, who formed the Hong Kong Rowing Association. They badgered the government for land and the Jockey Club for money for a boat house and boats, and set up a fine rowing centre which was able to use a course that might almost have been built for them. It wasn't actually. It was a river channel alongside the new racecourse in Sha Tin, but a dead straight, sheltered two-thousand-metre course could be set up. Gold medals for rowing have been won in the Asian Games.

The Academy for Performing Arts

Not all young people are of a sporting inclination and we wondered what less physically energetic activity could be devised for them. After consideration of a report by one of the external examiners for the Schools Music Festival, David Stone, we decided that it should be music. A Music Office was established in the Education Department and again it organized great musical gatherings, many of which took the form of introducing young people to instruments they had never played. On other occasions, musicians were assembled for group activities.

Again, the really talented had to be catered for. David Stone, who had been appointed Music Adviser, was asked to draw up plans for a centre for the teaching of music. He went round the world looking at various centres. In record time, he produced a full schedule of accommodation for a centre which would teach not only music but cover all performing arts. A piece of empty land near the Naval dockyard, right in the middle of town, was zoned as open space but we were able to persuade the Town Planning Board that a 'small' seven-storey building on part of the site would not be out of place.

The Jockey Club, which was headed by General Sir John Archer at the time, liked the idea and came up with the finance and John Halliwell, their engineer, supervised its construction under the guidance of a committee headed by a Jockey Club Steward, Aubrey Li.

The Jockey Club was particularly good at spotting good schemes which the government might feel a bit shy about spending public money on. They had the money. They had built Ocean Park, a splendid theme park based originally on a magnificent aquarium. They now took to the idea of this new academy. The plans were drawn up and construction was well under way before we recruited the director. The architect had produced an outstanding building with excellent facilities, but I was terrified that the director, when he arrived, would tell us we had got it all wrong. Happily, he was impressed with what was being built and quietly admitted that the quality and extent of the facilities were far beyond his wildest dreams. The opening performance was a full-scale opera which, we reckoned, embraced the whole gamut of the performing arts. The entire scheme for the Academy of Performing Arts proceeded at breakneck speed. From the first ideas to opening day was less than three years. You really could cut corners in those days if you had the right people on the job.

Gambling

Mention of the Jockey Club brings me to discuss the revolution in the regulation of gambling that took place in the 1970s. When we set up the City District Officer scheme in 1968, one of the City District Officers, David Lai, had written a review of illegal gambling taking place all over Hong Kong. It was a dramatic account of a disgusting situation that thrived in the days before the assault on corruption. In submitting it to the government, I argued that when people saw the law being flouted on such a scale, they could only draw the conclusion that collusion in the government reached right to the very top. They could see the government succeeding in all sorts of fields, such as the massive housing programme, but seeming to connive at this widespread illegal gambling. I am afraid I do not know how the report was handled in the Secretariat, but the Commissioner of Police did say to me, 'You seem to be pretty steamed up about gambling.'

Illegal gambling was in two basic forms — illegal gambling on horse-races and an uncontrolled numbers game called *tse fa*.

Horse-racing has been popular in Hong Kong since its earliest days but bets could only be placed legally on the racecourse and were confined to the tote. The Jockey Club, then the Royal Hong Kong Jockey Club, is a non-profit-making body. No profits are distributed. The Stewards receive no salary or dividends. No profit does not mean no surplus which has always been substantial. The surplus has always been devoted to charitable ends.

Illegal bookmaking was rife. Everyone had their bookmaker and could place bets by phone. The activity was scarcely disguised and led to a great deal of corruption among the police. Illegal gambling, together with drugs, were probably the chief sources of their corrupt income. No amount of persuasion could convince the most conservative Executive Council members that off-course betting should be allowed. Reports on gambling solemnly said that workers should not gamble, though the authors spent every Saturday round the mah-jong table. With the change in the Executive Council following the decease of one of the old stalwarts, and the accession of Y. K. Kan to the position of the Senior Unofficial Member of Executive Council, policy softened and legislation was enacted to permit the Jockey Club, but nobody else, to open off-course betting centres, again with bets going to the tote. Curiously, the subject was not raised in the Legislative Council immediately, but the Vice-Chancellor of Hong Kong University launched an attack against legal gambling, after the betting centres had been set up and were thriving. My maiden speech in the Council was all about the four vices — fornication, gambling, drinking and smoking — opium that is. Not a very maidenlike subject. I argued that in all these fields, a distinction had to be made between sin and crime. Sins were a matter between the individual and his deity, but crime was to be punished by the state. When the gap between the law and practice had grown as great as it had in the case of gambling, some change was necessary. The government did not purport to lay down moral guides. This was for other authorities. It did, however, have a duty to enforce the law. If this was so far from the public wish, then it had to be changed. This was not an easy speech to draft. One of my Chinese colleagues, Christopher Wong, said that we must never use the term 'legalize' in connection with gambling. The translation into Cantonese means to bring within the natural law of morals. This, my friend said, could never be done. I was to avoid the word. Instead, we used the term 'controlled' which had a much more satisfactory translation implying regulation, not a free-for-all — and it was more accurate. This is an area of policy to which there is never a clear-cut answer. To legalize, or to use a horrible word coined much later, to 'decriminalize', an unlawful activity, even one as widespread as off-course betting, always generates an increase in it. A judgement had to be made on the balance between recognition of a general practice and the moral stand taken by some people.

To make laws was one thing. To get the off-course betting centres off the ground was another. As soon as the laws were made, Bernard Penfold, a retired Major General, who was running the Jockey club then, went into action. Betting centres were opened up all over town. The Secretary for Home Affairs was the authority for licensing these centres and was expected to take local public opinion into account. We did keep distance between the betting centres and primary schools, but when a secondary school protested at a proposed centre it regarded as being too close, I ruled against the school. Everywhere else young men and women were exposed to the temptations of the betting centres. At least, the students of the school would have the guidance of their teachers which would not be available to youngsters of the same age working in the industrial workshops or on the streets.

The illegal bookies were eliminated almost overnight except for a few catering to customers with very large bets. These were very difficult to track down. Although eliminated, illegal bookies are still ready to supply a service wherever the Jockey Club has no centre. Today, it is District Boards who say whether public opinion is in favour or not. Because of the moral abhorrence of gambling, the public figures who sit on District Boards have great difficulty in refraining from opposing new centres. This has meant that there are some areas where a considerable population has no legal betting centre, the most notorious being Tsing Yi Island.

Another line had to be followed to deal with *tse fa*. This was a very old traditional numbers game like public lotteries anywhere. There were thirty-six numbers, each linked to some mythical animal or person. How anyone trusted the managers to make a fair draw when the whole operation was illegal, I have never discovered. It did not take much cleverness to make a fortune, so the operators were supported by gangsters — and the police. A seller of *tse fa* tickets was to be found at the foot of every staircase in every housing estate. They had no equipment and so were extremely mobile when chased. Our solution here was to create a government lottery. We were no good at running this sort of thing and so asked the Jockey Club to do it for us. The profits were to go to welfare. The anticipated profits were far more than could be spent on conventional social welfare, so we decided to impose a betting tax to divert some to general revenue. Again, the results were instantaneous and satisfactory. The prizes were much larger than in the illegal game and the public trusted the Jockey Club to run the lottery without fiddling. The draw was televised each week. And as time went on, the betting wizards in the Jockey club devised more and more clever attractions, such as rolling over the prize into a jackpot if nobody got the winning number. The profits went to the Lotteries Fund which became a source of welfare money. It was also a convenient account for the money people would bid for lucky car numbers. For this reason, I have often tried in vain to encourage those religious bodies, which are reluctant to take gambling money, to take money paid for a car number like 8888 — and we are talking about millions. Unfortunately, the lotteries authorities have not been able to keep their accounts in such a way as to convince some of the charitable bodies that are most hostile to any form of gambling.

It is my belief that by providing the off-course betting centres in sufficient numbers and decent premises, and running the government lottery, we not only eliminated a vast field of gangster-controlled activity, but also contributed to the suppression of corruption in the police who no longer had this source of funds.

The Committee on Widespread Unlawful Activities

Arising, I suppose from dealing with gambling, a thought occurred to me that there were other areas of administration where thousands of people, going about their ordinary business, were breaking the law of the land every day. I have mentioned hawkers and gambling but what about the thriving *pak pai* business in unlawful public transport? I suggested to the Attorney-General, the Commissioner Against Corruption and the Commissioner of Police that we might meet to discuss these matters with those responsible for the various areas of administration. So we established ourselves as the Committee on Widespread Unlawful Activities. We made some progress on hawkers and transport. Hawker permitted areas were established where any licensed hawker could trade, and licences were freely issued. School bus services took the place of the illegal use of private cars. Not great innovations but some progress was made in the aim to relieve ordinary citizens from having to break the law to earn an honest living.

Legislative Council

It may seem curious that at a time when all other colonies were seething with independence movements and were rapidly being given their independence, there was no parallel movement in Hong Kong. In the early postwar years, the whole place was a great refugee camp living without any outside support. People were struggling simply to survive. They had nearly all fled from the Communists and wanted no truck with the government in China. Though there were some who supported the new revolution in China, there were also substantial numbers who were supporters of the Nationalists in Taiwan. On the whole, people just did not want politics because of the dreadful experiences they had had in China. Except for a short period in 1956, the communists and the nationalists were kept from each other's throats. Nobody wanted any situation to develop in which people would have to declare their allegiance to either. One effect of this reluctance to be involved with politics was to stifle the growth of the trade union movement, for the very good reason that the unions were divided into those that supported the communists and those that supported the nationalists. Most workers wanted nothing to do with either camp. The government set up a Trade Union Office in the Labour Department and drew up laws that tried to keep unions on the straight and narrow in their electoral and money matters. In spite of some encouragement from the government, the unions never came to be a power in the land.

The same reluctance to be involved in politics also meant that there was no real pressure to set up elections for any organization that would run the government. We worked very hard to be accessible and to consult for we knew perfectly well that there is no guarantee against revolution. We had several hundred advisory bodies operating in all fields of administration so that there was a very wide public participation in policy formation though without formal elections. There was always a ready access to members of Parliament in London for those who felt strongly that the government was getting it wrong. And, of course, we could not lock up people we did not like — we just had to get on with them.

Until I retired in 1985, all members of the Legislative Council were appointed by the Governor or were officials. Whatever you may think of the appointment system, it existed. The Governor had to make these appointments. This job was taken very seriously by all governors. What was wanted was a group of men and women who commanded respect and who could be relied on to articulate strands of public opinion. Members were sometimes criticized for being 'yes-men', willing to accept everything the government proposed. This was never the case and the government did not always get its own way, as in the case of gambling legislation.

Among these Unofficial Members of Councils were found some outstanding political, or, if your prefer, community leaders. I have already mentioned Sir Y. K. Kan because I worked closely with him but his successor as Senior Unofficial Member of Executive Council, Sir S. Y. Chung also has an impressive record of public service. He was the driving force behind the major expansion of the original Polytechnic and then the founding father of the City Polytechnic and the University of Science and Technology. When he tried to retire, David Wilson got him to inaugurate and build up the Hospital Authority. I should not know where to stop if I was to try to recall all the able men and women who played such a pivotal part in the success of Hong Kong's political and social life. They may not have been elected but by any measure they have given Hong Kong more than many elected politicians in places with more liberal constitutions.

As Secretary for Home Affairs in 1976, I found that my recommendations were required. This was novel. When Hong Kong was a much smaller place than it was in the mid-1970s, the number of prominent citizens was also much smaller. It was possible for the governor to know personally a far greater proportion of the community leaders. The criteria for appointment were not recorded, just the governor's recommendations to the Secretary of State in London. I thought the system a bit haphazard and set about categorizing the sort of people we should look for. Murray MacLehose was determined to broaden the representative nature of the Council and try to make some appointments from the leaders at local levels in the districts. Having got the areas of society that should be represented, the next job was the identification of the individuals. The Governor was able to do this in many cases, but I had to make recommendations for people who were not seen in Government House. In turn, I asked each City District Officer to introduce me to the ten most effective people in their districts.

The 1976 appointments drastically changed the nature of the Legislative Council. The numbers were increased and drawn from areas in society that had never been considered before. I think all those appointed that year served Hong Kong well and are owed a great debt of gratitude for the service they performed. I can remember thinking about one particular man, Wong Lam, who was always at the forefront of activities in Kwun Tong, not a rich man but someone who could get rich men to support local activities. Nobody outside the district had heard of him but he was an outstanding example of a public-spirited citizen. His whole life would be changed. He would be lionized by the press, feted throughout the town and generally thrust into the public glare. He took it all with great aplomb. For years afterwards, he was able to bring us down to earth when discussions were straying too far into imagination.

Royal visit

In May 1975, there were five thousand and one notable visitors to Hong Kong. The five thousand were the first tranche of refugees from Vietnam and the one was the Queen of England. All arrived on the same day. The Queen's visit had been meticulously planned to the last detail. The Vietnamese arrived out of the blue on a container ship, the *Clara Maersk,* which had picked them up at sea.

Little did we know that we should be running refugee camps for the Vietnamese until 1998. We were completely unprepared but had to find shelter for the five thousand. By a stroke of luck, there was a nearly finished new hospital close to the container port. It was not operational but it was possible to house the refugees there for the time being. When the Governor had said good night to the Queen, he went over for the same purpose to the unfinished Lai Chi Kok hospital.

My job at the time was to manage the arrangements for the royal visit. Planning had started some months before. I had never been involved in the sort of meticulous detail that such an event requires. It was great fun. In the normal way, I was supposed to spend my time away from detail, brooding on great policies, leaving the detail to lesser minions. It was refreshing to immerse myself in detail again — real detail. For instance, one of the events was to be a reception. It had to be under cover, but what was the largest covered space in Hong Kong? Government House was far too small. We wanted to send out the largest possible number of invitations. We decided on the Ocean Terminal. That would take several thousand guests, other than those invited to the formal arrival or civic luncheon. On such an occasion, the Queen cannot speak to everybody but we should try to arrange for her, and for Prince Philip, to speak to as many as possible. Even the casual encounters should be stage-managed. We drew out two routes along which the Queen and Prince Philip would walk. These we marked out with little bits of sticky tape on the ground. The miracle was that people understood that these marked a narrow path and stood back leaving the tracks open. At ten points along each route, a City District Officer was to assemble ten citizens from various representative groups. I gave them money to invite their particular guests to lunch beforehand so that they would get to know them. Of course, we made no attempt to prevent conversation with anyone else, but I think the care we had taken did give both the Queen and Prince Philip an opportunity to have a few words with people from a great many walks of life, from religious leaders to street hawkers, film stars to sportsmen.

I thought it would be entertaining to show off the fishing harbour at Aberdeen which is always such colourful mayhem. To structure the visit, I asked the fisheries people to arrange for an informal procession of vessels of as many different sorts as possible. I had no great hopes of this being anything more than very slightly organized confusion for the boat people were quite uncontrollable. Imagine my dismay when we had brought the royal party on the Governor's launch to a floating restaurant from which to view the spectacle to find that the whole place had been closed down. Not a boat was to be seen on the glassy water of the empty fairway. After what seemed to me to be ages, a fishing boat eventually appeared and then, one by one, more and more paraded in unaccustomed regulated order. What we took for granted, the spectacle of the moored boats, the washing hanging out, the crowds leaning over the rails, the game of mah-jong on the deck of a cargo barge, were all novel to the visitors. What really made the event was the return trip to Hong Kong. To avoid road closures, which would cause inevitable traffic jams at rush hour on roads across the island, we arranged for the royal party to return on one of the Yaumati Ferry's shiny new hover ferries, made, of course, in England. This was to pass to the south of Ap Lei Chau Island but the sea there had got up in an unexpected blow. Instead, the ferry had to go back through the anchorage which had by now been restored to its usual chaotic state — much to the delight of the passengers on the craft.

We nearly had a catastrophe involving the presentation of the first gold coin struck in Hong Kong. This was to take place at the end of a civic lunch in the City Hall. During the preliminaries, the Secretary for Monetary Affairs saw the coin being prepared for presentation. He was dumbfounded. This was not the Queen's coin. It was the Governor's — the Queen's being of proof condition while the Governor's was of the slightly less prestigious mint condition. The Queen's coin had been sent down to the City Hall in advance and was safely locked in the manager's office. When he was found, he had forgotten the combination of his safe. My assistant and he spent the lunch period trying dates of birthdays and anniversaries to no avail until the last moment when the safe opened.

The coin was slipped onto the table just as the Governor was making his speech of presentation.

Our thinking was that we should include the minimum pomp and circumstance. This sort of thing was done so much better in London. We were not at all certain that Chinese residents of colonial Hong Kong, other than those hoping for invitations to functions, would greet the visit with much enthusiasm. The major public appearances were therefore to be in places where there would be crowds anyway. This was not difficult in Hong Kong. A parade down Nathan Road, of a sort that we then had from time to time, a visit to a swimming complex near a housing estate, an unannounced walk down a crowded hawker street in Central. All these went well and attracted far greater crowds than we had expected. As the visit went on, the crowds grew bigger. Perhaps the most significant turnout was for the departure drive from Kowloon pier to Kai Tak Airport. The route was announced, but no great crowds were expected for a drive past so early in the morning. On the day, the route was packed along its whole length, reflecting a surprisingly warm interest from ordinary people of Hong Kong.

15

Overseas Posting

After that glorious summer's sailing in 1977 I took up a new post, not in Hong Kong but in London. I was very surprised when Sir Murray MacLehose sent for me and asked how I should like to represent the Hong Kong government in London. The job of Hong Kong Commissioner had generally been filled by people who had retired after long service from some senior job here. I was nowhere near ready to retire and asked for an assurance that I could depend on returning after a limited time, which he gave me.

Colonial plenipotentiary in the metropolitan capital

Hong Kong Commissioner in London was a curious job. I was a plenipotentiary from a colony in the metropolitan capital, not an ambassador. Business between the Foreign Office and Hong Kong was conducted directly, but still a representative of the largest remaining colony in the British Empire, not a UK civil servant. It took me a little time to get used to living in England. I found that first winter cold.

Doing the East

This was in 1977 towards the end of the long period of Labour government which did not really like our successful corner of unbridled enterprise in the empire. Backbench members of Parliament often criticized labour conditions or social services, usually from ignorance. I felt I could not begin on this job without slightly better knowledge of the Far East than I had, so it was arranged that I should do the East in a period of ten days. Of course, this could be no more than a cursory glance, but it is surprising how much can be packed into a short visit when it is aided by the British ambassadors and high commissioners. I started with visits to Manila, Singapore and Kuala Lumpur. At each place, the ambassador or high commissioner gave me a penetrating analysis of affairs there and introduced me to a variety of local residents who enlarged on this background. Back to Hong Kong for the weekend and then to Seoul and Tokyo. I had not looked carefully at my itinerary and was alarmed to discover that we were due to make a stop in Taipei. In Hong Kong, we were enjoined to eschew any contact with the Nationalist authorities there, lest we be accused of fostering a two or three China policy. There was no question of ever visiting the place. It was with some trepidation that, on landing, I found that we were all required to get off the plane during refuelling. I duly set foot in this forbidden territory with no disastrous consequence other than some rather poor coffee. Again at Seoul and Tokyo, the ambassadors were kindness itself, the latter having been political adviser in Hong Kong during our 1967 excitements.

These visits were enough to fill in the picture I had formed that our social services were better than anything else in Asia with some exception in regard to Japan. I felt more confident to meet criticism in England — at least I had been to these places which was more than most of those I would meet.

Members of Parliament

I felt that my principal job was to tackle members of Parliament — friendly or hostile. In this respect, my work was completely different from that of the British civil servants who worked in the Foreign Office. They were not supposed to lobby members of Parliament or even speak to them except through one of their ministers. I had to tackle them direct. I could not have started on this without the help of the Anglo-Hong Kong Parliamentary group and, in particular, its chairman, Sir Paul Bryan. The group comprised members from all parties for there was no split on party lines on policy towards Hong Kong. This did not mean to say that some were not more critical than others.

It is much easier to contact great politicians who are in opposition than those in the government. The latter are usually busier and have a phalanx of civil servants to protect them from the advances of outsiders. Those in opposition are much more readily approachable and much more ready to listen to outsiders or anyone else who wants to lobby them. We had no very sophisticated techniques but we did have our offices in a charming listed building in Mayfair. The conference room could readily be turned into an elegant luncheon room, so we installed a small kitchen which outside caterers could use to produce good meals. MPs and others would accept our invitations to lunch. For an hour or so they could be filled with Hong Kong information — I almost said propaganda. Paul Bryan also arranged for us to meet groups of MPs for dinner in the House of Commons. I was surprised to find that nobody took offence if we paid. I soon found that you could not hold the interest in Hong Kong of anybody for anything like an hour. They were much more interested in affairs going on all round them. The only way to maintain a conversation was to become knowledgeable about affairs in Britain. But what did I know about what was going on in Britain? Practically nothing.

I spoke English like a native, I looked like a native, but I was ignorant of many of the things that people take for granted. I had spent all my life except for schooling, university and National Service in China or Hong Kong and was last in London as a student in 1950. Everyone expected me to know what was going on and to understand the social scene. Well, I didn't. In order to catch up, I read newspapers voraciously. Every morning I went pretty thoroughly through *The Times, The Telegraph, The Guardian,* and *The Financial Times.* It took a long time to get through them all. It was worth it for it was not long before I could hold my own in conversation with the politicians and other great men in London. They were very knowledgeable about their own specialist areas but no better informed about many other matters of the day than any other newspaper reader. It was an exciting time to be there during the last days of old Labour and the first of Thatcherism.

Another important coterie was that of the diplomatic press corps. These are the people who write about Hong Kong in English newspapers. They would often call when there was a Hong Kong story and I got to know them reasonably well. I found that they had nowhere to hold the Annual General Meeting of the Diplomatic Writers Association, so I offered them the use of our dining-room, with a bottle of sherry to aid their deliberations. They invited me to their lunch afterwards and a very pleasant occasion it was. When I was to return to Hong Kong, they very kindly gave me a lunch and a copy of the new *Oxford Dictionary of Quotations* which I found handy in speeches when I got back.

The UK press was, on the whole, not much interested in Hong Kong but occasionally I had to do some rescue work. One such occasion was when some paper got hold of the story that the barmen in the House of Commons were being given shirts made in Hong Kong and not in Britain. I was able to go on the radio and argue that, since all imports of shirts from Hong Kong were subject to a strict quota, the fact that some thirty barmen in the House of Commons were given Hong Kong shirts meant that thirty other men in England would be deprived of them. The decision involved no threat to the shirtmakers of England. I did not add that at the time the quota was sufficient for every man and boy in the country to have a new Hong Kong shirt every year!

Conflicts with British interests

I soon found that our interests and those of the UK government did not always coincide. I arrived during one of those periodic battles we had with the Common Market — not the UK government you understand, the Common Market — on the import of textiles. The British were among our fiercest antagonists but insulated from us by the shield of the Common Market. We had some pretty hot meetings in Whitehall. I can remember the Secretary of State for Trade asking Murray MacLehose in some puzzlement just who gave him his orders. How could a bureaucrat argue with a Secretary of State?

In some quarters, there really was a belief that it was the job of the colonial government to promote the interests of the UK, even when these conflicted with those of the colony. This view got short shrift from MacLehose and, indeed all Hong Kong civil servants ever involved in such situations. This old-fashioned attitude to the colony seldom showed itself, but I have heard stories of colleagues being threatened with blighted career prospects unless they furthered UK interests over those of Hong Kong. I remember Murray MacLehose saying shortly after his arrival that he could not understand why we always seemed to be in battle with the Foreign Office. Not long afterwards, he said to me in the car one day, 'I cannot understand those people in the Foreign Office — they seem to regard me as a cross between Makarios and a bandit chief.' 'That,' I said, 'is par for the course for a colonial governor.'

We did have one confrontation when I was in the Executive Council considering the question of a pre-emptive bid by the Japanese for the contract to design and construct our underground railway. The consortium included all the best names in Japan. The price was far lower than anything we could expect — but there was a strong British interest in the same construction. We went for the Japanese, but I fancy MacLehose got a roasting from the Foreign Office for doing so. As things turned out, the Japanese bid coincided with the 1973 oil embargo by the Middle East oil producers. This so changed their economy that, in spite of having signed a letter of intent, they withdrew. In the interval, the Mass Transit Railway staff had been built up and felt able to manage their own design, raise their own money and let their own contracts. As a happy footnote, even though the tunnels were largely built by Japanese contractors, the trains have 'Metro-Cammel' stamped firmly at every entrance door.

The Commissioner had a small, but nice, Chelsea house but it was too far from Westminster and also too small for our rather large family. I was authorized to find something more suitable. After some desultory browsing through estate agents' advertisements, I was beginning to realize that the requirements were not easy. One of our staff did, however, see an advertisement for a fine Queen Anne house in Westminster, not five minutes' walk from the House of Commons. The price was in our range, so I closed the deal and we found ourselves neighbours of the Bishop of London, the owner of the *Daily Telegraph* and a couple of MPs. We were able to get a Division Bell installed in the house. This bell was connected to the House of Commons and rang loudly whenever members had to vote. MPs could know of any call to vote in the middle of dinner and rush round to do their stuff. Meetings between visitors from Hong Kong and MPs at the house and at the office became routine. When we did not have important Hong Kong visitors to entertain, we arranged musical evenings. At any time, there are numerous very able music students from Hong Kong studying in Britain who would happily enjoy an expenses-paid trip to London to entertain our guests. The object of these functions was partly to draw the attention of the English music world to Hong Kong talent, but also to introduce some of our roughest critics, who thought of Hong Kong as nothing but a sweatshop, to an aspect of Hong Kong life they were ignorant of. Of course, we also sought out our friends on both sides of parliament. I could not have put on these musical evenings on my own. David Stone, the Hong Kong music adviser, not only knew who and where the students were, but which leaders of the music establishment we should invite and how to arrange a coherent programme.

The 1979 election

The last days of the Labour government were exciting times. They lost one division by one vote due to a member being asleep in his cups — none other than the man who had been persuaded by the guile of the Heung Yee Kuk to argue for less socialist policies in our land dealings. The government survived but not for long. On the night of the election, it was the custom of the owner of the *Daily Telegraph* to give an all-night party for the conservative faithful in his house next door to ours. In order, I suppose, to anticipate any complaints from the neighbours, we were very kindly invited to attend. It was a fascinating evening to be in London and no more interesting place could be found at this juncture. The great of the Conservatives, who were not in constituencies too far away, dropped in, one after the other, to congratulate themselves on the great triumph that they had achieved. Margaret Thatcher won a convincing victory and, as her press secretary from that time, Bernard Ingham, said recently in a BBC interview, 'She changed the nature of Britain.' I found that the new government contained some seventeen members, who I had previously sought out, and to whom I could send a personal letter of congratulation.

During the 1970s, Hong Kong had been under fairly constant criticism from backbench Labour MPs. We did our best by inviting them to visit Hong Kong, by introducing them in London to distinguished visitors from Hong Kong and sending them literature, but Hong Kong really was a place that flew in the face of much of what these men and women believed in. With the new Conservative government, it was quite the opposite. It was just the sort of place they wished Britain to be like. Ignoring the fact that nearly half the population lived in public housing, they thought we were the embodiment of *laissez-faire* capitalism that they hoped they could introduce into Britain.

I remember two encounters in particular — both connected with textiles. The first was when I was asked to address the annual meeting of a textile association in Leeds. The invitation took me by surprise. Surely, they were inviting me to the lion's den to make a meal of me. But I studied the statistics more carefully. My hosts were exporters of fabric, not garments. At that time, the world's largest importer of fabrics was Canada followed closely by Hong Kong. We were the world's largest exporter of garments, but the fabric to make garments had to come from somewhere. Hong Kong was, in fact, one of the biggest export markets the UK had for the excellent textile fabrics they make. I approached the ordeal with much greater confidence.

I was somewhat awed by the fact that the guest of honour was the newly appointed Secretary of State for Industry, Sir Keith Joseph. I spoke about Hong Kong's low unemployment, its balanced budget, its small civil service, its modest proportion of GDP going to the public sector, its low infant mortality and high life expectation at birth, in spite of having, technically, no National Health service, the high proportion of youngsters aged over sixteen staying at school, the proportion of university age group students going to university. In all these areas, I was able to show that the Hong Kong figures were better than those of the UK and furthermore our social services were far ahead of anything in Asia with the possible exception of Japan.

Afterwards, Keith Joseph was quite embarrassing in his praise. And, looking at me, said, 'Surely you were brought up here, like our civil servants, yet you are so different. I wish I could hear something like this from our people.'

When a delegation from Hong Kong visited London on textile matters, we called on Cecil Parkinson, the Minister for Trade. Our men from the Commerce and Industry Department did their battling for trade and Parkinson expressed much sympathy. But he said he really could not do very much against the strong textile lobby in Britain. At this point, I trotted out my recently acquired knowledge of Hong Kong's huge imports of fabric and asked him why the UK textile manufacturers did not do more to sell to Hong Kong. The shirts in British Home Stores might be made in Hong Kong, but there was no reason why they could not be made of British cloth. A seed must have been planted because a few years later he did mount a textile-selling mission to Hong Kong.

I was invited to join the Department of Trade's Hong Kong Trade Advisory Group to think of ways to stimulate greater exports to Hong Kong. I felt able to do this knowing that the Hong Kong government favoured nobody in its regime for imports and that exporters would sell nothing unless they could convince the Hong Kong importers of the merits of their goods. I saw no harm in encouraging them to sell hard in Hong Kong in the hope that we should get more imports of better value. Membership of this group involved me in several trips to the provinces. I was most interested to see what a variety of industries did, in fact, export to Hong Kong. More could be done. I suppose I began to feel that some of the agents in Hong Kong did not do all they could to sing the praises of what they were selling. I did exercise one little effort at export promotion. UHT milk was just coming in but at that time cream just was not available in Hong Kong. I like cream. Imagine my excitement when I found that UHT cream existed, though not in Hong Kong. I wrote to the makers saying this delicious commodity was not available in Hong Kong and urged them to try the market. They replied rather stuffily that they had good agents in Hong Kong and felt sure they would be kept in touch with demand for all of their products. I gave up.

Air route to Hong Kong

Hong Kong was not very often involved in parliamentary excitement apart from debates on textile imports. These textile debates seemed to follow a set pattern. As each speaker sat down, several members would jump up and the Speaker would call on one to speak — and what more natural than for him to spot a man with masses of textile industry in his constituency. They were all textile men from both parties singing the same tune. Towards the end of the debate, the Speaker called a member whose constituency had no textiles but a great many people who liked good cheap garments. He enthused about Hong Kong's excellent products. The textile men on both sides were horrified. Who was he? The men on the front benches leaned across to consult with each other in indignation. The good member who liked our garments had been one of the more supportive of my contacts and had good material for his speech.

We did have one very difficult issue — the question of flights between London and Hong Kong. British Airways had a monopoly of this route which was in the gift of London, not of Hong Kong. Cathay Pacific Airways, the Hong Kong carrier, just could not get in. With the new Conservative government keen to stimulate competition, an opportunity appeared. It was not going to be plain sailing. There would be pressure in parliament from the established interests in British Airways. We had to get ready for battle. Here Paul Bryan's advice was of the greatest help. He discouraged any public relations effort. The way to succeed was to tackle individual members, quietly, without fuss. This we did. We even managed a lunch with the minister when the Governor and Commander British Forces were in town. It turned out that the Hong Kong general had been at school or university with the minister. The cabinet minister said, 'Who would have imagined that you would finish up as a general?' To which the general replied, 'Who would have thought you would finish up as a cabinet minister!' Shortly before the government's decision was to be announced in parliament, British Airways did try to mount a public relations gimmick with Scottish bagpipes and pretty air hostesses parading outside parliament. It was too late. We had done our lobbying quietly long before. The decision was to be announced one afternoon which happened to be on the day of our Dragon Boat Dinner, given every three years by the Hong Kong businessmen in London. The guest of honour was to be the minister who had to make the decision. You can imagine with what anxiety we awaited the decision for it would be an embarrassing evening if the decision went against Cathay. Happily it did not, and a good time was had by all.

Living in Westminster

Living in London was, in many ways, a delight. We were extremely fortunate in our circumstances, living in the very centre of London. In the evenings and at the weekends, it was marvellous. The crowds that fill the place during the week disappear. The theatres are round the corner and you can park anywhere. Next door to the office was an outlet of the Medici Galleries, a dangerous place to enter but a marvellous source of gifts forgotten until the last moment. A drive to the Maritime Museum at Greenwich on a Sunday afternoon was only a matter of minutes along wide empty roads built for commuters. To reach the office, I usually took a the twenty-five-minute walk through St James' Park and Green Park with only a few yards of city street at each end. The evenings were not so cluttered with social engagements as in Hong Kong because everyone disappeared to the suburbs and seldom did the hour-long journey into town for dinner. In August, the place seemed to close down. Tourists abounded but traffic dropped to a trickle. An unexpected bonus of living in London was anonymity. In Hong Kong any walk through a street, any social occasion, involved bumping into someone you know. In a London street nobody knew who you were or cared a rap. It was relaxing.

And nobody worked on a Saturday. Even Friday afternoons were pretty slack. Parliament practically stopped on Thursday. All this took a little getting used to, but I soon began to enjoy that enormous feeling of freedom creeping up on you after lunch on Fridays. I found in dealing with workmen on the house that if a job had not been finished by Wednesday, they started talking about 'next week'. It took much longer to get used to Saturday working, when I got back to Hong Kong, with the corresponding weekend feeling held in check until lunchtime on Saturday.

In spite of all the pleasures of living in London, I found the job itself not very satisfying. To be frank, nobody in London really cares much about what goes on at the other side of the world. It was my sole interest but I could not say that even our staunchest supporters did not have matters of greater concern to hand. This is perfectly understandable. Few in Hong Kong cared much about what went on in London, even in colonial days. It is easy enough to understand the position but not so easy to get used to the unconsciously casual attitude to matters of the greatest concern to me. I looked forward to my visits back to Hong Kong. The first was after an absence of eighteen months. I arrived in the early summer. It was overcast and raining. The clouds never lifted. But the smells were there. The life was there. In London I missed the mass of acquaintances that you bump into here all the time, not people you know well, but people you often see and chat to. In London, there were no casual acquaintances. I also missed my enemies. I did not have many in Hong Kong but had none at all in London. I found that my enemies in Hong Kong were not such bad chaps after all. I really felt I was back at home when a hawker in Lee Yuen Street said, 'I thought you had gone back to England.'

So it was not without pleasure that I heard I was to return to my old job after an absence of three years.

16

Relations with China

As the last five years of my service were dominated by our relations with China, I could perhaps give some account of the impact that China had on us during the thirty-five years of my service. In one sense China dominated our lives, but in another sense we were practically unconscious of China's existence.

Advent of the Chinese People's Government

I started work in Hong Kong in the summer of 1950, just after the start of the Korean War. The Communists had recently triumphed in their civil war with the Nationalists, much to the relief of the Chinese themselves and many well-wishers outside. The KMT government had become a byword of corruption. The People's Liberation Army (PLA), in the last days of the civil war, swept into its embrace army after army of the Nationalists. It was a very small rump that landed in Taiwan. Unlike the normal conquering army, the PLA paid for what it took and was welcomed by ordinary people of the land. Even so in Hong Kong itself we were flooded with refugees, as we had been in 1937 and 1938 when the Japanese got down to the south. As a government, we would not admit to having any refugees at all. In Europe and Palestine, refugees were put in camps where at least they were fed but where they stagnated. We had no camps. We did not want to set up these dumps of despair from which it seemed to be impossible to escape. Our refugees got to work. The only exception was our treatment of a group of largely handicapped Nationalist soldiers. These were transported to the new huts in Rennie's Mill. I described their adventures when writing about my time in the Social Welfare Office.

In 1950, the world was still a pretty warlike place. At night, we could hear the Chinese artillery practising not far off. In the District Office in Tai Po, we had, on the verandah, a large number of black wooden boxes ready to receive the land records in the event of an invasion. We were all expected to do some form of national service. Our border with China was manned, on our side, by the police. There was a fence and we restricted access to the area near the border. A defence line of barbed wire extended right across the New Territories not far back. We had nearly a division of the British army camped in the New Territories, complete with artillery and tanks. There was a substantial Far East Fleet of the Royal Navy and the Royal Air Force had some fighters based in Hong Kong. On the Chinese side, they had PLA soldiers in a garrison which made us so jumpy that we thought an extra large kerosene smuggling operation in December 1950 was the start of the invasion.

Refugees and industrialization

As the Communist ascendancy in China settled in, thousands who could do so migrated down to Hong Kong. Among these refugees were industrialists from Shanghai who were disillusioned by the treatment they had received. Hong Kong had a little workshop industry and a small ship-building base, but it was the Shanghai industrialists that showed us what industrialization meant. In the twenty years after their arrival, Hong Kong became the world's largest exporter of garments, toys and watches. Our textile exports so worried the English that they imposed a voluntary quota on our exports. It was called voluntary because we imposed it on ourselves to avoid arbitrary controls by the British. This quota was in volume terms and had an unexpected advantage. Our manufacturers soon found that for the same volume you could make more money by selling more expensive goods of higher quality. Exporters who had performance when the quotas were imposed were able to cash in on their effective monopoly position. They might be limited in growth in volume terms but had no limits on the profits they could make by going up-market.

There was practically no traffic across the border except our imports of food. We had always been great consumers of pork: the pig trains from central China continued throughout. Vegetables and freshwater fish also came in. We deliberately insulated ourselves from dependence on China for staples such as rice and firewood. The import of these commodities was restricted to a few traders in return for their undertaking to maintain large stocks in Hong Kong. The press maintained a constant interest in what was going on inside China but nobody went there. It was said that we probably knew more about what went on through the occasional arrival of a provincial newspaper than the press in Beijing. Even so, we really were as completely cut off from China as if we had been an island in the Pacific. As government officials, we were forbidden to visit China.

Stories of the horrors of the Great Leap Forward of the late 1950s trickled through, but the subsequent starvation which led to millions of deaths in China did not. A few devoted communist farmers in the New Territories did actually go in for very deep ploughing which was being practised in China as part of the great leap. They suffered the same disastrous results.

Kowloon Walled City

It was only in handling affairs relating to Kowloon City that we had to proceed with caution. This enclave had been excluded from the New Territories lease but, soon after it was signed, Britain simply annexed it. The Chinese never recognized this. As a result, the reach of Hong Kong law in the Walled City was uncertain. The police did not enforce any law inside though they would occasionally raid drug dens and smash them up. Dog meat was readily available; unregistered dentists practised at the side of the street; there was no water supply from the mains nor was there legal connection for electricity; there were no refuse collection or street sweeping services. No building law was enforced. The place was a slum and a disgrace to the common sense of both China and Britain. This unsatisfactory state of affairs was greatly improved after the trial of a man accused of murder in the Walled City. His defence was that the courts had no jurisdiction. It was thrown out. There followed a massive clean-up of crime and filth. Ostentatious illegal activities ceased though the place was such a warren that it was difficult for the police to eradicate every illegal activity. The dentists continued but dog meat was scarcer.

Street sweeping and refuse collection services were introduced, some water was supplied in standpipes. Somehow China Light was able to find its way through the mass of illegal wiring. There was no attempt at enforcing any building legislation.

This was the state of affairs in 1957 when two ancient cannon were found while foundations were being dug for a new building. They straddled the boundary of the building plot and there was some danger that by pulling them out the adjoining building would collapse. It was decided to send in government engineers to extract the cannon. I was in the Urban Services Department at the time, so I suggested the ancient cannon should be mounted for display in an adjoining park outside the Walled City. This was agreed and work went ahead. Unfortunately, we did not move as fast as the New China News Agency. They protested that the cannon did not belong to us but to China and managed to escalate to Beijing. Little demonstrations were organized. We persisted in our extraction but then said that having ensured the safety of the adjoining building, we had no further interest in the cannon. It was not worth an incident. They were carried off and mounted prominently outside the former magistrate's *yamen*, by then an old people's home.

Water from China

In 1958, the Chinese built a reservoir near our border and offered us water. We were always short of water. Although we welcomed this offer, we still tried to maintain an independent water supply of our own on which we could rely if supplies from China were cut off. The reservoir was built and we built the pipeline from the border to the Tai Lam Chung reservoir in the western New Territories. The need to acquire the land speedily, and the landowners' reluctance to accept cash at the rates we offered, led to the beginnings of a way of issuing promissory notes for land surrendered, the latter to be redeemed by a private treaty grant of land somewhere else.

In the following decade, the unbelievable madness of the Cultural Revolution did seep over the border, but we never had the scenes of mayhem that took place in China. It was during this confrontation that we had one of the rare direct negotiations with Chinese officialdom when we tried to secure the release of a police inspector who had been abducted in a scuffle on the border.

Food and water crossed the border but not much else. We exported practically nothing except money. The border area on both sides was barred to ordinary citizens. Farmers continued to farm. The countryside in 1976 looked much as it would have done in 1876.

The opening up

In 1976 Chairman Mao died. At first, change in China came slowly but it was not long before Deng Xiaoping came to power and started his opening up of China to the world. The effect on Hong Kong was dramatic. The sleepy village we called Shum Chun, but which we now have to call, in the national language, Shenzhen, became a metropolis almost overnight. Land was cheap. Labour was plentiful and cheap. The industrialists of Hong Kong swarmed over not only to the border area but to all parts of Guangdong Province from which their ancestors had come. The industrialization of south China was the mirror image of the industrialization of Hong Kong in the 1950s and 1960s.

With the opening up of China and the relaxation of travel restrictions, we began to live on easier terms with our neighbours. Since my retirement, it has only been time and money that have restricted my travel around the country. It has taken a long time to get used to the idea of easy travel in China. It was strange to see this place run in such a different way. Since making some fleeting contacts with officialdom, I have found that they encounter many problems similar to those we had. Whether it was squatters in the back of Kowloon, or ethnic Tibetans on the Himalayan plateau of Qinghai Province, housing was the problem. The Party Secretary in that desolate place, a squat broad-shouldered jolly man, was very similar in outlook to Hong Kong District Officers I had known.

17

The Last Five Years

On arriving back in Hong Kong from London, I found the office of the Secretary for Home Affairs had been moved from the tenth floor to the thirtieth floor of a waterfront building and that my office commanded the most magnificent view of the harbour. I learnt that the windows were normally curtained with thick curtains and the desk positioned to face into the office. Although I never asked, I concluded that the man who had done the job when I was away had allowed a *fung shui sin sang* to look at the office. *Fung shui* is a form or geomancy that I had become familiar with in the New Territories. I began to grasp the basics of village locations but never knew how it was applied to offices. Many of my colleagues would not think of using a new office until it had been passed by a *fung shui sin sang* and the necessary modifications made. Even Government House planted a tree and built a pool to counteract the threatening knife-edge of the new Bank of China building. I always thought I could arrange my office as I liked it and was afraid that if I let a *fung shui sin sang* in, he would upset my notions. In this case, I dared not turn my desk to face the harbour for fear of ceasing to do any work at all. I put it at right angles to the window so that, during those long boring telephone conversations we are all afflicted with, I had some alternative diversion. I think this office was second only in quality to that of the District Officer of Tai Po during my service.

One of the first files to be presented to me was a proposal to reverse a reform I thought I had succeeded in achieving before I left for London. The perennial problem of licensing places where you could get a meal or buy a drink had come up and two of us, a barrister in private practice Oswald Cheung, and myself, were appointed a committee of two Executive Councillors to look into the matter. We found an odd situation. To get a restaurant licence, you naturally needed to have premises with proper kitchens and so forth. The premises had to be inspected and eventually a licence would be issued. If you wanted to sell alcoholic drinks, you had to get another licence. In practice, the only requirement was that you had a restaurant licence. There were all sorts of provisions about the applicant being of good character and so forth, but nobody had been turned down for being of bad character. Our conclusion was that liquor licensing should be abolished and the sale of liquor confined to licensed restaurants. Pubs would have found a way of getting a restaurant licence for they all sold food. This was fairly radical stuff. The sale of liquor in Hong Kong had followed the British custom of confining it to a few premises which could only open during restricted hours. My predecessor but one, Donald Luddington, had got rid of the opening hours. He found they ran from 6 a.m. to 2 a.m. the following morning. Even so, the police were continually having trouble with after-hours drinking dens. He got rid of opening times altogether. We wanted to go one further and the Executive Council agreed. The Urban Council did not. They got considerable revenue from liquor licensing and did not want to lose it. They protested. Their appeal was considered in the Executive Council when I was in London and thrown out on the grounds that the licences were not primarily intended as revenue-raising measures. They were for control. If the control was no longer necessary, the licences should go. Three years later when I got back to Hong Kong, I was presented with a fully drafted and agreed Executive Council paper arguing that the original decision should be reversed. I think I must have been jet-lagged to let this pass. I always had the feeling that the provisions in the legislation relating to licensees being of good character etc. were an open invitation to corruption or the niggling posturing of do-gooders. I was overwhelmed by my own staff, who said the police were adamant. I let the paper go forward. By the time we met to consider it in the Executive Council, I did mutter some uneasiness but my colleague in the original committee was no longer on the Council and the paper went through. Afterwards the Acting Governor, Jack Cater, did say to me that the Official Members of Executive Council were not really supposed to speak against government papers — especially those put up by their own organizations! I felt duly admonished — and you still need two licences if you want to sell a can of beer with a meal.

Immigration control

More serious developments were afoot. We never admitted it, but immigration to Hong Kong from China was always controlled by China not by us. Developments in China were leading to an impossible situation. Until the triumph of the Communist revolution in 1949, passage across the border with China had been unhindered by any restrictions. You could go across to Shenzhen, a village in China at the border, for an evening's gambling or up to Guangzhou for a weekend. Any Cantonese could enter Hong Kong freely. In practice, many came to work and would go home at Chinese New Year or when they retired. In 1949, we closed the border and started to require papers even from the people of Guangdong. In the Urban Services Department during the late 1950s, we were still converting dormitories for these labourers into married quarters for we could no longer rely on casual labour coming across just to work. An exception was made in respect of farmers who owned land in the New Territories, but everyone else had to have papers. There was a restriction of fifty a day who could cross to stay in Hong Kong. In practice, movement in China was so restricted that it was impossible to get anywhere near the border without good reason. The daily quota of fifty was never taken up. The Chinese would accept people we wished to deport in accordance with our legislation. In early postwar days, a great many criminals were deported. Any illegal immigrants who were caught were returned the next day. Chinese control was vividly illustrated in 1962 when the authorities freely issued permits to travel to the Hong Kong border. Thousands came down. They simply leaned against the chain-link fence at the border until it toppled over. What could we do? You can't shoot refugees. The police caught as many as they could and bundled them into camps where they were given a meal and spent the night. The next day they were loaded onto trains and sent back. There was no problem about their reception. They were simply turned loose and came round for another try. If they got through the patrols in the border area and made it to town, they were not hunted down. After a week or two of this chaos, during which I think some eighty thousand or more people got in, the Chinese relented and again imposed their control of movement, restricting permits to travel to the Hong Kong border to the few.

This state of affairs continued until the Cultural Revolution and the troubles we had in 1967. The Chinese then refused to take back anyone we wished to deport — illegal immigrants or criminals or, and this was the point, film stars who were creating mayhem among their following during our disturbances. The two luckless actors spent a few nights on the border bridge before they were allowed into China, but deportations of anyone ceased then. There was still pretty strict control over movement in China, so their decision not to accept any deportees from Hong Kong did not result in an immediate influx of immigrants. Some did come. Gradually it became known that if you could get into Hong Kong, you could stay. Security at the border was not very effective and we had a pitifully weak fleet of police launches to catch the boats of illegal immigrants. Departmental launches were drafted into the anti-illegal immigration patrols. As things quietened down after the Cultural Revolution, travel in China became easier. We started to get hundreds of arrests of illegal immigrants every night. We could not send them back, so they stayed.

The matter was taken up by the embassy in Beijing. It was agreed, after negotiations, that the Chinese would accept back any illegal immigrants caught in the immediate border areas while we would not seek out those who made it to the big city — a policy that became known as the 'touch base' policy. The negotiations had to be conducted in secret to prevent a rush to beat the deadline. This was imposed at midnight one night in the autumn of 1973. Rough and ready but we really had no infallible means of identifying illegal immigrants in town and could not have hunted them down if we had wanted to.

For the most part, our deliberations on immigration matters took place in the calm of offices with statistics and telegrams. Occasionally, we would come face to face with the real-life consequences of these policies. I was cruising with several sailing friends and had spent the night anchored in Long Harbour, bordering on Mirs Bay, whose shores marked the border between Hong Kong and China. It had been a bitterly cold night with a strong north-east wind. In the morning as we got under way, I noticed what looked like a home-made child's paddling pool drifting down wind. As we drew nearer, we saw that it was indeed a home-made, waterlogged rubber dinghy with two men in it. Neither moved. One had fallen forward with his face, and most of his head, under water. He had been dead for hours. The other had fallen backwards and was still breathing though completely unconscious. We pulled them on board, carried the live but unconscious young man below and covered him up. Fortunately he could not swallow the brandy we offered — the worst possible thing to give anyone suffering from this degree of hypothermia. Alongside the pier at Wong Shek, I went ashore and set off on the very long walk for a phone.

Fortunately, I soon came across a man from a construction team in a Land Rover. He took me to his site office. A phone call eventually produced an ambulance. The ambulance crew took the still unconscious young man off. The corpse was left on the pier to be picked up later. It was some time afterwards that I learnt that the one who had been rescued alive had come round but had suffered permanent heart damage. Because of this, and only because of this, he was not deported. Some years later, I received a photograph of a strapping young American Chinese who said he was the youngster we had rescued. Little did he know that if there had been a little less east in the north-east wind that night, he and his friend would have been blown clean out of Mirs Bay into the South China Sea.

After Chairman Mao's death, and the advent of the more relaxed regime of Deng Xiaoping, it became much easier to travel to the Hong Kong border. The number of illegal immigrants reaching base began to increase. Again, arrests in the border areas started to mount until hundreds were being caught every night. As many again made it to the big city. This time we realized that nothing short of conventional immigration arrangements, with deportations of all illegal immigrants were necessary. The Chinese did not demur. Who was entitled to stay and who not? In theory everybody was supposed to have an identity card, but thousands did not. Illegal immigrants who had made base, and who bothered to apply, could get cards. There was no real sanction for not having one. A most elaborate operation was mounted to give everybody a few days to come forward for an identity card if they had not got one. Thereafter, tough new legislation required everyone to carry their cards wherever they went.

The operation went surprisingly smoothly. The crowds applying for new cards did not exceed the numbers expected and the logistics had been well planned. Before the new arrangements were introduced, I had feared the growth of a new underclass of illegal immigrant who had no identity card and could hide in the community. These people would be subject to exploitation by anyone threatening to report them. They could not get any form of government service without producing their cards. They were subject to being asked to produce their cards by any policeman. Any trifling crime that brought them to notice would reveal their illegal immigrant status. In practice, the new arrangements worked well. The underclass did not develop. People without cards were soon spotted and sent back over the border. Illegal immigration came to a halt — at least for a while. There were some hard cases of pregnant women who, on admission to hospital, were found without cards. They were treated but not allowed to stay. To this day, illegal immigrants are found among casual labourers on construction sites, but I do not think there is any large body of illegal immigrants buried, undetected, in the community and living in constant fear of discovery.

The old identity cards were not difficult to forge, so a new card was produced. Everyone would have to be issued with a new card. This was an enormous undertaking. When the first postwar cards were issued, people had to queue for hours in the sun at the racecourse to get them. I argued that people would not tolerate anything like this in the circumstances of the 1980s. Every man, woman and child would be required to attend twice at offices of the Immigration Department. They would, I said, come away with either a good impression of the government, or bad. We had to make it good. I suggested that the offices where the interviews would take place had to be of a similar welcoming standard to that of a good branch bank office. We went to look at one. The Immigration Department officials were all for it. They did not want to get the opprobrium attaching to a thoughtless procedure. In the end, they got everything the branch bank had except the ornamental fish tank. Individual appointments could be made. Interviews and photographing were done in moments. I would not say this operation marked a turning point in polite reception by government departments, but it came pretty near it. Certainly, the haughty handling of supplicants became a thing of the past.

District Boards

While I had been in London, steps had been taken to introduce a degree of formality to the informal arrangements that District Officers used to maintain contact with and to consult the people of their districts. I arrived back in time to take part in the planning of this innovation for the urban areas. In the New Territories, the arrangements for Village Representatives and Rural Committees had left out all those who were not indigenous villagers. New towns had been constructed over all the accessible areas of the countryside. The old guard would not agree to absorb these newcomers into their arrangements. In any case, there was no similar organization in town. There the informal District Committees that District Officers set up comprised good men and true, but they lacked any representative status. David Akers-Jones, who was now District Commissioner in the New Territories, had started the ball rolling with a District Board in Tsuen

Wan. It was decided to extend the system of District Boards to the urban areas. Most of their members would be elected by the people of the districts. This involved the momentous decision to compile a register of voters. Everyone was to be included and the procedures were extremely simple. No prolonged investigations were required. The identity card number and address was all that was needed. All very well but if there was complete adult suffrage for the new register of electors, why should they not elect the Legislature and the government? There could no longer be any logistical objection. That debate continues to today but in the meantime we had to decide just what the new District Boards were to do.

There were, I think, to be nineteen District Boards so they could not be given any meaningful administrative responsibilities like education or transport. Administration of these affairs could only make sense when applied to the whole territory. On the other hand, such matters as local refuse collection, which could be administered locally, were not very glamorous. We decided to do exactly as we had done when we set up City District Officers and give them no executive powers at all. On the other hand, we enabled them to discuss and give advice on 'any matter affecting the welfare of the people of the district'. We did not want to see a repeat of the endless arguments we had with Urban Councillors who wanted to debate matters outside their terms of reference. District Boards could not order government departments about, but they could discuss their affairs and could expect departmental officials to attend meetings and answer for their activities. Later, they were given funds for simple local improvements.

The advantage of proceeding like this was that we could get going without delay. The most time-consuming part was the administrative organization for getting voters registered and practical arrangements for elections. We did not dispense immediately with the appointed members. They had, after all, served for some time and shown that they could make a useful contribution. They had gained experience from working on District Committees, knew which departments dealt with what and generally were able to participate usefully from the outset. Many turned out to be a good deal more useful to their communities than some of the elected ones. There is still a politically correct objection to appointed members of District Boards on the grounds that they are not elected. This entirely ignores the benefit to be gained from the service of citizens of proven worth who are prepared to devote time, and indeed, money for the welfare of their fellow citizens. There is a Chinese tradition of community service which has always been able to find an outlet in Hong

Kong and we saw no reason to throw it out at this time. One little aim I was frustrated in was to secure a unique name for each electoral constituency. District Officers ran out of names and started using names like So-And-So North and So-And-So South. I said surely there must be some feature of the locality that would suggest a unique name for each area even if it had to be dug out from the history books. I made some progress but North and South still stuck.

Sir Murray MacLehose

I suppose Murray MacLehose was the Governor that I saw most of. Even so, none of us, except possibly the Chief Secretary, would see any Governor performing over the whole field of his activities. At first, I found him rather imposing. I think several of my colleagues found the same, but as we worked together I found a great fund of humour and a very penetrating mind. I think his greatest strength was to identify weaknesses in the system and set about dealing with them. I had only a minor role in the two greatest of the weaknesses he identified, namely housing and corruption.

He did not start public housing but he did identify the real weakness in the situation. There was no ultimate objective. There was no time frame within which an aim was to be achieved. Rules of eligibility for housing assistance were set without any conception of ever having enough housing for the eligible. The real strength of the 1972 Ten-Year Housing Plan was not so much the target figures as the fact that there was a clear target to provide adequate housing for everyone, a clear idea of what the minimum standard of adequate housing was, and an estimate of the size of the housing programme that was implied. I cannot help thinking that this clarity has been lost with the ever growing waiting list of those eligible for housing that is not there.

To attempt to eliminate the corruption that existed in the early 1970s seemed to many to be an unreal idealistic aim. What was required was not only new law and lots of money but determination and intelligent operational planning. Jack Cater had a messianic determination to root out corruption. John Prendergast, his Director of Operations, brought all his experience from running the Special Branch in the police in Hong Kong and elsewhere before coming to Hong Kong. They were the executioners, but without the equal determination of the Governor, the drive would have run into the sand.

These were the principal areas where this identification of a problem, and a determination to get the system to produce an answer, are remembered. But there were many others, some of which I have mentioned elsewhere.

It is perhaps forgotten now that only a few days before Murray MacLehose retired, he suffered a 'mild' stroke — if there is such a thing. Farewell functions were cancelled and he had to go very slowly until he left. He seemed indestructible but some years earlier had had to have a hip replacement and, after retirement, had to have the second done. These had taken more out of him than most of us realized. A Governor cannot take a few days off. He cannot take it easy for a while. He is either working flat out or sick in hospital. I last saw him two years before he died. By then, he could only walk round the house with the aid of a stick but his mind was as clear as ever. He was sympathizing with Tung Chee Wah being hit by the problems of the 1997 Asian financial crisis, which he compared with those of the oil crisis that had hit him in 1973 just as he was starting as Governor.

The New Territories lease

1981 saw the departure of the newly ennobled Lord MacLehose and the arrival in 1982 of Sir Edward Youde. In his welcoming speech, the Senior Unofficial Member of Executive Council, Sir S. Y. Chung, pointed out that there were only fifteen years left of the New Territories lease. The British, even under their interpretation of the nineteenth-century treaties with imperial China, would then be required to give up the administration of the New Territories. The question of what was to be done then was a common subject of speculation and gossip, but the Chinese were inscrutable. Murray MacLehose had been required to raise the subject with Deng in 1978, though in fact it was Deng who raised the subject before MacLehose could do so. MacLehose came back with Deng's Delphic exhortation to the businessmen to 'put their hearts at ease'. Soon after Sir Edward Youde's arrival, Margaret Thatcher, Prime Minister of Britain, and fresh from the triumphant battle over the Falkland Islands, paid a visit to Beijing. She had a rough time, but it was agreed that talks would start on the future of Hong Kong with the agreed aim of the preservation of the 'stability and prosperity of Hong Kong'.

The first little tiff we had was with the Foreign Office. It was to get agreement that the Executive Council should be consulted on all aspects of the negotiations. It may seem surprising that this was resisted. Diplomats were not accustomed to having to explain their secret negotiations to anyone, let alone ask for advice. The negotiations were between Her Majesty's Government and the Chinese People's Government. Neither the people of Hong Kong nor its government had any status. The mandarins met their match in Sir Edward Youde, an extremely competent mandarin himself. He had just left the prestigious position of Chief Clerk, second only to the Permanent Under-secretary, and was of longer experience in the Foreign Office than anyone there. What was at stake was not the future of the mandarins in London but the lives of the people of Hong Kong. Negotiations could not be conducted through the press, but the British side could not ignore their own Royal Instructions which required the Governor to consult the Executive Council on all 'important matters'.

From the outset, the Governor took the Executive Council into his confidence but the circle was extremely tight. It was essential that there should be no leaks for we did not wish to be accused by the Chinese of breaking our agreement to secrecy. Accordingly, it was arranged that all papers relating to the negotiations should not leave the Central Government Offices but would be made available in a special reading room for Executive Council members. As an Official Member of Executive Council, I was privy to all these discussions but as Secretary for Home Affairs I was not required to play a significant part in them. A special unit was set up in the Secretariat under Bim Davies to work on the issues with the Political Adviser, Robin McLaren. Teddy Youde took personal command, and Philip-Haddon Cave, the Chief Secretary, took a great deal of the day-to-day administration off his shoulders.

We really had no cards. Deng had made it clear that the Chinese did not recognize any of the treaties that had led to the establishment of the British presence in Hong Kong. They were going to have Hong Kong back with or without British agreement. All we could do was to argue that, whatever the past, Hong Kong was now a thriving metropolis of considerable regional importance and value to China, and that its 'stability and prosperity' were worth preserving. Although Mao had gone, memories of the Cultural Revolution were still fresh in the minds of Hong Kong people. They were terrified at the prospect of the Chinese government taking charge in Hong Kong.

At first, we proposed that since the British had made a success of Hong Kong and knew how it worked, we should continue to administer it while recognizing Chinese sovereignty over the land. This went down badly. Communist trade unions began to trumpet that sovereignty and administration were inseparable. The communist press had learned articles, as well as less temperate comment, to the same effect. It became clear that negotiations were not going well. The fear spread to the markets so that the Hong Kong dollar, which was a freely floating currency, began to sink. From a norm of about $6 to the US dollar it sank as far as, one Saturday morning in 1983, to $10.

Hong Kong's currency

Perhaps I should divert for a moment to say a few words about our currency. When I arrived, the Hong Kong dollar was a part of sterling. The exchange rate was $16 to the pound sterling and had been since the 1920s. We had no influence over this fixed rate. Our reserves were part of the sterling area reserves, and were not trifling. This continued until, of all times, the disturbances we had in 1967. It was not our troubles that upset the arrangements but troubles in Britain that forced it to devalue sterling. We were told, over the weekend, that we had freedom not to follow sterling down. This put us in a difficult position, having never had any control over our currency before. It was decided to follow sterling but within days it became obvious that the devaluation was so drastic that it was entirely inappropriate for Hong Kong. So on the Monday we were still exchanging our dollars at $16 for a much devalued pound, but by Thursday we had revalued to $14.55 or so and decided to link ourselves to the US dollar. As time went on, even this measure proved to be disadvantageous as our currency was strengthening all the time. In the end, we decided to float the Hong Kong dollar. Although a small currency, this worked well enough for a long time. International movements of funds were not as mercurial as they are now, but the panic of October 1983 was too much. We could see that political forces beyond our control would make a floating currency no longer viable. An ingenious means of linking the Hong Kong dollar to the US dollar was devised. The simplest, though probably technically inadequate, explanation of the scheme was that since all banknotes in Hong Kong were issued by private banks, they would be required to give a US dollar to anyone producing $7.80 in Hong Kong banknotes. The peg, as it has become known, stabilized the situation though at some cost from the pre-panic rate of $6 or so to the US dollar.

British administration will no longer be possible

After this crisis, it was obvious that we could not pursue our suggestion of continuing British administration of a sovereign part of Chinese territory. When you got down to it, just what could we do that a Chinese government could not? The real answer was that Hong Kong people trusted the current administration but was frightened of the Chinese one. This was scarcely an argument that we could produce in negotiation. The Chinese had flexed their muscles and demonstrated, if demonstration was necessary, that they held all the cards. Negotiations continued without much progress through the winter. By the spring of 1984, it was clear that we had to recognize that there would no longer be any part for British administration after 1997. After this was accepted by the Executive Council, the members of Legislative Council were informed, and then the conclusion was announced at a press conference by the British Foreign Secretary, Sir Geoffrey Howe, on Good Friday, 1984. It was a sombre day. I had arranged to take one of the British diplomatic writers, John Dickie, out to lunch. We had become good friends when I was in London. He was travelling with the Foreign Secretary's press corps. We went to the Yacht Club, which I thought might be more cheerful, only to find that everyone was away on the China Sea Race and we were the only ones in the bar and the dining-room.

I suppose the conclusion was obvious, but it took a good deal of getting used to. It also meant that an enormous amount of work had to be done quickly. In the Foreign Office, the main burden fell on Percy Craddock on his return from being ambassador in China. David Wilson led the UK group which negotiated the actual text with the Chinese during that hot summer in Beijing in 1984, while the ambassador in Beijing, Richard Evans, handled the face-to-face negotiations. Deng had said that negotiations could go on only until September, and that if no conclusion had been reached by then, he would announce the Chinese decisions on how things would proceed.

What was needed now was some statement embodying a framework of administration which would be acceptable to the Chinese and would not disturb the stability or prosperity of Hong Kong. It was not easy to write down on a piece of paper a whole way of life that was so different from that which was the norm in China. The negotiations involved sharp exchanges not only between Britain and China, but between Hong Kong and London. Eventually, the Joint Declaration was produced.

This document comprised declarations by Britain and China covering matters within their respective prerogatives, with nobody purporting to declare anything that was not their business. I do not think it included anything that we did not want to see. There certainly were additional things we should have liked to see, and details we should have liked to fill in, but the September deadline, and the need to reach agreement on every word in English and Chinese, meant some vagueness had to be left.

Constitutional reform and the Joint Declaration

In the meantime, we were looking afresh at our own constitutional arrangements. There were still no elected members on the Legislative Council. In a Green Paper of proposals published in July 1984, we suggested the gradual introduction of an elected element into the Legislative Council. Two sorts of elected member were proposed. One was a representative elected by voters on a geographical basis with a first past the post-voting method. There was discussion as to whether the members of the geographical constituencies should be elected directly or by an electoral college of some sort. The second type was novel. Appointed members had tended to include representatives from various walks of life — doctors, lawyers, social workers, businessmen, trade unions and so forth. It was proposed that instead of the government nominating these representatives, the bodies should elect their own. Although I was keen on the idea of these 'functional constituencies' as a useful halfway house to the more conventional geographical constituencies, I have since become less enthusiastic. A doctor or lawyer appointed by the Governor would be a man recognized not only in his professional circles but also as a contributor to society as a whole. If the doctor or lawyer is elected by his fellows in the profession, the person elected will be much more likely to be the person who can offer the most to his electors rather than the community at large. In practice, this danger has not been realized to any damaging extent, but the system has not been going long. It is just as well that the functional constituencies are not going to be a permanent part of the constitution.

Final agreement on the Joint Declaration was reached in time for the September deadline. It was initialled in Beijing by the Foreign Secretaries and published. The principal feeling was one of relief. China's absorption of Hong Kong was seen to be inevitable. Everybody looked for the bit that affected them — the airlines, the shipping people, the churches, the lawyers, and ordinary people. Everybody had an interest. The time-lag since the Good Friday announcement that Britain would no longer have any role in administration meant that people had got used to the idea of the resumption of Chinese sovereignty. Everybody saw that the declaration itself gave them good reason to view the future with equanimity. The joint declaration filled in a great many details that were causing anxiety. The phrase 'a high degree of autonomy', which was to characterize relations with Beijing, certainly eased many minds, even though some fingers remained crossed in uncertainty about implementation.

In November 1984, the government published its White Paper of decisions following the proposals in the Green Paper on constitutional reform. Members for the geographical constituencies would be elected by members of District Boards. On the question of direct elections, the White Paper says, 'there was strong public support for the idea of direct elections but little support for such elections in the immediate future'. This is my recollection too. Hong Kong people generally are cautious about constitutional development but can accept it in small doses. At that time, the idea of direct general elections was just a little too far ahead of the general feeling of the people.

Nevertheless, elections to the Legislative Council would take place in 1985. There would be ten members elected by District Board members, one each by members of the Urban Council and the Regional Council, twelve by members of nine functional constituencies comprising eleven representative organizations, twenty-two members would still be by appointment and there would be ten official members.

The Green Paper had proposed that the majority of appointed Executive Council members should be replaced progressively by members elected by the Unofficial Members of the Legislative Council, that is, members other than the officials. This was an obvious move towards a cabinet form of government which would evolve into a ministerial form. The Chinese did not like this nor was there much comment on the Executive Council from the public. 'The issue will remain open for further public discussion and consideration,' said the White Paper. It still is — but there has not been any follow-up.

Sir Edward Youde

Teddy Youde was the last Governor I served under. He knew he had a heart problem before he came to Hong Kong and had had a heart bypass operation. This, he said at the time, made him feel better than he had done for years. His public face was one of reticence, so much so that my colleagues in the public relations departments were sometimes in despair, for his personality was so difficult to present. Among us, he was friendly and anything but reticent. I remember one occasion when he was to start a small meeting about some recent barb from Beijing, sitting back with his feet on the table roaring with laughter at the insult. He had studied Chinese as an undergraduate and could read and write the language with ease. He would read a selection of the Chinese language press every day as well as the English. Another skill he had, which he seldom divulged, was an ability to write shorthand at spoken speeds. This he had acquired when he found himself on a troopship for weeks on end and wanted something to do. In the Foreign Office, as a junior man taking notes at meetings, he would sometimes be challenged as to just what the great men had said. He was able then to read back verbatim the exact words that had been spoken. He had served in the Beijing embassy during the civil war in China and earned an MBE for going behind the fighting to try to negotiate the release of a Royal Naval frigate, the HMS *Amethyst*, when she was bottled up by the Communists in the Yangtse River.

When he came to Hong Kong, he had retired as Chief Clerk in the Foreign Office. Having such a senior and experienced Foreign Office man in Hong Kong was to prove an immense advantage during the negotiations on the future of Hong Kong. These negotiations were never easy because Hong Kong had to fight its corner not only with the Beijing authorities but, from time to time, with London as instructions for the negotiators were being thrashed out. That the Joint Declaration was ever completed, that its contents were so comprehensive, that it included so many provisions important for the continued stability and prosperity of Hong Kong owes a great deal to Edward Youde and the team he led in Hong Kong. I had retired just after the signing of the Declaration but was able to admire the way in which he quietly secured solutions to many of the problems that had soured relations with China for years. The problem of Kowloon Walled City was dealt with. Hong Kong's independent status as a customs territory was established. He drove himself mercilessly and in the end it was his heart that killed him when on a negotiating trip to

Beijing. It says a great deal for man whose last years had found him in the uncomfortable position of being neither a British Civil Servant, nor a Chinese diplomat, but the Governor of Hong Kong, that when he died, leaders in both Britain and China paid such genuine tributes not only to an able man, but also a friend. The depth of sorrow in Hong Kong was palpable.

The two last Governors I served under, Murray MacLehose and Teddy Youde, made enormous contributions to Hong Kong. In MacLehose's case, he presided over a period of unprecedented economic growth during which he drove the bureaucracy to spend money. This may sound easy because most of us were more inclined to grumble about lack of funds rather than superfluity. Murray MacLehose's strength was to drive the planning and execution of ambitious schemes that tended, if not to encounter resistance, then to meet with cries that they were impossible. I think particularly of the establishment of the Independent Commission Against Corruption and the building of the new towns. The problems facing Teddy Youde were less physical. Here it was his skill as a negotiator that was demanded. Each man had the strengths that the times required, and deployed them without regard to the demands made on them personally.

The pace of reform

1984 was a pretty active year in the constitutional field with the continuing negotiations on the Joint Declaration and our internal proposals on constitutional development. The Green Paper was published in July, the Joint Declaration in September, and the White Paper in November. Throughout my time, we proceeded very cautiously with constitutional reform. All along, it was clear that Hong Kong was not moving towards independence. It was not at all clear how far we could move without bringing the wrath of Beijing on our heads. In the 1950s and 1960s, we were afraid that any form of meaningful election would be a battleground between the communists and the nationalists on ideological grounds that had nothing to do with domestic Hong Kong affairs. A communist win could lead to moves to unify with China. A nationalist, or any non-communist, win, which was far more likely, would infuriate Beijing. Chinese reaction to recent elections in Taiwan suggest that our fears were well-founded. We were never afraid of consultation and had an excellent system in the New Territories from the outset. That covered barely 10 percent of the population. In town we had the Kaifong Welfare Associations, which were neighbourhood organizations that were confined to purely welfare activities. They were a poor vehicle for local representations. In 1968, we introduced the City District Officer Scheme with the avowed intention of bringing local opinion much more actively into affairs. We did not do this by any form of local government, as advocated by some of the administrators transferred from Africa on the independence of their colonies. Instead, we built on the multi-functional District Officer system to establish, first informal, then more formal, local consultative committees. From this came the really significant establishment of the District Boards. They did not, it is true, have even menial executive responsibilities, but their remit covered everything affecting the welfare of their districts. By the time I retired, elections for some of the Legislative Council had been decided on.

Outsiders have criticized the sedate rate of constitutional change that we followed. This was entirely consistent with our treatment of reform in all areas. We would not move until we were sure of overwhelming public support. We moved slowly on housing in 1953 until convinced that the refugees would not return to China and the disastrous Shek Kip Mei fire demanded immediate action which the public would support. Our progress in education and labour matters followed only when practice in town had moved. Even our reform of marriage law followed public wishes. In 1967, when there were serious disturbances, we only escalated our actions in response to public pressure as, for instance, when we decided to raid union premises which were arsenals of home-made weapons and bombs. The fireworks ban, also in 1967, was only attempted when there was overwhelming public support for it. In economic affairs, we positively refrained from intervention except in the most unusual and limited circumstances.

I am not at all sure that the more precipitate transition towards a Westminster-style of government that was pursued in all other colonies, as they moved towards independence, has proved an outstanding success. The more sedate pace in Hong Kong has accommodated a continued respect for the rule of law, a free press and a comprehensive range of freedoms that are conspicuously absent in many other territories.

Time to go

During this last period, there was a good deal of travelling required of the Governor and the Chief Secretary. Neither post could be left vacant, so when either left Hong Kong, the posts were filled on an acting basis. Usually, this meant that I was to act as Chief Secretary in addition to being Secretary for Home Affairs and even as Governor as well.

Acting as Chief Secretary brought me into much closer relationship with the Governor. This was rewarding as I admired both Murray MacLehose and Teddy Youde. Both treated me with the greatest courtesy and frankness. When the Governor was away as well, there was nobody to appeal to. Presiding over the Legislative and Executive Councils, I was fortunately spared any very dramatic controversy. Formalities such as giving assent to ordinances and signing appointments of Justices of the Peace were easy enough. Riding round in a Crown car with a bodyguard was a little alarming at first. Another curiosity of the days acting as Governor was that the Inland Revenue solemnly refunded the tax I had paid on my salary for those days. The Governor was exempt from tax, though I never got any duty-free liquor.

My time was drawing to a close. The two extensions of service beyond the normal retiring age, then fifty-five, were about to expire. In my last month in office, I was asked to join the group of Hong Kong citizens going to Beijing to witness the formal signing of the Joint Declaration on the future of Hong Kong by the prime ministers of Britain and China. It was my first visit to China since I was a boy. I had never been to Beijing. The formal ceremonies were accompanied by receptions and dinners so that we had little time for sightseeing.

We did have one free afternoon. A few of us took a taxi to the Temple of Heaven. The drive was through a drab and dusty city. At the temple itself, we were overwhelmed by the tranquillity, serenity, elegance and massive scale of this fine edifice. It put our little modern affairs into a fitting context.

18

Epilogue

Retirement

In retirement, I soon found that I could not keep up with the minutiae of government activity. Once outside the government, you are outside the system of briefings and off the circulation of policy papers. I became much more an armchair critic, more interested in broader issues as seen in the media, or discussed in gossip. So my account of events after my retirement is less backed by personal knowledge and is bound to include more speculation.

Tiananmen

The glow of good relations with China that followed on the signing of the Joint Declaration replaced the more uneasy relations that had existed between China and Hong Kong during the negotiations. Sir Edward Youde gave priority to the clearing-up of old problems and some new ones such as identity card and passport issues.

These friendly relations with China took a disastrous turn after the Tiananmen troubles in 1989. People watched, with increasing unease, the prolonged demonstrations which were so damaging during the visit of Russia's Gorbachev. The whole of Hong Kong revolted at the news of the brutal suppression of the demonstrations. My wife and I were two among the sombre thousands at the Happy Valley Racecourse on 4 June. These crowds which gathered in enormous numbers, at first in Central, and then at the racecourse, were quiet and orderly without a policeman in sight. There was a very moving outpouring of grief which pervaded the whole community. There were elements of fear, but the predominant feeling was one of anguish at the appalling breakdown in human relationships in Beijing.

Britain broke off negotiations with China in the Sino-British Joint Liaison Group which dealt with details of relations between Hong Kong and China. Hong Kong people had sent considerable funds to support the protesters in Tiananmen Square which was covered in Hong Kong tents.

In October 1989 the Governor, now Sir David Wilson, announced impressive plans for the development that the building of the new airport would require. Outline planning for these major works had been completed. They now had to be announced so that detailed planning and the work could go ahead. The Governor had told the Chinese, on more than one occasion, what was planned and what he would say in his annual speech to the Legislative Council in October. He received no adverse response. We had not sought prior Beijing agreement for such major public works as the first cross-harbour tunnel or the construction of the MTR, but this project was different. It might just be completed before the handover, but it would leave considerable debt behind for the new government, even though the forecasts projected that there would be no trouble in meeting the obligations. Hong Kong's record in public investment of this sort was impressive, but the money could only be raised if China backed the scheme. Yet, this was so soon after Tiananmen that nobody was talking to the Chinese.

The bad feeling from Beijing was still so strong, and the suspicions so deeply held, that the Chinese could see nothing but evil in the plans. The communist press started to publish stories that the 'Rose Garden' plan was the last fling of the colonials to bleed the place dry, line the pockets of British construction firms, leave Hong Kong with enormous debts and an airport that would be a white elephant.

Long and rough negotiations led to an Airport Agreement with China which included Chinese support for the new airport. An important aim of the Chinese seems to have been to get John Major, the British prime minister, into Beijing to sign it. He was the first Western leader to make a call after Tiananmen.

David Wilson retired to the House of Lords, where, as things turned out, he has distinguished himself with such service to his native Scotland that he has been awarded the prestigious Knighthood of the Thistle, Scotland's highest award, as was Murray MacLehose. John Major would know that a general election was due the following year. He would probably lose some good men in parliament. He banked on being able to find a suitable politician for governor for the last five years of colonial rule.

The political governor

The man he chose had good credentials. Chris Patten had played a significant part in securing a Conservative victory in the election though losing his own seat. He was chairman of the party and a close friend of the prime minister. He has many pleasant personal characteristics and a great ability to woo the masses. When he made his first policy speech in October, he — predictably — infuriated the Chinese by trotting out a panoply of arrangements for Legislative Council elections without any previous consultation with them. This was not in the traditions of quiet soundings which the Foreign Office mandarins and Hong Kong governors were so skilful at. It was quite exciting. How would the Chinese react to this blunderbuss approach? The Chinese announced that there was no scope for discussion on these proposals and would not meet. It was not until the following spring that, after internal battles in Beijing, they agreed to start negotiations. Of course, they would be tough. Nothing less was expected.

The point of negotiating is to do a deal. True, the British side had no cards but then we had none in the negotiations on the Joint Declaration. This time Patten failed to do the deal. The contrast with the earlier negotiations is stark. Those politicians in Britain, who sneered so openly at what they saw as the Foreign Office mandarins' subservient acceptance of Chinese dictates, thought Patten was a hero who had taught the Chinese a lesson. He had done nothing of the sort. His arrogant rejection of any need for compromise that went beyond his imagination meant that the last four and a half years of British colonial rule were characterized by Anglo-Chinese bickering of the most undignified and petty sort. Thank goodness, there had been nothing like this during the much more difficult negotiations leading up to the Joint Declaration. If there had been, we should never have had a Joint Declaration at all.

The real tragedy of this quarrel was that it was unnecessary. Detailed arrangements for a 'through train' for the Legislative Council for the period from 1995 to 1999, non-stop through of the handover station in 1997, had already been worked out in secret discussions between London and Beijing in 1990, before David Wilson left. The drafting of the Basic Law, which contained the principal provisions, was, strictly, purely a matter for Beijing and the Basic Law Drafting Committee in Hong Kong, a body containing no government officials. It would only come into force after Hong Kong had reverted to China. In practice, it was clear to both governments that the chances of maintaining Hong Kong's prosperity and stability would be enhanced if the contents were acceptable to both governments as well as in Hong Kong. It is said that Patten did not know about these discussions or the documents exchanged during them. This almost passes belief. There were plenty of people in Hong Kong and London who knew all about them and there had been enough leaks in the press for everyone to know that something was going on. It is also extraordinary that Patten himself did not think to ask what had happened between Britain and China in the five years between the signing of the Joint Declaration and the publication of the Basic Law. In the end, it was the Chinese who told him that he was going over old ground that had already been settled between Britain and China two years earlier. He would not revert to agreements that had already been reached. British politicians are no fonder of losing face than Chinese.

Although I believe that the main thrust of Patten's policies was wrong, he did secure one important benefit for a significant minority. This was the UK government' agreement to grant British citizenship to those people of Hong Kong not of Chinese race. They could not become Chinese nationals for this is a racially determined status. They had lost the nationality status of the countries from which their forbears had come. He argued that unless these people, mostly originally from India, became British citizens, they would become stateless. His political skills were such that he did, in the end, secure this concession against the stiffest opposition from the Home Office in London.

I was in England during the handover itself. I was astonished at the universal apprehension that pervaded the media. I was told recently that the Foreign Office was just as frightened. I saw no reason why the days of easy relations that had followed the Joint Declaration would not return. The British politician had gone. The Beijing officials and those in Hong Kong understood each other much better. When we got back to Hong Kong in the early autumn, we found a new relaxed atmosphere everywhere.

Gone was the daily Anglo-Chinese quarrelling that had filled the press before we left. The People's Liberation Army had indeed come in but were nowhere to be seen. The street names were unchanged. The only change was the occasional red flag with a bauhinia in the middle, and the colour of the postboxes: they had been painted green.

The civil service

Hong Kong never stands still and of course there is constant change. There is, however, a continuity in that most important component of government, the civil service. Those at the top now were not quite so high up when I retired sixteen years ago but they were there. Most have matured in a most impressive manner. There have been problems and mistakes but this is not new. The general level of administration is as good as it ever was. Modern technology has produced a much more accessible bureaucracy through web sites and electronic telephone replies. Nothing like this was available when I was in the service.

The present crowd has the immense benefit of not having to answer to London all the time. In my early days, Hong Kong was a small, insignificant colony out of the mainstream of the empire. The important places were in Africa and the big change in the empire was the move towards independence. This absorbed all the attention that Whitehall could devote to colonial affairs. Hong Kong was left alone. We managed to stay a bastion of the free market economy during the years of socialist government in England with only occasional attempts to divert us. Even in 1980, when I was Hong Kong Commissioner in London, the Foreign Office department concerned with Hong Kong, and other remnants of empire, had only two people in it. It was a long time before telegrams became as common as airmail letters. Hong Kong was left to run its own affairs with the 'high degree of autonomy' that is so central to the Joint Declaration. In the 1980s, during the negotiations on the future, the Foreign Office began to take a greater and more detailed interest in us. This was accompanied by questions and suggestions that must have been irritating to my successors as they became more and more inquisitive and supervisory.

Governing Hong Kong as a Special Administrative Region of China is much more relaxing than operating under the watchful eye of London in the last days of the empire. There is no interference in the day-to-day work of the government. Even when major crises occur, the place has to manage on its own. I try to imagine the flood of telegrams that would have burnt up the airwaves when the money market made a concerted attack on the Hong Kong dollar's link to the US dollar, if this had happened in colonial days. The unprecedented action taken by the government would surely have been vetoed by the Bank of England. As it was, China was sympathetic, but left it to Hong Kong to tough it out. Donald Tsang, Joseph Yam and Raphael Hui triumphed over the money men by their bold intervention in the stock market — and made substantial increases in the government's reserves in the process.

The anomalous Legislative Council

Set against this are the increasing requirements of the Legislative Council. Much of this seems to be confrontational which must be due to the anomalous position of the Legislative Council. At election time, people think they are electing those who have something to do with the government. Yet, those who are elected are not required to play any part in policy formation and are not accountable for policies. They do their best to be seen to be requiring the civil service to account for their performance. But they are not the advocates of policies which they have formulated. Their only function can be to criticize. This must be as frustrating for the legislators as for the civil servants. The legislators have to demonstrate to the voters that they are doing something but they are denied any responsibility for administration. The civil servants have to work up their proposals without any but informal input from the legislators. Most of the points that are raised when the policies are published must have been considered during the process of policy development. The civil servants then have to go over the same ground all over again.

Some better method must be devised to involve the people elected to this important constituent of the government in the processes of policy formation. They should be expected to assume a measure of responsibility for policy. Only in this way can they play a more useful part in explaining the policy conclusions to the public. They may not all agree with the conclusions reached, but the public could see that it was their elected representatives who were responsible, and adjust their voting in future accordingly. Voting for members of a debating society is singularly unsatisfying.

I do not think I have heard any public defence of the present provisions by either the government or the legislature, except as a purely transitional arrangement. It follows that I hope we shall see some more coherent proposals for constitutional development soon.

Constitutional development

It remains to be seen whether the steady, albeit measured, pace of constitutional development we have followed will prove to be more successful in the long run than the more precipitate methods followed in former colonies or advocated by some reformers both in the past and at present.

The sedate pace of constitutional reform that we pursued throughout my years of service continued after I retired. It was interrupted only for a few months by a governor who tried to make things go faster. It continues under Chinese sovereignty.

There is an old Chinese story of the farmer who daily visited his paddy-fields. He could see the rice shoots growing but thought they were not growing fast enough. He pulled each one up — just a little bit — to help it grow faster. The crop withered.

We do not have complete formal electoral arrangements but we have always had a very wide range of consultative bodies and an effective machinery for maintaining close contact with practically all strands of public opinion. In some ways, in a small territory, this is an even more effective way of maintaining touch with opinion than great elections every few years with politicians free to do as they will in the interval. We were, of course, helped by a vigorous and free press. If we behaved too unreasonably, people always used to be able to go over our heads to parliament in London.

Present arrangements for producing the Legislative Council and the Chief Executive are a great advance on those in colonial days. Then the Governor was appointed by London without any consultation with Hong Kong at all. All members of the Legislative Council were appointed in a similar way, up to the time when I retired.

The Basic Law envisages steady progress in constitutional reform and lays down detailed provisions for the composition of the Legislative Council up to the year 2007. The 'ultimate aim' set down in Article 68 of the Basic Law is 'the election of all the members of the Legislative Council by universal suffrage'. Similarly, the ultimate aim for the selection of the Chief Executive is also by universal suffrage after nominations by a broadly representative nominating committee.

Present arrangements are clearly not good enough to last for long. There is beginning to be some discussion about constitutional development. I should think there is a good deal of thought being given to it in the Government Secretariat.

Functional constituencies

Some business leaders are said to be planning to push for retention of the functional constituencies after 2007. I am sure this would be a mistake. When they were introduced, there were no elections for the Legislative Council at all. Legislative Council members were appointed. The appointment process was not arbitrary nor was it a process of looking for yes-men who would simply back everything the government did. The aim was to find men and women from different social groups who would give serious thought to proposals and, if they were no good, to say so. Doctors, lawyers, bankers and the rest were not appointed to represent their narrow interests but because they were individuals who had demonstrated that they had a much broader view of the public interest. A similar balance in the representation of various walks of life was hoped for in an elected Legislative Council, so the circles from which appointments used to be made were enabled to elect their own representatives. Those elected from functional constituencies in the early years did not confine their work to the interests of their electorates. With the passage of time, and with the realization that it is only through the votes of their constituents, that members are elected to functional constituencies, we have seen a narrowing in their interests. This was seen most clearly in the election campaign for the year 2000 elections. And the farce of a Council member being elected by a few hundred voters, or less, clearly has to be ended. If we can survive one more Council with a few functional constituencies, it will be about as much as will be good for us. In Britain, it was not until after the Second World War that the functional constituencies formed by the graduates of Oxford and Cambridge Universities were deprived of their right to return members of Parliament. But then things do move more slowly there.

To end the functional constituencies does not mean the end of functional interests lobbying and bringing pressure to bear in the Legislative Council. One needs only to look at Britain or America to see that. After all, how many days in the year is it really necessary to have a representative of the tourist bodies, or lawyers, or the education establishment, or a social worker actually sitting in the Legislative Council to ensure that their concerns are considered? The many advisory bodies that exist may become more active in making their views known. Entirely, new pressure groups could spring up if the legislature was riding roughshod over any substantial body of interest. To try to pack the Council with representatives of all the vested interests in Hong Kong is impossible. Only a few can make it even now. It is ridiculous to suggest that it is only the wise heads of the functional constituency members that preserve us all from anarchy in the legislature.

Universal suffrage

What does universal suffrage imply? There has not been much discussion about this, yet it must surely be the most important constitutional issue to be faced not only in 2007, but by the whole population as they prepare to elect the 2004 Legislative Council. Arrangements after 2007 must have the backing of two-thirds of the Legislative Council and this means the Council elected in 2004.

The subservient status of the Legislative Council cannot survive the election of a Chief Executive by universal suffrage. Such a Chief Executive could only win election with massive public support. This support can only be generated by an organized appeal to the voters. In other words, the Chief Executive thus elected will have to have the machinery of a major political party behind him. No political party capable of getting the support of the population at large will be an organization ruled despotically by an individual. There will be a team. This team will contribute a substantial number of Legislative Council members, probably a majority. They will insist on taking part in the formation of, and accepting responsibility for government policy in a way that the present Legislative Council is prevented from doing. The suggestion in the 1984 Green Paper that the Legislative Council elect from among themselves the majority of Executive Council members might be one way of moving that way.

Talk about attempting to eliminate a political background from any candidate for the highest political office is clearly condemned to fail. The whole point of standing for election to the highest office must be to secure widespread public support for political aims, whether these are disguised as 'reforms' or 'new initiatives'. The electorate is not there to elect a god-like creature without any policy other than 'Trust me: I shall do the right thing'. He is not a judge who, although independent of the executive, is bound by the law. The government makes laws. It taxes and spends the citizens' money. Anyone elected to such a position will be the person who has convinced the great mass of the people that he will lead a government that has the best programme for the stability and prosperity of the population as a whole.

Universal suffrage, as promised in the Basic Law, will bring major changes. Some will view them with apprehension, fearing the advent of an irresponsible government manned either by venal politicians out for their own ends or by those making fanciful promises which they cannot keep. But are Hong Kong people really such simpletons? The place is full of all sorts of organizations of broader and narrower interests, but few of them are run by idiots or crooks. Why should Hong Kong people be fooled by incompetent people out for their own ends?

Hong Kong is just not equipped to be run by a repressive government and never has been. We cannot put people in prison unless they have been sent there by the courts which are independent of the executive. There is no government control of the media. Freedom of expression and assembly are enshrined in the constitution. We have a formidable machine for combating corruption. It is inevitable that Hong Kong will move towards a more conventional system of government based on general elections which produce the people who will take the important decisions of government policy — political decisions made by politicians. Of course, there are risks that some fools get elected, but we have to go through this stage until voters realize that votes are for matters that really affect their daily lives.

Evolution or revolution?

No system of government is immune to revolution. We never came anywhere near it. So long as steady progress towards the 'ultimate aim' is maintained, this should continue to be the case. Trouble would certainly arise if progress is halted or put into reverse.

To try to hold back the move towards a much more meaningful job for people elected by the general population runs the serious risk of something much closer to revolution than a few religious geeks sitting about protesting in yellow shirts.

Index